150365607 8

AF616610

THE BUSINESS INFORMATION MAZE: AN ESSENTIAL GUIDE

The business information maze: an essential guide

Edited by
Jo Haythornthwaite

Published by
Aslib, The Association for Information Management
Information House
20–24 Old Street
London
EC1V 9AP

British Library Cataloguing in Publication Data
Haythornthwaite, J. A. (Jo A.)
The business information maze: an essential guide
1. Business firms. Information systems
I. Title
658.4′038

ISBN 0-85142-250-0 hbk

Typeset, printed and bound in Great Britain by
Page Bros (Norwich) Ltd

CONTENTS

INTRODUCTION vii

1. Working with business information today 1
   Jo Haythornthwaite

2. The online revolution 15
   Jo Haythornthwaite (additional research by Diana Edmonds)

3. Newspapers: an undervalued resource 31
   Jo Haythornthwaite

4. British official publications 49
   Jo Haythornthwaite

5. 1992 and all that: business information from the EC 73
   Michael Hopkins

6. Management information 89
   Bob Norton and **Sharon Barker**

7. Company information 107
   Diana Edmonds

8. Marketing information 127
   Jo Haythornthwaite and **Diana Edmonds**

9. Worldwide market resources 147
   Jo Haythornthwaite

10. Banking information 163
    Olivia Freeman

11. Patents and standards 187
    Jo Haythornthwaite and **Diana Edmonds**

12. Paying for information 197
    Jo Haythornthwaite and **Diana Edmonds**

13. Business information: quo vadis? 213
    Diana Edmonds

Biographical notes to contributors 221

Index 223

INTRODUCTION

This book grew out of a series of lectures given as part of an elective course on business information which I taught at Loughborough University, Department of Library and Information Studies, from 1985 to 1989.

I hope that it will prove to be not only a useful text book for teaching purposes but also a practical introduction for any information professional who ventures into the fast-changing world of business information. The information scene changes so swiftly that some of the material may well be out-of-date by the time this book is in print. I can only say that it was correct at the time of writing.

My thanks are due to all the contributors who were both prompt with copy and enthusiastic, and especially to Diana who collaborated on several chapters and read and commented on much of my material. I should also like to thank Graham Clements for much patient proofreading and Irene Martindale for her speedy and accurate word processing.

Jo Haythornthwaite

July 1989

Chapter One

WORKING WITH BUSINESS INFORMATION TODAY

Jo Haythornthwaite

Business information is the most exciting and rewarding area of work open to the young information professional today. It is an area of growth, continuing change and enormous variety, such variety that defining business information is, in itself, no easy task. Business information is, in essence, any information that the businessman or woman needs to further his or her business objectives.

Whether the information specialist works in a public library, an academic library or a company information centre, the provision of accurate and swift business information renders a very real service to society, for, 'After people and finance, information will emerge as the most powerful determinant of relative economic performance'[1]. This speaker, Justin Dukes of the *Financial Times*, went on to point out that the results would be cumulative, since the better informed company will make better decisions and therefore tend to pull ahead of its competitors; and that would apply to countries as well as companies.

We are constantly being told that we are moving into an information age, an age in which the information professions can play a crucial role if they have the energy and expertise to do so. Britain must compete with Japan and the United States, both of whom are nations which value information and disseminate it more efficiently than we do, and we must also meet the challenge of a frontier-free Europe in 1992.

This book hopes to provide answers to some of the questions which are central to any discussion of the importance of information to the business community in a changing economic climate and, in addition, to examine some of the sources of information that are available. Initially, certain questions must be addressed. What subject areas does business information include? From where can this information be obtained? Who are the information providers or, to put it another way, what sort of jobs are currently available in the world of information and libraries? Finally, are the information professions supplying the information that the business community wants in the form in which they require it, and why is it vital that they should do so? Justin Dukes has already provided part of the answer to that question.

What is business information?

> *Business information* is the published data, facts and statistics needed for decision-making in business organisations, private or public, as well as in government. It includes marketing information, financial, bank and company information, laws and tax regulations, economic, commercial and trade information, as well as factual information about the environment in which businesses and other organisations operate[2].

The problem about business information is that it can mean totally different things to different people. It is a subject without a structure, there are a multiplicity of sources of variable quality and there is a total lack of co-ordination between the sources, which leads to duplication, overlap and yawning gaps in provision.

Finally, in Britain, there is the added problem that the business and commercial centre of the country is in the City of London. The main sources of business information are therefore also located in the South East, mainly in London, although technology has now rendered this centralisation less significant.

Business information includes a wide variety of information categories. First, quick reference information, including addresses, telephone numbers, biographical data, timetable information, hotel prices – the list is endless. A business librarian recently told me that her duties frequently included booking theatre tickets for visiting overseas directors and her only failure of late was an inability to obtain two tickets for the cup final!

Company information will always be of prime importance and may include addresses of head offices, background data on companies and names and addresses of directors. Product information and financial information can be seen as part of company information or as separate but closely related areas.

There has been a remarkable increase in information centres based in banks and finance houses and banking information is now, therefore, an important field.

Depending on the type of organisation the information centre serves, it may also include marketing information, material relating to advertising and information about potential markets at home and overseas.

Statistical data from both governmental and non-governmental sources may be crucial for, for example, forecasting long-term consumer trends. Standards and patents must also be considered.

Finally, management information should play an important background role in all companies and the information scientist will provide a valuable service by making all that is new and relevant in management theory available to those who have to make decisions. Later chapters will examine these subject areas in some detail and, in addition, the role of the freelance information broker, the fee-based information sector and the implications of the new technologies for business information.

Where, then, can the business community obtain the information it requires?

If a company is large enough, it may have its own information centre or library with its own trained staff. If, however, the company cannot afford its own information centre, there are many other sources of information.

At the national level, business information is supplied by all sections of the British Library but especially by the Business Library of the Science Reference Information Service (SRIS). The Department of Trade and Industry's Export Market Information Centre (EMIC) can also claim to provide a national service. There is also the Business Statistics Office in Newport, Gwent, and a host of small firms, information centres and development agencies. The European Business Centres set up by the EC are a reliable recent addition to the range of business information resources available to us.

Public local authority services include, of course, the business libraries of the major cities; good examples include City Business Library in London and the business libraries in Birmingham, Sheffield, Nottingham, Liverpool, Manchester, Aberdeen, Glasgow and other large industrial centres. Local authorities also frequently provide business advice centres and these, ideally, work closely with the local library service and with other business information providers in the area.

Academic libraries are now pressurised to generate income and in order to do so are seeking to provide a service for business.

Who are the information providers? Where are the jobs in information?

A great many information providers work in the types of organisations that have just been mentioned: public libraries, national libraries, academic libraries, information centres, the traditional workplaces of the librarian. Some of today's information scientists, however, are grasping the new opportunities for computer-literate, information-conscious personnel in banks, insurance companies, market research organisations and in a variety of other areas of business, industry, commerce and the media. Many are also working for the new non-library information providers: database producers, software houses, online hosts and publishers.

In the last 10 years, non-library sources of information have proved to be a substantial growth area. There are basically two types of services which the user or the information centre can buy in: information services on demand and online information services. Information services available on demand include subscription-based information services such as those provided by London Business School and the *Financial Times* and market research organisations who, in some cases, will not only provide data which has already been published, but will accept commissions to undertake specific projects. The in-house database is now frequently the central pivot round which the company library revolves, while online searching of commercial databases provides the bulk of the professional work done by the information officers. This is especially the case in business information since the growth of online information has not only revolutionised the provision of business-related data but is also the most substantial growth area in the online industry. Thus, more and more of the information science graduates of the future will be employed by, or have frequent contact with, these non-library based information services.

Finally, the increase in freelance information specialists seems to demonstrate that many organisations do not see a full-blown information centre as a cost-effective way of providing information, and prefer to buy the information they want on a 'one-off' basis. All the same, most young graduates at present find their first experience of business information work either in commerce and industry, in a public library or in an academic library.

Working for a merchant bank is very different from working for an advertising agency or in the library of a multinational company, and it is also different from working in the business information department of a large public library or the business studies section of a college or university library. It may be helpful to examine how the work differs in these varied environments.

Working in commerce and industry

An awareness of the value of information has, at last, penetrated many sections of the British economy. Organisations which have in the past not been information-conscious are becoming more and more aware of its importance and, as a result, many are establishing information centres and appointing staff.

One consequence of this growth of libraries and information centres in the private sector is that it may often be the case that a young and comparatively inexperienced information scientist will be expected to set up an information service where none has existed before. Often, this has to be done with very little support, in every sense of the word. The information scientist is usually a 'one-man band' whose value and function is insufficiently understood by the company management team and other sections of the organisation.

In order to set up a relevant information service, it is vital to find out as much as possible about the operation of the company. What does it do? How does it go about accomplishing its objectives? Reading about the company is valuable here. It is difficult to use time better during the first few days in a new organisation than by reading internal newsletters, house magazines and recent press comment on the company. There is probably one better way of utilising those first few days and that is by talking to people, since the best way of getting the 'feel' of an organisation is always by talking to colleagues. Anyone who seeks to develop a new service within an organisation must ascertain as soon as possible where power lies. Who are the key people who can help and support the establishment of the information centre? They must be convinced that it will be beneficial to them personally and to the company.

After obtaining an informal overview of the organisation, it is time to move on to a structured user survey. After interviewing the key people and ascertaining their information needs, it should be possible to compile a user profile of the organisation which will illuminate both company objectives and those specific user information needs which can be satisfied. By now, it should be possible to plan the sort of information centre which will contribute effectively to the work of the organisation, and the librarian should document a proposal which shows his or her understanding of the company's needs and justifies the space, shelving, files and terminals in terms of their utility to the goals of the parent organisation. Sadly, it is not enough to put all of this on paper, however eloquently! A proposal must be sold to the key people. No plan or proposal, however well written, markets itself and the best way to sell something is always face-to-face.

Accept every opportunity to publicise your information service, both when it is in the process of development and later when it is established. Too often when a business experiences a setback, it appears easy to save a little money by closing the information centre. If the information officer has a high profile in the company and is seen as indispensible, this is far less likely to happen. So, once the information centre has achieved the status, space and staff which the proposal suggests, it is vital that marketing should continue to be an essential part of the job. Talking to people, even in a social context, is never a waste of time; it is a way to learn more about the company and to win friends and influence people.

Especially in the needle-sharp, smart world of the City, image can be crucial, it is, therefore, vital to look smart, attractive and pleasant, as a friendly manner and a good appearance leave a favourable impression on the user and create confidence. If you look efficient, most people believe that you are efficient. No opportunities should be lost to make presentations at departmental meetings, to show visitors round the information centre or participate in induction sessions for new staff. User education should be made available, especially when new databases are acquired; it is always a good idea to give demonstrations of any new technological toys which may impress the users. It is helpful to write a column in the company newsletter and to produce a current awareness bulletin, since, at the very least, such endeavours constantly remind colleagues that the library exists and may be of service.

While 20 years ago, a business library usually consisted of a few shelves of reference books, some journals, files of cuttings, some in-house reports and perhaps some material in microform, the modern information centre is likely to hold very few books, and terminals and databanks have largely replaced the abstracts, the indexes and some of the periodicals. There will certainly be a selection of journals, both house journals and commercial ones and there may be a few newspapers. It is probable that the annual reports of competitors, suppliers and customers will be filed, as will all in-house reports if the company produces any. Trade catalogues may be important to the company and, in some cases, a selection of standards and patents will be held. In addition, there may be substantial files of clippings, unless these have been replaced by an in-house database. Appropriate storage facilities will need to be found for microfilm, microfiche, video tapes, audio tapes and compact discs, depending on which of these media are purchased. Most modern information centres subscribe to a number of hosts and will require the appropriate hardware and software to facilitate their use. They may also use some videotex services.

The services that such an information centre can provide have changed radically over the years. Loans of books and periodicals and the circulation of periodicals now play a minor part in the work of most business information services. Probably the three most important services which the information officer provides in most business environments are speedy replies to quick reference enquiries, either by telephone or in person, online searching and current awareness.

Answering relatively simple reference enquiries swiftly, efficiently and accurately and in a pleasant manner is not only a service to the company, it is also excellent public relations and an immeasurable creator of goodwill.

Online searching still has a certain mystique for the uninitiated and, therefore, the trained information intermediary can impress the end-user by demonstrating the system with practised skill. It is, however, a mistake to make a great mystery of the business of online and prevent the end-user from learning to interrogate a relevant database. If the command language is complex, there are cost factors which make it preferable for information centre staff to undertake searches, but if the database is user-friendly, the information specialist should teach those who are interested to do their own searching. It may well be that searching may lead the information specialist to utilise the available software to produce a graph or chart which displays the requisite data in a clear and attractive manner.

Current awareness is a valuable service in the special library context. Many information officers produce a weekly current awareness bulletin listing new books, periodical articles and reports of interest to company personnel. Such a bulletin is best if it is not merely a list of titles but is rather a brief selection of short abstracts. A long list of mere authors and titles is likely to travel very swiftly to the waste paper bin! Photocopies of contents pages are also frequently disseminated. Individual current awareness services are very time-consuming to provide but can reap golden rewards. Such a service is usually provided only for a few key managers and may depend on a regularly updated card index listing their interests or on the utilisation of a database with a Selective Dissemination of Information (SDI) facility. Abstracting material in a succinct and informative way is also an art at which most special librarians and information scientists become adept.

A press cuttings file remains a seemingly old-fashioned service which has not entirely been superseded by the new technology. The alert information specialist can clip material from newspapers and journals relevant to the company and its competitors. Such clipping is time-consuming, the files take up space and they must be regularly weeded. An in-house database can replace the vertical files but this also needs constant updating and weeding and cannot accommodate pictorial material. BIM produce a useful fact sheet entitled, *Maintaining a press clippings file*, which is well worth obtaining since it provides sensible advice on how long to keep material and provides a list of subject headings used by the Management Information Centre of BIM[3].

In the ideal situation, the information office or library should be the central repository of information resources in the company. This should mean that the information centre staff not only compile and update the company's in-house database but also that the librarian knows exactly who does what in the firm; for example, who speaks Japanese, and who is likely to be looking for news of a competitor in the disposable nappy business. It is often important to build up a list of people willing to provide translations and, with the approach of 1992, information scientists with language skills will be highly marketable.

From time to time, the information centre will be asked to undertake lengthy and complex research projects. Such projects can be the most satisfying and rewarding part of the job. If the research project involves investigating a company (which the organisation sees as a possible acquisition) or a possible new product line, the information centre may acquire valuable prestige if the research is satisfactorily completed. It may be, however, if the centre has a staff of one, that the best way to handle such a project is to utilise a fee-based information service, such as *Mintel* (if it is marketing research) or the FINANCIAL TIMES BUSINESS INFORMATION SERVICE (if the enquiry is for mainstream business and/or company information). Another possibility may be the use of a freelance information consultant. The trend in industry and commerce is now to minimise the headcount as far as permanent staff are concerned and buy in additional expertise as and when it is required.

There are other, less tangible, ways in which the image of the information service can be enhanced. The information specialist is too often seen as a loner; someone working away steadily but detached from the mainstream of the company's activity. It is important to identify with the company's objectives and give those objectives every support. In order to do this, it is valuable to take every opportunity to become involved in the company at every possible level. If there are internal management courses, it is worthwhile to attend them and if there is a social club, it is important to join. If the librarian plays badminton, opponents on the court will probably visit the library. All professional and social contacts within the company are worth fostering, while contacts outside the company with other information scientists can be an invaluable source of information and can also help to ameliorate the professional isolation of the lone librarian in industry.

The information centre should be an active rather than a passive source of information. The role of the modern librarian/information scientist is not simply running a well-organised information office with neat rows of books, vertical files and racks of periodicals. The information specialist should be a dynamic force within the company, uniquely placed to be infinitely knowledgeable about the activities and objectives of that company, committed to those objectives, and ready to assist the company in any way possible. This will mean getting the right data, to the right person, at the right time and in the right form. Few managers have the time to read long articles from journals, but a crucial passage, mentioning a possible market opportunity, in the middle of the desk, highlighted to catch the eye, can be of great value and has immediate impact.

Thus, despite diversities of products and objectives, there may be some common threads which can be perceived as running through the work of information managers in business libraries in the manufacturing industry, in advertising and in the world of finance. All live in a highly competitive world in which they must not only do a good job but be *seen* to do a good job. The business information centre must be high profile. Time and effort must be given to marketing and public relations and then the service must live up to its own publicity.

Working in a public library

The nature of the stock, the clientele and the enquiries in a public library business information service are markedly different from those in some libraries in commerce and industry.

Public libraries tend to have a much more extensive stock of reference books, company directories, international telephone directories, trade catalogues, technical directories, government statistics, abstracts, indexes, maps, street plans and timetables. By having this wide and varied stock, they can answer most of the quick reference enquiries which come their way.

The clientele of the library in a company are all from that organisation, whereas the users of a business reference library come from all walks of life and may use the library for their own purposes or on behalf of their company. Many come in themselves and seek to find information swiftly and without seeking assistance[4]. A recent research project demonstrated that most of the users in three large business libraries did not want to ask for help. Their perception of a good business library was one in which the library had the data they required and the arrangement and guiding of the library made it easy for them to find the material themselves. In general, the clientele thought highly of the service they received and valued it, but the evidence also suggested that some users left the library with their queries unsatisfied either because they did not like to bother the staff or because they did not realise that the staff were well qualified to help them. The CRUS (the Consultancy and Research Unit) report and other research confirms suspicions that the public sometimes finds library staff unapproachable and often doubts their ability to be of use. This highlights the necessity of being friendly and approachable at all times and also the crucial image problem which seems to dog most librarians and information scientists. Tom Wilson was not far wrong when he suggested humourously that if everyone who answered the 'phone at Sheffield City Business Library (CBL) called him or herself Angela, this might help to overcome the difficulty that every public information service faces in trying to project itself to its clients as a trusted personal contact[5].

Much of the enquiry work done in a public business library is of a quick reference nature and a great deal of it relates to company information, but longer and more detailed enquiries are also received.

The quality of the service provided in some public reference libraries has been called into question recently as a result of a survey carried out by students from the Department of Library and Information Studies at Manchester Polytechnic. A set of questions was presented to 20 public reference libraries, and the responses were very disappointing. A request for biographical information about Robert Maxwell produced a hair-raising reply: 'We've nothing on Robert Maxwell. Would a book on Rupert Murdoch do?'[6]. Where specifically business libraries are concerned, however, the CRUS survey and a similar survey undertaken by Capital Planning Information suggest a much higher degree of reader satisfaction[7].

Changes in the library and information world have had a dramatic impact on business information provision in large city libraries. The three major developments which have affected this service have been the advent of the new technology, especially online, the debate as to whether or not to charge and the trend towards co-operative information services.

New, and not so new, technology has certainly altered the work of business library staff. Back runs of journals may now be on microfilm or even on compact disc, stock market data may well be displayed on a video screen via PRESTEL and the invaluable Companies Registration Office *Directory of Companies* now appears only on microfiche or online. Online has obviously revolutionised the work of the business librarian and many business libraries, for example, Birmingham, subscribe to a large number of databases.

Online, however, is an expensive medium and the problem of how much to charge, and how to charge, has accelerated the process of discussion as to what should or should not be charged for within the public library system.

The third factor which is radically changing the face of business information is the growth of co-operative groupings. Some co-operation is simply at the level of selective book and journal buying, for example, Nottingham Business Library does not buy some items to which Trent Polytechnic subscribes, and users who need this material are referred to the Polytechnic and vice versa. In Newcastle, the Business and Technical Library is a member of NETWORK, an information co-operative which includes the central public libraries of the region and the universities and polytechnics in the area. Such co-operation obviously saves money and makes a wider range of information resources available to the user.

Working in academic libraries

Universities and polytechnic libraries are now much more business information conscious than in the past. Until recently, business information received more attention in polytechnics than in universities since polytechnics were founded with the intention of forging close links with local industry and usually offered business studies degrees, diplomas in business studies and various management qualifications. Now universities also are under pressure to make closer contacts with local industry and, in some cases, have decided to offer a specialised information service to the business community. Services like the University of Warwick Business Information Service, the London Business School Information Service and HERTIS are discussed in another chapter. Even universities and polytechnics who do not offer such ambitious packages are investigating the possibility of offering a subscription service or are now at least encouraging external users to join the library on the payment of a fee. The old days of trying to exclude the public are over!

Apart from these external users, the business specialist in an academic library, in general, performs a rather different role from the business librarian in other types of organisations. The quick reference enquiry about a company or an individual, which is the staple information diet of the public library, and is also commonplace in the private sector, is less common in the academic environment. If the library is a subject specialised one, the business librarian liaises with the relevant academic departments on the selection of books and journals, and will catalogue and classify them and be responsible for the administration of that section of the library. Liaison with the Business Studies Department is usually close. The Business Librarian is often a member of the Departmental or Faculty Committee and is on Course Boards. When new courses are developed, again the subject specialist is usually included on the Course Development Board or Committee.

Service to the staff and the students on business studies, economics and management courses is the main responsibility of the business librarian, and activities usually include the checking of reading lists, helping students with projects, the production of book lists and informational leaflets and the provision of stimulating user education programmes which are fully integrated into the courses. It can be especially stimulating to provide user education for mature part-time students on DMS and MBA courses, who are always highly motivated and to whom the wealth of information available is frequently a revelation.

Co-operation may result in more conventional business information work being done in academic libraries. Certainly, such co-operation can only be beneficial to the staff of all the organisations concerned who, all too frequently, do not know about the resources both of materials and staff expertise which are available just down the road. Contacts are often the most valuable source of information and they are a source which diffident information scientists often fail to tap.

Thus, the work of the business librarian in the academic context has, until recently, been very similar to that of any other academic library subject specialist. Trends towards the rationalisation of resources and the provision of co-operative business information services, greater involvement with local industry and pressures on the whole of academia to get out into the marketplace and make money seem likely to diametrically alter their work. To be a business specialist in an academic library in the future will involve meeting the challenge of change.

Are we supplying the information that the business community needs?

Are we supplying the data in the form in which it is required? If we are not doing so, is it sometimes because it does not occur to industry to ask us to do so, because the service that libraries give has a reputation for being too slow and the information too out of date? Do we fail to convince industry and commerce of the value of information? Do we fail to market our own skills effectively? Frequently, even when a company has an information centre, a low value is placed upon it within the parent organisation and consequently the information officer is also inadequately valued and therefore enjoys low status and low pay. It is essential that the new information managers should market themselves and their service differently and more actively.

So, what can the information profession offer the business community? We can offer skilled staff with a knowledge of information-seeking techniques, access to a wide and growing range of information resources, access to online systems via experienced, trained intermediaries and a network of contacts inside and outside the organisation. The large city business library can offer all these services and also, usually, a far larger selection of printed sources, since company libraries today tend to carry less and less books.

The real commercial value of information tends to be underestimated by businessmen and women and industrialists but this may well soon no longer be the case. In 1983, the Cabinet Office produced a report *Making a business of information* which suggested that more and more information provision would be available on a commercial basis[8]. A recent Office of Arts and Libraries report on the growth of privatisation and the encouragement of joint enterprises indicates that the day is coming when free information may be as rare as 'food for free'[9]. A greater respect for the value of up-to-date information may come with payment. Businessmen and women, especially, tend to value what they pay for but, of course, they will also expect greater efficiency – real value for money.

It was not a crusading librarian but Sir Monty Finniston who declared,

'Part of the trouble with our society is that Government, the Treasury and industrialists are working on outmoded information, so they cannot get to grips with absolutely up-to-date facts'[10]. Once your organisation has obtained that absolutely up-to-date and relevant information, how can it be translated into productive decision-making?

This will only be the case if the organisation becomes truly information-conscious and aware of the commercial value of information. All organisations need to have an information strategy and this must be linked to a system of communication within the organisation. Only if communication is good within the organisation can information be utilised efficiently. Effective communication does not just *happen*; it has to be *planned* and managed. An organisation must have a system of communication which is appropriate to its structure, and that communication system must transmit information to the whole of the organisation. It is also crucial that specific pieces of information should be targetted at those people who are able to use the data. The importance of information within the organisation must be acknowledged at the very top of the organisational structure if its transmission and utilisation is to be efficient. The information manager of the future must not only supply current data swiftly and efficiently but must also tirelessly promote the value of information within the organisation.

References

1. DUKES, J. The issue of ownership and control of information, a paper delivered at the Aslib/IIS Joint Conference: *The nationwide provision and use of information*, held in Sheffield, 15–19 September 1980, 95.
2. VERNON, K. Management literature and business information. In: Vernon, K. (ed.) *Library and information services of management development institutions*, Geneva: International Labour Office, 1986, 18.
3. BIM. *Maintaining a press clippings file*. Fact sheet. n.d.
4. ROBERTS, N. et al. *Use and users of public sector business libraries*. Sheffield: CRUS, 1987.
5. Call everyone Angela, says Tom Wilson. *Aslib Information*, August 1985, 188.
6. LEA, P. and JACKSON, L. The exception or the rule? The quality of the reference service in public libraries. *Library Association Record*, 40, 10 October 1988, 582-585.
7. CAPITAL PLANNING INFORMATION. Qualitative assessment of public reference services, by Kennington, D. and Edmonds, D. BLRDD, 1987 (BL Research Paper, 21).

8. CABINET OFFICE: Information Technology Advisory Panel. *Making a business of information*, HMSO, 1983.
9. OFFICE OF ARTS AND LIBRARIES. *Joint enterprise*: roles and relationships of public and private sectors in the provision of library and information services: report of the Library and Information Services Council and British Library Research and Development Department Working Party. HMSO, 1987 (Library Information Series, No. 16).
10. FINNISTON, Sir Montague. Information for a dynamic economy, a paper delivered at the Aslib/IIS Joint Conference: *The nationwide provision and use of information*, held in Sheffield, 15–19 September 1980, 396.

Further reading

BAKEWELL, K. G. B. *Business information and the public library*. Gower, 1987.

CAMPBELL, M. J. *Business information services*, 2nd ed. Bingley, 1981.

CAMPBELL, M. J. (ed.) *Manual of business library practice*. 2nd ed. Bingley, 1985.

ROBERTS, N. et al. *Use and users of public sector business libraries*. Sheffield: CRUS, 1987.

WEBB, S. P. *Creating an information service*. 2nd ed. London: Aslib, 1988.

Chapter Two

THE ONLINE REVOLUTION
or are books and librarians obsolete?

Jo Haythornthwaite
(with additional research by Diana Edmonds)

The world of business information has changed radically within my professional lifetime and is continuing to change at a bewildering speed. The major reason for this revolution is the development of online information retrieval and the importance it has assumed in relation to business information.

In the last 10 years, the rate of growth in the online industry has been phenomenal and the area of greatest growth within the industry has been business information. This is hardly surprising since the information required in business is seldom historical information and frequently what is required is data that is current and, indeed, has only been released in the last few days. Online databases are uniquely able to produce such current data, although it must be said that the information available via some databases is not as current as the producers would like us to believe. Secondly, business and commerce have embraced the potential of online because they are better fitted than other sectors to afford to pay for it. Online remains an expensive way of obtaining information but this is not a problem in the affluent commercial sector, where time is money and where what is paid for tends to be valued more highly than what is free.

In writing this chapter, I am assuming some basic knowledge of computers and of the terminology and practice of online searching. I plan to concentrate, therefore, on the decision-making areas relating to online: the advantages and disadvantages of online as compared with hard copy; how to decide what source to use; the obstacles met in going online; how to choose hosts and databases; and, finally, to look briefly at current and future trends in online business information.

The advantages of online searching for business information retrieval

Searching manually for information is very satisfying to the dedicated researcher. It satisfies the 'terrier' instinct in all of us and makes us feel that we are demonstrating the skills which we have been taught at library school and are utilising the collections available on the library shelves.

When swifter routes to larger numbers of references are now so readily available via online services, such attitudes are hardly tenable. There are a number of reasons why online searching may be the best way of searching for information swiftly and comprehensively.

First, online opens doors to a tremendous amount of information. The biggest growth area within the online industry is the business sector and within that financial information services. Not only, therefore, is there a wealth of information available online, but much of it is directly relevant to the work of the business specialist. No library, however large and wealthy, is likely to have the range of sources now available online.

Carol Tenopir, in her paper on decision-making by reference librarians, writes, 'Online databases should be used to expand the coverage and scope of the reference collection. They allow a library to access reference materials they would not otherwise have'. She goes on to point out that few libraries can afford to subscribe to hard copy versions of reference books or bibliographies which they seldom consult and so 'it makes sense to access these online in the rare times they are needed'[1]. It is a cost-effective medium for seldom used material since most online databases are now 'pay-as-you-use'.

Secondly, speed is vital in business information and saves both time and money. Most of us have encountered the busy executive who wants the data within the hour. An online search can produce material in minutes which it would take a researcher hours or days to assemble. Thus, time is saved: the enquirer's time and the information officer's time. Time saved is money saved. The information officer's time is valuable and the time he or she saves by searching online rather than manually can be set against the costs of going online. The online enthusiast can claim that online searching saves further money because information found swiftly may, for example, help the marketing department to draw ahead of the competition. Subscriptions to a number of reference books, indexes, abstracts and journals may be rendered unnecessary and this will also save space, a horrendously expensive commodity, especially if the company headquarters is in central London.

Thirdly, flexibility is a great advantage. It is possible to search under several closely related terms at the same time by using truncation and it is possible to link terms or exclude some concepts by the use of Boolean logic. Boolean logic can involve the use of 'and', 'or', 'not' and similar terms depending on the search language being employed. It is an invaluable method of making a search more precise. Databases now also offer greater flexibility as to the routes by which the searcher can access the information. It is possible to interrogate most databases via author and subject, but many business databases are also hospitable to entry via SIC codes, company names, product names, trade names, advertising slogans, directors' names and a multitude of other starting points depending on the subject content of the specific database, for example, whereas an advertising database may allow searching under slogans, advertising agencies, product names, manufacturers and personalities featured in advertisements, a company financial database may provide access under company and also under specific balance sheet headings.

Fourthly, and increasingly, the information simply is not available in any other form. More and more data is now available either only online or, although available in other formats, would be almost impossible to assemble, for example, PROFILE provides the full text of articles from a wide range of world newspapers and, although theoretically it would be possible to obtain all these newspapers and amalgamate the material oneself, it would be immensely time-consuming.

Undoubtedly, database producers would claim that the need for up-to-date information was one of the strongest reasons for using online. A recent survey of public business libraries found that, while users had very few criticisms, they did make the point that out-of-date reference books and the consequent misinformation they contained was worse than useless since the user was actually misled[2]. Publishers have not, in fact, found that hardback sales have decreased appreciably. Libraries still buy *Who owns whom?* but they also subscribe to it online in order to have up-to-date details as to take-overs. Do not assume, however, that the database is always up to date. Find out how frequently the files are updated. It may be sensible to check *Who Owns Whom?* online but then also to have a look at REUTER TEXTLINE, including NEWSLINE, and flick through the RESEARCH INDEX. Information derived from newspapers, whether on paper or online, will always be the most current information resource. The original sources of newspaper information, that is wire services and press releases, can be invaluable when current data is required and many wire services are also now available online.

Up-to-date financial information is certainly an area where databases can be seen to have an edge over other sources of information.

Another and final advantage of online databases is that they provide a way of answering enquiries that cannot easily be dealt with by any other means. Complex questions that require the combination of several factors can be answered swiftly and efficiently via online: Carole Tenopir cites the example, 'How many software companies in San Francisco employ more than 50 people?'[3].

Online offers more and more ways in which the material it generates can be utilised. Enquirers will almost certainly want the material printed out so that they can take it away. They may well require software to be utilised in order to display the data via spread sheets, graphs and reports. Arguably, the hardware end of the business is facing a leaner time than in the past, as the giants in the field have been under-cut by the smaller manufacturers. Many online database producers know that, at present, they are unlikely to get rich marketing databases and, therefore, both hardware manufacturers and database producers see the production of more and more sophisticated and flexible software as the way to expansion. Thus, software is currently the great growth area in the computer world. It is likely that there will be substantial growth in this market and the only problem will be how to select the most suitable software packages for our own needs at a price within the budget.

Other features which are available from some hosts include a document delivery service which can be linked to an electronic mail service (PERGAMON FINANCIAL DATA SERVICES and DIALOG provide this facility) and the possibility of using the online service to generate a current awareness service. Such a service is often referred to as Selective Dissemination of Information, or SDI.

There are still undoubtedly some situations in which hard copy is superior to online. It is easier to browse in a book than on a database. Hard copy is exceedingly 'user-friendly' and because it is a familiar and unthreatening information resource, both end-users and librarians are at ease with it. There is usually no need to teach either information staff or end-users how to use a new paper reference source, although there are some complex exceptions, for example, the Citation Indexes. Reference books are still probably the swiftest way of answering one-dimensional questions, for example, 'Who manufactures Mars bars?'. Finally, printed sources currently remain the best source for illustrations since online can at present only reproduce text.

How to choose the right source with which to answer an enquiry[4]

If hard copy can have advantages in some circumstances while online is far superior in others, then it may be useful to consider whether it is possible to develop a tentative strategy for the evaluation of sources.

First, it is vital to analyse the nature of the enquiry, to establish exactly what is being asked. Here there is no substitute for talking to the enquirer in order to find out exactly what is wanted. Is it an author/enquiry, a fact-finding query or a material-finding one? Does it require a straightforward factual or statistical answer or does it involve collecting a portfolio of background material? Once the nature of the enquiry and its scope are clearly identified, it is possible to consider what type or types of sources it would be appropriate to interrogate.

Secondly, it is essential to check on the hard copy resources available in the library or information centre and decide whether they are likely to provide an adequate answer to the query.

Thirdly, the online resources which are available should be considered.

A fourth line of enquiry should be consideration of any in-house sources of relevant information. It is at this point that the inestimable value of knowing what goes on in your organisation and who does what within it becomes apparent.

Next, there is the possibility of external sources of information. The informal network of local information scientists, friends and ex-colleagues can be an invaluable source of free assistance.

Finally, external commercial sources may be the best way of satisfying the enquiry if finance allows. The librarian should consider whether contacting a fee-based information service, or information broker, or a professional association might produce a better, more complete and more authoritative answer than can be generated in-house. It could even be the most cost-effective route in the long run.

Of course, it is not quite as simple as that. Such decisions are impacted by various factors, of which ideally the paramount factor should be the needs of the enquirer. Is speed important? Is the enquiry vital to the user; that is, is it a clue in a crossword, or data on which the company's marketing strategy may depend? Does the information need to be the most up to date possible? Where business is concerned, this is almost always the case. Is there a need for confidentiality? If there is, for example, if the company is researching a new product, the use of external sources may not be admissible.

Internal constraints may influence the choice of sources utilised to answer the enquiry. Few information scientists can embark on a search without considering the costs involved. Hard copy versus online decisions often come down to a question of passive costs versus active costs. If the library has the books, abstracts, indexes, etc., it may seem wasteful to interrogate a database even if the staff time devoted to manual searching may be extensive.

Staff time, therefore, must also be considered. Is there staff available to undertake the work? What are the hidden costs of using a member of staff, or more than one, to answer the enquiry?

If an in-house source is to be approached, the information manager must decide if this is advisable. Will the person be delighted at having been asked and impressed that the information centre staff knew that he or she might have the information or will the person be irritated at being asked for assistance? Confidentiality may also be a factor here. The enquirer's department may not wish the staff of other departments to be approached.

Similar factors come into play when asking for help from an external source. If it involves a personal contact, this is often a pleasant and straightforward matter, especially if your library is able to reciprocate the assistance from time to time. If this is not the case, however, and requests for help tend to be all in one direction, it may become a cause of annoyance to the originally willing contact. If an impersonal organisation or an association of which your company is a member is approached this is often easier since there is no question of reciprocity or gratitude involved.

External commercial sources can be assessed on their merits, in terms of cost and convenience. Here it is a case of 'horses for courses'. If an external commercial source is chosen, the librarian must be sure it is the right one, the service which is tailored to answering that type of question: for example, the BBC is excellent for background information about people. The cost of using such a service may be significant but may be outweighed by the library not having access to either hard copy or online resources which will answer the enquiry or simply not having the staff available to undertake the searching involved.

It may be helpful to illustrate the decision-making processes involved when evaluating a specific type of question: searching for directory information provides a relevant case study.

When searching for directory information currency is obviously vital and online has a definite advantage providing the file is regularly updated. Search facilities are superior online because Boolean logic can be used to combine various record elements. If you are unsure of a company name online is likely to cope better, especially if you use truncation. Online also avoids idiosyncratic filing rules and enables the searcher to use range searching and to sort by rank. The results of the search can be printed out and, therefore, note-taking is unnecessary. There are also great advantages in speed of access and savings in staff costs and time. From the costs point of view, there is a saving resulting from the cancellation of subscriptions to some hard copy directories and the resultant saving of space.

Hard copy has some advantages, however. If the directories are already held in the library, they can be used at no additional cost although, of course, staff time is a factor. Books have an undeniable advantage over online for the browser, for example, a user may wish to get an indication of the approximate size of a certain industry section, the companies involved, the regional concentration and the approximate size of the industry in terms of capital and turnover. A range of directories also allow a number of people to look at different directories at the same time. Finally, some of the smaller and more specialised directories are not yet available online, although more and more are becoming available all the time.

More and more business information queries can now be answered using online sources. The recent CPI study of business information queries received by Nottingham and Leicester Business Libraries revealed that over 50 per cent of the enquiries received could be answered from online sources[5]. Even so, 'Just as computers no longer appear to promise planned obsolescence for librarians, we have come to appreciate that online databases are neither a universal panacea nor a substitute for reference work'[6].

Obstacles to going online

It is sad to have to acknowledge that the greatest obstacle to going online may well be existing staff. There are still many people who are afraid of computers and who, therefore, have a psychological resistance to going online. If they are nervous about working with online databases, only practice will change this. 'Hands-on' experience with a very easy-to-use database which is 'menu-driven' will work wonders. The term 'hands-on' is self-explanatory but 'menu-driven' possibly needs to be explained. This is the term used to describe a database which displays a menu from which an option is chosen at every stage of the search. The opposite of 'menu driven' is, of course, 'command driven' which indicates the need to learn a command language, which may be very simple, for example, PROFILE or more complex, for example, DIALOG. Library catalogues are now frequently held on a computer and displayed to the reader using OPACS which operate in this way. TEXTLINE is an example of a 'menu-driven' database which is very easy to use and is therefore a good service on which to introduce the nervous or antagonistic member of staff to online. Later, when they are 'hooked', they can learn the bad news about all those different command languages used by other hosts.

So, staff resistance can be overcome by giving them experience on the more 'user-friendly' databases, sending them on training courses and by communication and discussion. The second problem, which many information specialists encounter, is that while there are terminals in the building, the information centre either does not have one at all or does not have enough of them to provide an adequate online service. Many companies subscribe to certain databases but house them in what they see to be the relevant department to which the information manager does not have ready access.

A third obstacle may be lack of staff training and, where there is lack of training, often there is psychological resistance to online. The only way to overcome this is by obtaining training either 'in-house' or by sending staff on courses run by library schools, Aslib, TFPL or by the databases and hosts themselves.

Cost is the most usual reason given for not going online; the sheer expense of purchasing terminals, printers and software and then the added costs of subscriptions to the chosen hosts. Some hosts ask for an 'up front' annual subscription, while others operate a 'pay-as-you-go' policy by which users are billed according to the time spent online. It is now becoming common for hosts to offer a choice of methods of payment so that the user can decide which method is suited to his or her needs. If the organisation is likely to be a heavy user, obviously the annual subscription is the better bargain, whereas 'pay-as-you-go' is now generally the more common method of payment and is, when available, the most cost-effective for the infrequent user. Whichever way payment is made, it must be clear that this is not the end of the expense which will be incurred. There will also be telecommunications costs, electricity, discs, paper and maintenance and repair bills relating to the equipment.

Earlier, I talked about the savings to be made by using online searching but these probable savings must be weighed against the cost of going online. A library which has plenty of space, is well staffed, has long runs of journals, abstracts, indexes and government statistics and a good collection of reference books may see it as a deplorable waste of already available resources to invest in online as well.

There are, of course, ways in which costs can be somewhat reduced. The staff should take advantage of all the free training which is available as this will improve the speed with which they operate. They should also be encouraged to use all the 'free' time which many hosts offer each time they launch a new database. Staff must be taught to plan searches before leaping on to a terminal with gay abandon. A search which is thought through first and prepared offline saves money.

Costs may also be reduced by purchasing frequently used databases on CD-ROM when this format is available. CD-ROM allows unlimited use of the file once it has been purchased. CD-ROM, therefore, makes it easy to allow both library staff and end-users to spend time learning to use the database without worrying about online costs and password security. The knowledge that they are not running up enormous bills greatly reduces the nervousness of the unaccustomed searcher. The major drawback of CD-ROM is that recent information cannot be made available in this form. Information relating to the current year will almost always have to be sought online, although more flexible discs to which information can be added are at the developmental stage.

One of the cost-related problems which has perhaps delayed the wholehearted use of online in public business libraries and academic libraries has been the problem of who pays for the search. Does the library shoulder this burden or pass it on to the user? In view of the

Government Green Paper, it now seems certain that libraries, both public and academic, will have very little choice but to charge for online services either at a rate that will at least cover their costs or at a price which generates a profit[7].

Many librarians are deterred from subscribing to a host because they are uncertain which to choose. The proliferation of hosts and databases bewilders some would-be users. To a librarian trying to make the right decision, there are too many hosts, too many databases and too much overlap between hosts: for example, ICC and PREDICASTS appear on more than one host. It is genuinely very difficult for the busy information professional to find the time to assess which host or hosts will best suit his or her organisation. Many, therefore, put off the decision to invest. It is, therefore, no surprise that information about hosts and databases, which is unbiased and does not emanate from the manufacturers, is a recurrent request when librarians and information scientists are asked what seminars and courses would be useful to them.

It also cannot be denied that technical problems do deter some people from becoming online enthusiasts. There are some people who have only to touch a terminal for the system to go down! Technical problems can be of many types. Incompatibility dogs some users and telecommunications problems add to the frustrations. Power cuts, which are prevalent in some developing countries, can impede searching as do thunder storms but, worst of all, from the point of view of the user's blood pressure, is the frequency with which systems still inexplicably go down. Here again, CD-ROM has advantages since the user is not dependent on telecommunications and, unlike an online database, a CD-ROM does not go down.

Many users are also irritated by the proliferation of command languages. It seems complete nonsense that the user has to learn three different command languages in order to interrogate three different hosts. It is, therefore, all too easy to make mistakes when one changes, for example, from DATA-STAR to DIALOG. It has been suggested that the inevitable rationalisation of the industry, which is likely to result in fewer and bigger hosts, may lead to the elimination of some command languages. The 'menu-driven' approach, which is prevalent in the sector aimed directly at the business community, eliminates the need to learn commands but is, of course, slower and, therefore, more expensive in terms of time and money, especially if the system is 'pay as you go'. The growth of gateways, i.e. systems which allow the user access to a range of databases via a simple menu, also overcomes this problem, for example, INFOSEARCH, BIM HELPLINE.

These, then, are the obstacles to going online and the problems which can be encountered by online users. In spite of such obstacles and problems, online remains a tremendous advance in the retrieval and dissemination of business information.

How to choose hosts and databases

The choice of hosts and databases can be difficult since it would be unusual if all the databases that would be useful to a given information centre were on the same host. Many databases are available on more than one host, and the difficulty is choosing which of these hosts will be the best choice in the light of various factors.

In evaluating a database, obviously the first and most essential factor is subject coverage. Does the database offer the information you need? The best way to establish this is to check both the subjects covered and the sources indexed. If the major journals in your company's field of operation are not abstracted, it is unlikely that it is a good choice. Access can be difficult from certain parts of the country. Never take the word of a salesman or woman regarding ease of access. Ask other librarians in your area whether they have problems. See how you feel about the command language. Is it easy to learn? Do you feel comfortable with it? How is the database loaded? Remember that it is easier, quicker and cheaper to search if there are merge files rather than separate ones. Are the available search files the ones that you want? Search files enable the user to interrogate the files in a range of different ways, for example, under authors, subjects, managing directors or SIC codes.

Every database has special searching features: these are the extra features which facilitate the searching process and may include online thesauri and the ability to use truncation. If you want to be able to offer your users a SDI service, it is crucial that you make sure that the host to which you plan to subscribe will facilitate this.

Costs have already been discussed and may well be the vital deciding factor.

The amount of training offered by the host can be a substantial inducement. Hosts and individual databases now see training as a vital selling point. Free demonstrations and practical 'hands-on' sessions usually form part of the pre-sale marketing offensive. Once the agreement has been signed, there is usually a free training course, often in a classroom setting with a practical element. This may be supplemented by free demonstrations and training in the buyer's own environment. Many hosts also offer additional free classroom sessions when they load a new database.

In addition, most hosts offer a range of sophisticated self-teaching aids. These include free time on some databases, (especially when new files are acquired), training databases (these are very useful for practising finding your way around the database but, understandably, only provide access to a limited range of information) and training CD-ROMs which are training databases in a cheap and convenient form. All hosts offer some printed aids to their users. The most important of these is the user manual which can be a great asset in increasing sales if it is well-written, clear, easy to use and not too large. Most hosts and some individual databases produce a newsletter. These alert the user to new databases which have been loaded, new files which have been added to an existing database, changes in the command language, forthcoming training courses and generally combine information and public relations. The existence and quality of user support is an area where it is wise to talk to other users rather than to the salesperson. Hosts normally have a help desk and other information scientists may be able to tell you if it provides swift, efficient and pleasant assistance. If the host you are evaluating is American, or indeed, any nationality but British, it may be important to find out whether or not there is a UK office. This is essential both for swift assistance with problems and for rapid document delivery, if this service is provided.

Current trends

The cost of purchasing hardware has decreased in the last few years and the use of microcomputers may decrease the hardware costs of online still further. Many information producers are now also marketing software packages to complement their databases but some software remains relatively expensive. The usefulness of data is obviously greatly enhanced when it can be displayed on spread sheets, edited, added to and generally manipulated.

Telecommunications networks are now cheaper to use than the telephone and, thus, provide swift, cheap access to hosts, for example, a local telephone call can connect a user to a database in California via a network. Great improvements in telecommunications throughout Europe are envisaged in the near future to prepare for the advent of the Single European Market in 1992.

There are other developments which relate to the databases themselves and trends in the information industry which produce them. There has been substantial growth in source databases; these are databases which display the information itself rather than a bibliographical reference to a periodical article. Over 90 per cent of the market now comprises source databases and a growing number of these are either full text or nearly full text.

Discussions on the future of online often involve speculation on the potential of the end-user market. At one time it was fashionable to believe that this could lead to the end of librarians, at least the end of librarians fulfilling the sort of roles they had undertaken in the past. Many database producers in the business information sector are currently gearing their products to the growing end-user market. This has involved making their products easier to interrogate either by the use of very simple command languages or by the menu-driven approach. Despite the endeavours of the producers, the expected enormous increase in direct use by business people in the UK has failed to live up to expectations, although this is not the case in the United States. In Britain, it seems, there are still many people who prefer to have searches done for them. Where financial and economic data is involved, however, (where the figures on the screen can often only be adequately interpreted by an accountant) there is probably no real role for the librarian as an intermediary. In such cases, the best person to interrogate the database is the individual who will utilise the statistics. Statistical hosts, such as I.P. SHARP (now part of TEXTLINE) and DATASTREAM, are not initially easy to use but can become so for the user who accesses them regularly. Other databases that are frequently used by the information seekers themselves are often the menu-driven type. There is some evidence also that laymen and women prefer viewdata methods of presentations to the terminal screen, whereas information scientists tend to prefer to use a terminal as the screen can accommodate more information.

At a recent UKOLUG/COPOL seminar 'End-users – a new challenge', there were interesting and wide-ranging discussions on the subject of end-users. Allan Foster reported that in the US end-user searching has become popular and has led to an increase in usage. The end-users, however, did not develop the sophisticated search strategy skills that were needed to fully exploit the systems. Staff would still be needed to establish the system, provide initial training, disseminate information on new databases, keep the documentation up to date, negotiate with hosts and database producers, assist in problem solving and do some searching[8].

A current trend, which no-one can fail to observe, is the number of changes of ownership in the information industry. In the past, hosts have been eager to add new databases to their stable but now some hosts are dropping uneconomic databases. Some hosts insist on exclusivity as regards the databases they include, while others are happy to allow their databases to be available on other hosts. Many observers of the information scene believe that in 10 years, there will be fewer and larger hosts, and this prediction is borne out by the current increase in mergers and acquisitions. Such a development may well provide the librarian with a less daunting task when selecting a host, and the amount of overlap and duplication may well also decrease. It is a possible, but perhaps not a probable, idea that costs may fall. Certainly, flexibility in the way in which the user pays for and can receive services will, hopefully, continue to grow. A choice between an annual subscription and the 'pay-as-you-go' method is obviously desirable as is the growth of choice in the methods by which data is delivered. It is becoming more common now for the data to be available either in hard copy on a terminal screen, on CD-ROM, or via viewdata.

A few years ago, it was fashionable for the information professions to suggest that the growth in customer proficiency online, together with the increase in menu-driven databases, would lead to there being less and less need for trained intermediaries. In other words, there was a theory that librarians and information scientists who taught their clients how to use databases might be doing themselves out of a job! So far, there is really no evidence of this and this argument is now heard less often. Some hosts are too difficult for the average layman or woman to interrogate unless he or she does so on a regular basis. An inexperienced searcher will always be slower, less efficient and, therefore, may produce an unsatisfactory search at a high cost. An information manager recently told me of a user who searched on TEXTLINE for several hours with no real success. The information manager then took over the search and produced a substantial body of valuable material in a few minutes. This was especially surprising and revealing since TEXTLINE is very easy to use and, therefore, should be a database which can be as effectively interrogated by an end-user as by a trained information specialist. Encouraging businessmen and women to do their own searches using a slow menu-driven host may be a very expensive exercise. The trained searcher will always produce more information more swiftly and therefore more cheaply than will the amateur, so there will always be a role for the expert when speed and skill are required. The information specialist will also be responsible for teaching the non-specialists who wish to do their own searching and will, therefore, be able to advise the organisation as to which hosts, which databases and which software should be purchased and what new developments may be relevant. There are theories which suggest that, in the near future, the status of the expert in industry and in society is set to rise dramatically. If this is so we, the information experts, could be in a very strong position.

The challenge for the information scientist

This, then, is the challenge for the information specialist. Information is a commodity of immense potential commercial value in business, but its potential has not, as yet, been inadequately recognised. The librarians or information scientists of the future must grasp the opportunities offered by online since their role as the expert in this field, unlocking immense databanks of knowledge, renders them uniquely placed to rise to the business information challenges posed by 1992 and by the next century. It seems inevitable that the amount of information available to us in a multitude of forms will continue to increase and information scientists, trained to retrieve and disseminate this data, will become key personnel of increasing value both to business and to society as a whole. All that is necessary is that information scientists should both be proficient and knowledgeable about online resources and that they should market their skills effectively.

References

1. TENOPIR, C. Decision making by reference librarians. *Library Journal*, 1 October 1988, 66.
2. ROBERTS, N. et al. Uses and users of public sector business libraries. Consultancy and Research Unit, Department of Information Studies, University of Sheffield. British Library Board, 1987. (CRUS occasional paper no. 14, BLRDD Report 5942).
3. TENOPIR, C., op. cit 66.
4. 'How to choose the right source' section is based on notes supplied by Diana Edmonds.
5. CAPITAL PLANNING INFORMATION. Qualitative assessment of public reference services, by Kennington, D. and Edmonds, D. BLRDD, 1987 (BL Research Paper 21).
6. STIEG, M. F. and ATKINSON, J. L. Librarianship online: old problems, no new solutions. *Library Journal*, 1 October 1988, 48.
7. *Financing our public library service: four subjects for debate*. HMSO, 1988. CM 324. *Green Paper*.
8. FOSTER, A. The Librarian's tale, paper given at a UKOLOG/COPOL seminar entitled, *End-users – a new challenge?* held at Thames Polytechnic, London, on 29 November 1988. Reported by Nigel May, *Online News*, Jan/Feb 1989, 13–15.

Further reading

ARMSTRONG, C. J. and LARGE, J. A. (eds) *Manual of online search strategies*. Gower, 1988.

FOSTER, P. and FOSTER, A. (eds) *Online business source book*. Cleveland: Headland Press, 1988.

GILLMAN, P. Computer systems in library and information services. In:

VERNON, K. (ed.) *Library and information services of management development institutions*. Geneva: International Labour Office, 1986.
HENRY, W. M. et al. *Online searching: an introduction*. Butterworths, 1980.
NORTON, R. The impact of online services on business information workers. *Business Information Review*, 2, 2 October 1985, 30–36.
WALSH, B. P. et al. *Online information – a comprehensive business-user's guide*. Oxford: Basil Blackwell, 1987.

Chapter Three

NEWSPAPERS: AN UNDERVALUED RESOURCE

Jo Haythornthwaite

> Never believe in mirrors or newspapers
> (John Osborne: *The Hotel in Amsterdam, Act I*)

While approaching the contents of popular newspapers with a healthy scepticism, newspapers are an essential, indeed indispensible, source of up-to-date and usually reliable business information. It is therefore a mistake to dismiss all newspapers as ephemeral and lightweight. Anyone who aspires to a successful career in business information must cancel their subscription to the *Sun* and start buying the *Financial Times*. It is desirable to make time to read one of the the other quality dailies, i.e. the *Daily Telegraph*, *The Times*, the *Independent*, or the *Guardian*; and the *Observer*, the *Sunday Times* or the *Sunday Telegraph* at the weekend.

The importance of newspapers

In his *Manual of business library practice*, Malcolm J. Campbell wrote with some truth:

> It might be said ... that a business information service of some kind could be provided without any books at all, given a telephone (or telex), an extensive knowledge of outside sources and the *Financial Times* and/or *Wall Street Journal* exploited intelligently[1].

Newspapers remain the best source of material on recent events and new developments: indeed, they are often the *only* source of information relating to something which has happened very recently. They also provide an excellent method of establishing the date of an event, e.g. via the use of the *Times Index* and *The Times*. Frequently, newspapers provide an account of a technical advance at the layman or woman's level and such accounts are just what is required when all the client needs is a brief and simple resumé.

All the quality newspapers also feature special reports. These often occupy around four pages in the centre of the newspaper and can be removed and filed. They usually focus on specific countries at regular intervals: usually countries with whom the UK has strong trading links. *The Times*, for example, may well cover Hong Kong almost every year while countries of less interest to British exporters are surveyed less regularly. *The Times* and the *Financial Times* are especially highly regarded for their special supplements. In addition to special sections on countries, specific parts of Britain, e.g. Tyneside, Scotland, Wales, are featured, as are industries, e.g. pharmaceuticals, construction, road haulage. These supplements are well worth filing but, if they are not retained, they can be traced very easily via the RESEARCH INDEX and via the online news services, TEXTLINE and PROFILE.

In *Business Information Review* in April 1987, a paper by Carmel McGrother focused on the business news coverage of the four leading national dailies: the *Daily Telegraph*, the *Independent*, the *Guardian* and *The Times*[2]. When the writer looked at the weekly number of business pages as a percentage of the total pages, the *Telegraph* led with 30 per cent, *The Times* provided 25 per cent, with the *Independent* close behind at 23 per cent and, finally, the *Guardian* with only 11 per cent. Specific areas of business information revealed interesting variations within the overall picture. The *Telegraph* owes its lead over *The Times* partly to business advertising but is very strong on share prices and personal finance. The *Guardian*, while taking less interest than the other three in business in general, shows concern for industrial policy, law and industrial relations. The *Independent* is an effective source of company news and competes with *The Times* strongly in this field. *The Times*, itself, remains an excellent source of business information and is particularly strong as regards finance, economics, share price comment, statistical information and management. None of these four newspapers, however, can compete with the *Financial Times* which is, in essence, a business newspaper; although it should also be noted that the *FT* is an excellent source of general news and of arts reviews.

It is also important not to disregard the major regional newspapers. If the librarian is seeking material on a company located in the west of Scotland, the obvious place to look would be the *Glasgow Herald*. Thus, when researching a company in the regions, it is sensible to utilise the local newspaper.

Problems relating to newspapers

Newspapers are both a blessing and a nightmare to the librarian to whom they present a number of problems relating both to exploitation and to conservation and storage.

The exploitation of information in newspapers is greatly impeded by the absence of a comprehensive printed indexing service, even for our quality newspapers. Secondly, differing editions present difficulties when a specific item is being sought. Newspaper publishing is a continuous process from the first to the last edition, with new editions appearing throughout the day, e.g. *The Times* produces six editions per day. The *Glasgow Herald* has four or five as do most of the other serious dailies. Newspapers, therefore, frequently miss out some important events from some editions, for example, if a piece of news breaks late, it may only be found in editions five and/or six of *The Times*. Conversely, a story featured prominently early in the day may be ousted by some new drama by the time the last edition surfaces. Newspapers can anticipate important government announcements, as they receive press releases in advance, but they cannot do anything about sudden unforeseen events, like a diplomatic incident or a police siege. It is important that the information manager knows that *The Times* indexes the sixth edition *only*. Usually, indexing services use the latest edition, therefore, items ousted in the course of the day are frequently hard to trace.

Local newspapers are a valuable source of local business news, and are especially valuable in the context of the public library business information service. Here again, different editions of a local newspaper can create problems when the researcher is trying to locate a news item. Local newspapers usually operate on a map of concentric circles so that the outermost circles represent remote areas and the innermost the city or town itself. The country areas get the earlier edition and the town receives the latest edition. Later editions may omit some news items which have been dropped to make room for more dramatic news stories and the late city edition will often omit some of the material that relates specifically to the rural areas.

The storage and conservation of newspapers has been a nightmare for libraries in the past. They are bulky and take up valuable space: if they are bound they are inconvenient to use and terribly heavy to move around. The paper itself also tends to discolour and becomes brittle. Luckily, the business librarian seldom requires to keep extensive back-runs of national newspapers.

In a company library, relevant material from newspapers may well be clipped and filed or even included in an in-house database. If longer runs of national newspapers are required they can be purchased in microform. The public library may feel the need to keep local newspapers from the local history point of view. These can be microfilmed, and guidance is provided by a British Standard, BS 5847.

Microfiche is rather easier to handle, store and use than microfilm but shares some of the same advantages and disadvantages. The main advantage of microform is that it takes up very little room. Secondly, it has a reasonably long shelf life. Until recently, it was thought that microform did not deteriorate significantly, but tests now reveal that such a view was over-sanguine. Microfilm, especially, is easy to tear and microform is adversely affected by climatic conditions. There are, of course, disadvantages. Newspapers often microfilm unsatisfactorily because the quality of the original newsprint is frequently poor and the pages are awkwardly large. If a high reduction ratio is used, the resulting image may be difficult to read. Many readers seem to dislike reading microfilm or microfiche, and there are also expense factors: the process is not cheap and, while readers are cheap and reasonably satisfactory, reader-printers tend to be very expensive and not wholly satisfactory. CD-ROM may well prove to be a storage medium with which readers will feel more at home.

In the business context it seems likely that, in future, most information specialists will rely on commercial online services for newspaper information since the available databases now provide a swift and efficient route to material reported in the newspapers.

The exploitation of newspapers

In most libraries or information centres with an interest in business information, one or more members of staff scan the *Financial Times* and the business sections of the other quality daily and Sunday newspapers. They may also encompass some periodicals in their regular scanning routine, probably *The Economist* and those journals which relate to the work of their parent organisation. Relevant material may well be clipped and filed. Despite the ready availability of online services, many information officers, especially in a company context, still feel it worthwhile retaining their own press cuttings file. If staff time does not allow the provision of this service, an alternative is a subscription to a press cuttings service. The *McCarthy Information Service* provides a service by which articles are available on paper – daily, weekly or on an ad hoc basis. The user can specify the area of business required and the data can be provided on paper or microfiche or online.

Some information units may also feel that the most cost-effective way to handle news-based enquiries is to subscribe to a fee-based service and, in this context, the FINANCIAL TIMES BUSINESS INFORMATION SERVICE would seem to be a probable choice. However the information is obtained, what really matters is how it is disseminated.

Material obtained from newspapers may be included in the current awareness service which may take the form of a weekly list of references or a selection of abstracts. Since the value of newspaper information is dependent on its currency, it is better if a photocopy of the feature itself, mounted and highlighted, can be delivered promptly to the appropriate desk.

How to trace information about newspapers

If you want information about newspapers, i.e. the address of the publisher, the price, the name of the editor, there are three major sources which will provide the required information: *Willings Press Guide*, *Benn's Media Directory* and *BRAD* (*British Rate and Data*). Which of these suits your information centre will depend on the type of enquiries that are received and since none of them are completely comprehensive, it may be worthwhile to have more than one.

Willings Press Guide is a probable choice for the small library or information centre. It appears annually and describes itself as a guide to the press of the UK and to the principal publications of Europe, the Americas, Australasia, the Far East, the Middle East and Africa. Especially useful features include an index which lists newspapers by county and by town within the county. *Willings* is very easy to use in that the UK entries are simply arranged A-Z by title and, although the entries are not as detailed as those in *Benn's* they are adequate for most purposes.

Benn's Media Directory is published in two volumes. In 1986, this directory changed its name from *Press Directory* to *Media Directory* in order to reflect more accurately the comprehensive media coverage which it includes. The UK volume of the directory includes material on broadcasting, including cable and satellite, and electronic publishing. Useful features include an index of publishers, a section on newspapers and another featuring periodicals. *Benn's* provides the most detailed account of the coverage of the publications and the best lists of the names of journalists. The second volume is an international one and provides invaluable coverage of the media all over the world. Since 1986, a free information hot-line gives subscribers access to *Benn's* media files. This could be most helpful in providing details of new periodicals and newspapers, defunct publications and changes of title.

BRAD (*British Rate and Data*) is the only one of these three publications to appear monthly. It is, therefore, very bulky, expensive and, one would hope, more up to date. *BRAD* is aimed more at the advertising industry than at libraries, although it is a very useful library resource. *BRAD*, therefore, includes some features which are not available in the other sources: these include the cost of placing advertisements and some mechanical data, for example the width of pages. Surprisingly, although it appears monthly, *BRAD* is not always as up to date as the user might expect.

A comparison of the information offered by these three sources was made by Susan Turner in November 1986[3].

What kinds of material do press directories cover?

(× = inclusion)	*Benn's*	*BRAD*	*Willings*
National newspapers	×	×	×
Regional newspapers – priced	×	×	×
Regional newspapers – free	×	×	×
Periodicals	×	×	×
Publishers' addresses (as a separate sequence)	×		×
Radio stations	×	×	
Television stations	×	×	
Other advertising media	×	×	
Annual publications	×		×
Directories	×		×
Suppliers of services to the media (e.g. press agencies)	×		×
Media organisations (e.g. trades unions)	×		

It also revealed that all three directories contained a good deal of out-of-date information. *The Times* moved to Wapping on the 30 January 1986, yet the old address was given in all the directories, including *BRAD* for September 1986. Richard Ingrams left *Private Eye* in March 1986 and yet was given as the editor in all three directories, including *BRAD* for September 1986.

The Advertisers Annual is a very useful small directory which, as far as newspapers are concerned, contains the same type of information as *BRAD*. It is divided into three volumes: media, advertising and services. Since it is annual and much smaller than *BRAD*, the entries are shorter and the coverage of journals is less comprehensive. The coverage of newspapers is good and, like *BRAD*, it indicates advertising rates and mechanical data.

PRESTEL, British Telecom's viewdata system, also contains some press information. It does not include national newspapers but does cover regional newspapers, both free and priced. Since the material is submitted by the advertisers, the entries tend to be inconsistent and are not always very informative. *Benn's* hotline facility has been mentioned and since annuals inevitably become swiftly out of date, the potential market for online access to the compilers' files is obviously considerable. Ulrich's directories are available via several hosts including DIALOG and on CD-ROM, while *BRAD* is accessible via MAGIC.

Indexes to newspapers

Indexes to newspapers fall into two main categories: indexes to specific newspapers, and indexes which cover a range of newspapers.

Three British national newspapers produce their own indexes: *The Times*, the *Guardian* and the *Financial Times*. In addition, some libraries may subscribe to the excellent *New York Times Index*.

The Times Index has been in business since 1906. It now indexes *The Times* itself (the late London edition), the *Sunday Times*, the *Times Literary Supplement*, the *Times Educational Supplement*, the *Times Education Supplement Scotland* and the *Times Higher Education Supplement*. The *Times Index* is a reliable source of information on items from all the publications listed above.

Entries are admirably specific, citing not only the date of the issue and the page but also the column in which the item appeared. Unfortunately, the monthly issues usually appear at least two months late. This greatly lessens its utility for the business librarian who is all too frequently asked to retrieve a feature which appeared in the last couple of weeks.

Until January 1977, the *Times Index* was produced quarterly but, from that date, the much more practical monthly paper issues began to appear. The annual bound volumes also appear rather slowly, nearly six months after the end of the year.

From the point of view of usability, however, the *Times Index* is superior to most other newspaper indexes. It contains a sensible list of subject headings and tries to use this consistently throughout and, therefore, it is a clear and predictable reference tool.

The *Guardian Index* commenced in January 1986 on a monthly basis with an annual cumulation. In general, the level of indexing has been judged as inferior to that of the *Times Index* and it is probably of less relevance to the business information specialist since the *Guardian* carries less business news than does *The Times*.

The *Monthly Index to the Financial Times* is certainly the most valuable of the printed indexes to daily newspapers in the business field, since the *FT* is the only purely business-based daily newspaper. This index appears monthly, has an annual cumulation and is also available on microfiche. It used to be in three sections: corporate information, general information and personalities; but now there is one general sequence. Like its competitors, it appears rather late; maybe it is a conspiracy to make us all subscribe to online! My most recent visit to the relevant bookshelf revealed that the August 1988 issue had arrived in my local library on the 30

January 1989. It is a pleasant and well-produced service to use. The indexing is consistent, the typeface is clear and elegant. The information given is basically the same as in the *Times Index*: that is, date, page and a column reference. The entries are compiled from the final London edition but the *Index* also contains entries from the international Frankfurt edition.

It is especially useful for tracing the fluctuations of fortune of major companies and it is also invaluable for information about people, as the *Financial Times* may often be the only source of biographical data about a newly-risen star in the business field.

The *Glasgow Herald* has had a printed index since 1906, but the time-consuming and therefore costly exercise of producing an index was discontinued in 1968. In 1984, the *Herald* approached the Department of Information Science at the University of Strathclyde, seeking funds and expertise to index the newspaper from 1969 to 1984[4]. The project was completed with aid from the Manpower Services Commission. The project has now reached the end of 1987, but current material, which would be of the greatest use to the business community in Scotland, remains unindexed at present.

Indexes which cover a range of newspapers are obviously invaluable to the business researcher but would also be more useful if they appeared with greater speed: they do, however, appear a great deal more swiftly than do the indexes of individual newspapers.

The *Research Index* is probably the most widely used and powerfully loved and hated of the tools available but a comparative newcomer also has considerable merits. This is the *Clover Newspaper Index* and *Company Data Supplement*.

The *Research Index* appears fortnightly and lists articles of financial and business interest appearing in over 100 periodicals and the national press. It is divided into two sections. Section One contains industrial and commercial news listed under subject headings, arranged alphabetically and is on pink paper. Section Two is on blue paper and is in alphabetical sequence under the names of companies. This is an invaluable source of up-to-date material about company takeovers, new directors, share prices and other swiftly-changing news items. The company section and the subject section are both produced as three-monthly amalgamations so the business librarian ends up with 12 months of fortnightly issues and two volumes of amalgamations in three-monthly sections. The binders which Business Surveys issues to *RI* subscribers are too fragile for the weight of a year's contents; the large, ungainly volumes are impossible to keep tidy on the shelves, the binders often being broken. The physical appearance of the product leaves much to be desired in other ways since it is produced on cheap paper and is difficult to read.

Nevertheless, the *Research Index* is an indispensible tool for the business information specialist. It covers a very wide selection of newspapers: the *Daily Express*, *Daily Mail*, *Daily Telegraph*, *Financial Times*, *Guardian*, *Independent*, *Observer*, *Scotsman*, *Sunday Times* and *The Times*.

The virtues of the *Research Index* include the speed with which it appears. The editors aim to publish issues only seven days after the last date of material indexed. In fact, it seems that recently this has not always been possible since many of the 1988 issues did not reach the library shelves for two weeks.

Width of coverage is the *Research Index's* other great strength. Not only does it cover all the major national daily newspapers, it is also an excellent source of citations from trade journals as well as from the general run of economic and business journals, including *The Economist* and *Business Week*.

A helpful small feature is the use of asterisks to indicate any item that is longer than one page. This provides an excellent key to substantial items and, where countries are concerned, often signals the presence of a four to six page special report. The *Research Index* provides the user with other causes for irritation apart from its sheer ungainly bulk. The indexing is very hit-and-miss because it is done at great speed.

Students at the Department of Library and Information Studies, Loughborough University, have produced analyses of the coverage of newspapers in the *Research Index* with regard to thoroughness and accuracy. The *Research Index* claims to be comprehensive but, in fact, this seems not to be the case. One student, who undertook a computer analysis of two weeks' worth of financial and business orientated items in *The Times*, revealed that 20 per cent of the relevant financial articles were omitted and that 3.3 per cent of references cited were inaccurate[5]. Coverage of the *Guardian* during a similar period found that coverage in one week was poor but in a later one excellent[6]: in other words, there was a high degree of variation in both coverage and accuracy. In spite of its faults, however, it is an enormously useful, indeed invaluable, source of up-to-date references to items in the news.

The *Clover Newspaper Index* and *Company Data Supplement* is inexpensive and swift in appearing. There are 46 issues per year and it aims to send the issues out within eight days of the last date of entries. It includes the *Daily Telegraph*, the *Guardian*, *The Times*, the *Financial Times*, the *Independent*, the *Observer*, the *Sunday Times* and their colour supplements. The main part of the Index does include some business information. It is arranged under very broad, and therefore frequently unhelpful, headings, for example, book reviews. Diana Dixon, surveying the *Clover Newspaper Index* in *Refer*, Spring 1987, discovered some omissions when she compared the *Clover Newspaper Index* and *The Times Index*; although it was claimed that the colour supplements were indexed, several articles from one issue of the magazine were omitted, including an article on tourism in Italy and one on railways[7]. The *Company Data Supplement* consists of references to companies in alphabetical order.

Omissions, lack of cross-references and some eccentric indexing are obvious problems with this publication. Its faults are much the same as those of the *Research Index* for much the same reasons; the *Clover Index* is produced as swiftly and as cheaply as possible. It is also difficult to read as the print is small and faint, but the readability has recently improved somewhat. The whole publication has a rather amateurish look but is very good value for money, easy to use and appears with commendable swiftness.

If it is not absolutely current news that is required, it may be worth including the *British Humanities Index* in the search. The title is somewhat misleading, as this publication does include material relating to economics and some business information. It is published by the Library Association and appears quarterly with annual cumulations. The newspapers indexed include the *Financial Times*, the *Independent*, *The Times*, the *Sunday Times*, the *Observer*, and the *Guardian* but, oddly, not the *Daily Telegraph*. The *Independent* and the *Financial Times* were added to the BHI list in 1988. BHI is good for references on banks and banking, a subject area for which the *Research Index* is not always very good. Unfortunately, the quarterly issues take three to four months to appear. The indexing is excellent and the layout and appearance of the pages is pleasing. It is, of course, only of peripheral utility for this subject area.

If the user requires background information about world affairs, current events or political changes in another country, it may be that a news digest service can provide a helpful addition to the pile of newspaper items you have retrieved. The two best known publications of this type are *Keesing's Record of World Events* and *Facts on File*.

Until 1987, *Keesing's* was entitled, *Keesing's Contemporary Archives* but it has now acquired the less archaic title, *Keesings Record of World Events*. *Keesing's* produces monthly news digests accessed by a system of regularly replaced indexes. The indexing has recently been greatly improved and contains entries for countries, subjects and names in one sequence. Each section begins with a summary of major world events and goes on to specific news stories relating to various countries. What appears is, in fact, a very full précis, almost an amalgamation of what a selection of relevant newspapers from all over the world have said about an event. There is now also a bi-monthly publication called *Keesing's UK Record* which concentrates on UK current affairs.

If your company does business with a number of developing countries, even though *Keesing's* is emphatically not a business information source, it may well be worth keeping, since it does record the political and economic state of a country from reliable sources. It is especially good for the UK, Europe and the Third World and background material on developing countries can sometimes be very difficult to find. At the end of each article are listed the newspapers from which the article has been condensed; thus, *Keesing's* can be used both for its summaries of news and as a source of further, more detailed, information.

Facts on File is an American news digest service with a cumulative index. Although it claims world coverage, it has a definite American bias so would only be worth purchasing by a business library if the company had a great deal of business in the United States and, therefore, wanted a reference tool which summarised American news. It is weekly and thus scores from the point of view of topicality over *Keesing's*. It has good indexes which appear twice monthly, three to four weeks after the issue concerned.

Since June 1986, it has increased its European coverage and now has a European section in each issue and a section on developing countries. *Keesing's* still, however, provides superior coverage of these areas. Diana Dixon found that, while Third World coverage had improved, a study of the coverage of Africa in October 1986, revealed only items on Tanzania, the Central African Republic and Nigeria[8]. Unlike *Keesing's*, *Facts on File* does not give the sources of the reports. Apart from news items arranged under the names of the relevant countries, it does include a 'People' section and a section of brief obituaries.

While neither of these reference resources are directly business-orientated, they are worth remembering for background information on world events and countries. A coup in a far-off land can radically damage sales!

Newspaper libraries

If all else fails and you cannot trace the elusive piece which your boss insists was in the *Guardian* two or three weeks ago, be brave and telephone the newspaper's own library.

Almost all newspapers, even the tabloids, have libraries, and many have kind and efficient staff who will be especially helpful if the person at the other end of the telephone line is also a librarian. I have found it necessary to telephone a newspaper library when the news item was removed from the paper before the last edition appeared and hence did not appear in the printed index. A word of warning here! Whereas, until a few years ago, most newspaper libraries would give the general public and other information officers information free, there is now a growing tendency to charge.

The *Financial Times* found their staff spent so much time answering enquiries from the City and the public that they developed a very successful fee-based information service. The *Daily Telegraph* has now also started to charge. These developments will be described in more detail in the chapter on fee-based information services.

Many newspaper libraries not only clip and file stories from their own newspaper but also from their main competitors, but the printed indexes and the rows of filing cabinets may soon largely give way to terminals. News International is currently developing an ambitious database which will eventually include all the News International stable of newspapers; that is, *The Times* and all its subsidiaries, the *Sunday Times*, the *Sun* and the *News of the World*. This development is called the ELECTRONIC LIBRARY SERVICE. *The Times* is already available on PROFILE in full text, but it is envisaged that, ultimately, the Electronic Library Service material will be marketed via several hosts, and that some of the material will also be available on CD-ROM[9].

News online

Since printed indexes to newspapers either lack comprehensiveness and consistency or appear rather slowly, online can be seen as the best medium through which to obtain material from newspapers. Online has the facility for swift updating of material and since most newspaper articles are not of great length, it is possible, via some of the available databases, to obtain the full text of the relevant article. More and more business information specialists who have access to online sources are going straight to, for example, TEXTLINE for their information.

In a book which aims only to offer an introduction to business information, it is neither possible nor necessary to provide a comprehensive and detailed account of all the databases which provide news online especially since changes of ownership in the online industry may render any information out of date by the time of publication.

I propose, therefore, to describe only a selection of the major databases in this area and, fortunately, they also illustrate the different types of news databases which are currently available.

TEXTLINE is probably the most heavily used database in the country. It is used both by information specialists and by end-users since it is menu-driven and thus easy to use. TEXTLINE's coverage is really extensive. It includes national newspapers, business journals, press releases, corporate financial reports, news tapes, newsletters and some stockbrokers' surveys. Material is translated from French, German, Italian, Japanese, Spanish and Danish, and there is excellent coverage of European newspapers and sources from all over the world. Thus, UK news receives thorough coverage and it also provides a good source for overseas news.

In June 1988, they rather belatedly added the *Independent* to the database which effectively gives them coverage of all the quality daily and Sunday papers as well as the *Daily Mail*, the *Daily Express* and the *Standard*. They also index all the major regional dailies, including the *Aberdeen Press and*

Journal, the *Western Mail* and the *Belfast Telegraph*: a service of immense value, since material from these sources is often difficult to locate via other means.

The entries on TEXTLINE are sometimes virtually full text, while in other cases, they are detailed abstracts. This database should not be overlooked as a source of recent financial data about companies since indexers always include any financial data that appears in the original. Reuter also owns DATALINE, a small database which provides corporate financial analysis and is marketed with TEXTLINE.

NEWSLINE is Textline's up-to-the-minute service and is ideal for answering that query about an event which happened yesterday or even earlier on the day of the search. NEWSLINE consists of headlines only of news items which have appeared in the last few days. Only a small selection of newspapers and journals are scanned for this service but, for most of the titles included, NEWSLINE boast that the headlines of the day's stories are available by 9 a.m. on the day of publication.

Since Reuter bought TEXTLINE, they have incorporated the full-text of all Reuter articles into the service. They have also made a substantial investment in additional computer capacity which, it is hoped, will improve the quality of the service.

TEXTLINE's strengths are its excellent coverage, its timespan – being the oldest of the British news databases, it goes back to 1980 – and its ease of use. The disappointing factors, especially from the point of view of the experienced online user, are the slow and cumbersome search software and the very slow response time. A detailed analysis of TEXTLINE can be found in *Online Business Information*, January 1987[10].

NEXIS, the American equivalent of TEXTLINE, is a much more sophisticated product. It provides full text swiftly, using far more advanced software than its British counterpart, but can be very expensive to use, nonetheless. From the British point of view, however, it obviously does not include the wide range of UK sources available on TEXTLINE but it does offer the full text of the *Financial Times* as well as the *The Economist* and many useful overseas sources.

A company which was involved in a great many business transactions in the US might well find that a subscription to NEXIS would be a good investment in spite of the expense. There is now a London-based offline print facility so that search results can be mailed first class to UK subscribers or sent by courier rather than arriving several days later from Ohio. MEAD DATA CENTRAL owns NEXIS and LEXIS, a full text legal database, and claims that the two facilities combined are the largest full text database in the world.

Like TEXTLINE, it is a comparatively old database and, therefore, most publications are held since 1975. It is strong in the business area and in high technology and prides itself on providing excellent coverage of technical innovation and of personalities. It is updated daily from the previous day's newspapers. While it cannot compete with TEXTLINE's comprehensive coverage of UK data, it is currently infinitely superior as regards search software and response time.

PROFILE BUSINESS INFORMATION is the major full text online news information service in the UK. There have been many changes of ownership in the online industry in the last two to three years and one of these was the *Financial Times*' acquisition of DATASOLVE, which hosted the database which used to be called WORLD REPORTER. Now renamed PROFILE, the service has added the *FT*'s Business Reports to their database list and have continued to enlarge their list of newspapers. In December 1988, the *Independent* was included so that PROFILE can now claim to be able to display the full text of all the UK quality daily newspapers. It also hosts *Today* and claims that this is the first tabloid to be available in full text online. The *Sunday Times* and the *Sunday Telegraph* are also on PROFILE as is the Associated Press newswire service. In addition, PROFILE also hosts MCCARTHY ONLINE, the online version of McCarthy's old established full text press cuttings service, and the Department of Trade and Industry's new European database, SPEARHEAD.

PROFILE's strengths are the fact that it is full text and that the commands are so simple and easy to remember: the three basic commands are Select, Get and Pick. Most hosts and databases offer training and competition in the training field is fierce. Many training courses are free and others are very cheap. PROFILE are very conscious of the marketing value of good training and have now produced a training disc which was reviewed by Sheila Webber in *Online Newsletter*, January/February 1989[11].

There are a number of other sources of newspaper-based information online but TEXTLINE and PROFILE are certainly the two services which librarians and information specialists in the UK are most likely to use. Other services available will be mentioned only briefly in this chapter. PREDICASTS includes F & S INDEX which claims to have the broadest coverage of business subjects of any online database. It is very useful for tracing material in business journals, financial newsletters and newspapers, and indexes many international sources including the *Financial Times*, and *Le Monde*, but it is obviously strongest when indexing American material. PREDICASTS databases are hosted by both DIALOG and DATA-STAR. NEWSNET, another American service, concentrates on business newsletters and wire services.

BIS INFORMAT NEWSFILE includes abstracts of over 500 newspapers and trade journals, material from a range of wire services, broadcasts and the publications of institutions, including banks, and a very useful selection of European newspapers. It is available on PERGAMON FINANCIAL DATA SERVICES.

It seems logical that access to databases, whether online or on a videoscreen, will replace the storage of piles of bound and unbound newspapers and even the cabinets of microfiche and microfilm. Most of the news-based services are easy to use and can, therefore, be used by the end-user, that is, the person who actually requires the data.

Some of these services are rather slow but most of them can be interrogated more swiftly and with superior search results by a trained online searcher: for example, TEXTLINE allows the experienced researcher to use 'short prompts' which circumvent the long and tedious repetition of the menus. Thus, in spite of their ease of use, these databases are often still best utilised for maximum efficiency by an information specialist.

Most news-based databases not only include material from newspapers but also cover a selection of the major newswire services, for example, Associated Press. This material is invaluable especially for stories relating to the smaller developing countries which often are inadequately covered in the national newspapers of the developed world.

Information from newspapers in whatever form remains a crucial resource for the business information specialist as a great deal of business information is disseminated solely via this medium. Remember that a few minutes scanning the business pages of a good newspaper is never time wasted. Knowing the way around the business information sections of the national newspapers is a skill no true business information specialist can afford to be without

References

1. CAMPBELL, M. J. *Manual of business library practice*, 2nd ed. Bingley, 1985, 128.
2. McGROTHER, C. Business news coverage in national daily newspapers. *Business Information Review*, 3, 4, April 1987, 23–31.
3. TURNER, S. E. *A guide to UK press directories*. Department of Library and Information Studies, Loughborough University of Technology, 1986–87. *Unpublished project*.
4. BAIRD, P. et al. A newspaper's index finger. *Times Higher Education Supplement*, 20 September 1985, 17.
5. BROWN, S. *The 'Research Index': just how good is it?*. Department of Library and Information Studies, Loughborough University of Technology, 1985–86. *Unpublished project*.
6. NEALE, I. M. *An Analysis of 'Research Index' with particular reference to the 'Guardian' and 'Campaign'*. Department of Library and Information Studies, Loughborough University of Technology, 1985–86. *Unpublished project*.

7. DIXON, D. I think it happened a few weeks ago ... access to recent news, *Refer*, 4, 3, Spring 1987, 7.
8. Ibid. 8–9.
9. WITHEY, R. *The Times* database, a paper delivered at an Aslib Midlands branch meeting held at Birmingham Central Library on 9 November 1988. *Unpublished.*
10. RYAN, F. Testdrive-Textline revisited. *Online Business Information*, January 1987, 2–10.
11. WEBBER, S. PROFILE information training disc package. *Online Newsletter*, 59, Jan/Feb 1989, 22–24.

Further reading

DIXON, D. I think it happened a few weeks ago ... access to recent news. *Refer*, 4, 3, Spring 1987, 6–9.

McGROTHER, C. Business news coverage in national daily newspapers. *Business Information Review*, 3, 4, April 1987, 23–31.

WHATMORE, G. Newspapers and other material on recent events. In: HIGGENS, G. L. (ed.) *Printed reference material*, 2nd ed. Library Association, 1984, 196–218.

Guides to newspapers

Advertising Annual, 1925, Annual. British Media Publications, Windsor Court, East Grinstead House, East Grinstead, West Sussex RH19 1XE.

Benn's Media Directory, 1846, Annual (Formerly *Benn's Press Directory*). Benn's Business Information Services Ltd, Sovereign Way, Tonbridge, Kent TN9 1RW.

BRAD (*British Rate and Data*), Directories and Annuals, Bi-annual. MacLean Hunter Ltd, MacLean Hunter House, Chalk Lane, Cockfosters Road, Barnet, Herts EN4 0BU.

Willings Press Guide, 1874, Annual. British Media Publications, Windsor Court, East Grinstead House, East Grinstead, West Sussex RH19 1XE.

Indexes to newspapers

Research Index, 1965, Fortnightly. Business Surveys Ltd, PO Box 21, Dorking, Surrey RH4 2YU.

Clover Newspaper Index, 1986, 46 issues per annum 32 Ickwell Road, Northill, Biggleswade, Beds SG18 9AB.
British Humanities Index, 1962, Quarterly. Formerly Subject Index to Periodicals 1915, Library Association Publishing, 7 Ridgmount Street, London WC1E 7AE.

Background information on world affairs

Facts on file, News Digest, 1941, weekly. Formerly Facts on File Weekly. Facts on File Ltd, Collins Street, Oxford OX4 1XJ.
Keesing's record of world events. Formerly Keesing's Contemporary Archives, 1931, monthly. Longman Group UK Ltd, 6th Floor, Westgate House, The High Harlow, Essex CM20 1NE.

Useful addresses

Databases and hosts

BIS Informat Newsfile, VO-TEC Centre, Hambridge Lane, Newbury, Berkshire RG14 5HA.
Data-Star (UK), Plaza Suite, 114 Jermyn Street, London SW1Y 6HJ.
DIALOG Information Services (UK), Woodside, Hinksey Hill, Oxford.
Financial Times Business Information Service, Financial Times, 10 Cannon Street, London EC4P 4BY.
McCarthy Information Service, Ash Walk, Warminster, Wiltshire BA12 8BY.
Mead Data Central (UK), (NEXIS and LEXIS), MDC International, 1 St Katharine's Way, London E1 9UN.
Pergamon Financial Data Services, Achilles House, Western Avenue, London W3 0UA.
Predicasts (UK), 8–10 Denman Street, London W1V 7RF.
Profile Business Information, Sunbury House, 79 Staines Road West, Sunbury-on-Thames, Middlesex TW16 7AH.
Reuter Textline, 85 Fleet Street, London EC4P 4AJ.

Chapter Four

BRITISH OFFICIAL PUBLICATIONS
(or a route through the minefield)

Jo Haythornthwaite

No category of material appears more daunting to the young business specialist than those rows of command papers, the annual collections of impenetrable statistics and the seemingly endless flow of *Hansards*. Actually, once one gets over the feelings of panic engendered by the sheer bulk of material, those dull-looking tomes often provide the answer to a business query and frequently contain a distractingly fascinating wealth of interesting if, at the time irrelevant, information.

Non-statistical publications

Undoubtedly, statistical publications will be the category of government publication which you will consult most on a regular basis. It is, however, a mistake to forget or discount the considerable value of the non-statistical material which emanates from government departments. Some of these publications provide background material which supplements the statistics, while others provide information and guidance. It is these non-statistical publications which I shall describe first.

A brief account of how official publications are generated seems necessary at this point.

HMSO publishes around 9,000 new titles per year but the bulk of UK Government publications are not published by HMSO. Each year, more and more are being published by the government departments themselves. Government publications are divided into:

Parliamentary publications: publications which have been presented to,

or arisen from, Parliament and are needed by Parliament to conduct her day-to-day business, for example, bills.
Non-parliamentary publications: publications which do not arise directly from the business of Parliament, but rather set out to provide the public with information, for example, *The General Household Survey*.

HMSO is responsible for all Parliamentary publications but only some non-Parliamentary ones.

Parliamentary publications include:

Hansard: the record of what is said in Parliament.
Command papers: papers presented to Parliament by command, for example, reports of Royal Commissions. It is useful to remember that Royal Commissions are composed of people other than MPs 'The great and the good' and because these are very busy people often take years to produce their reports; whereas parliamentary committees are made up of MPs only, who accept written and verbal evidence from organisations and the public and produce results rather more quickly.
Bills
Acts

Non-parliamentary publications include:

Statutory instruments: regulations made by a Minister under the authority of an Act.
Publications of departments of an informational kind: These can include leaflets aimed at farmers or small business men or women and also the many collections of statistics.

How to trace UK official publications

HMSO publications

HMSO publish a range of catalogues and publicity material which make it relatively easy to trace their publications.

The *Daily List* appears every day except Saturdays, Sundays and public holidays and can be posted out to subscribers daily or, at a rather cheaper rate, in weekly batches. It includes parliamentary and non-parliamentary publications, some publications of international organisations, Statutory Instruments and all Northern Ireland publications.

The *Monthly Catalogue* excludes Statutory Instruments, for which there is a separate monthly list, but otherwise has the same coverage as the *Daily List*. It is indexed and, therefore, is a very useful reference tool but delays in its appearance cause great inconvenience to official publications librarians.

The *Annual Catalogue* also appears rather slowly and, like the *Monthly Catalogue* excludes Statutory Instruments. Despite attempts to improve the standard of indexing in these catalogues, they still display a certain eccentricity. The searcher must scan their indexes with persistence and imagination! There is also a separate *International Organisations Annual Catalogue* which lists all the international publications received by HMSO. It must be understood that this is by no means a comprehensive catalogue of the publications of international organisations, it is simply a catalogue of the publications of those organisations for whom HMSO acts as a UK agent.

PRESTEL lists current HMSO publications, usually on the day of publication. This can be a useful service if you need to find out about a publication the day before the *Daily List* comes by post. International organisations' publications are listed on the day that they go on sale from HMSO. It is also possible to order HMSO publications via PRESTEL.

HMSO in print on microfiche is available quarterly via an annual subscription. The fiches do not include international organisations' publications or publications relating to Northern Ireland.

Sectional Lists record all the in-print publications of specific government departments. They are currently being reorganised and very few are in print.

HMSO has now become far more publicity-conscious and is producing a range of useful subject catalogues and leaflets on topics which include *Social Issues*, *Business*, *Information Technology*, and *Central Statistical Office Titles*. These are available free as are the lists of forthcoming books, *New books HMSO*, which look very much like commercial publishers' catalogues, since they include photographs and two or three paragraphs of enthusiastic prose about each forthcoming publication. In these brochures, HMSO tries to bring to the attention of booksellers, librarians and the public, those titles which they believe are of general interest and, therefore, worth serious marketing.

HMSO's bibliographical services database is also available online via BLAISE-LINE. The database is a cumulation of the monthly and annual catalogues published by HMSO since 1976 and is updated monthly.

The file was launched in April 1989 and includes items published and distributed by HMSO on behalf of government departments, other British bodies and international organisations such as the EC. BLAISE claim that the files will have a multiplicity of users beyond the purely bibliographical and should be invaluable to official publications libraries and business people who wish to answer questions on subjects as diverse as 'What are the duties of company directors?' or 'What EEC and government initiatives have been issued in preparation for the Single European Market in 1992?'.

Official publications not published by HMSO

Until 1980, tracing official publications other than those published by HMSO was exceedingly difficult. In 1980, however, Chadwyck-Healey began to produce their *Catalogue of British official publications not published by HMSO*. This invaluable bibliographical tool appears bi-monthly with annual bound volumes and has made the librarian's life far easier since it provides access to information about the less easy to trace items of official publishing. A document delivery service is available on microfiche, and the *Catalogue* is also available online via DIALOG.

There is now a new development, *The catalogue of United Kingdom official publications* (*UKOP*) published on CD-ROM by HMSO and Chadwyck-Healey. This combines HMSO and non-HMSO publications in a convenient bibliographical file on compact disc. The material will appear on discs every quarter and each disc will be issued within four weeks of the end of the three month period it records. The first disc appeared in March 1989.

Current awareness

In addition to the government's own current awareness services and the Chadwyck-Healey catalogue, it may be worthwhile subscribing to publications produced by other publishers which provide a specialised current awareness service. Two publications that spring to mind rather confusingly share the same title: *Business and Government.*

The longest established of these is published by Key Facts and was established in 1981. It is a slight monthly newsletter which provides two or three paragraph abstracts under a variety of headings including business opportunities, education, statistics and industry. It scans the publications of HMSO government departments, nationalised industries, research organisations, quangos, the EC, Eurostat, OECD, Council of Europe, GATT, IMF, FAO, IAEA, WHO, UN and Unesco.

In 1989, a second newsletter of the same title was launched. It is a bimonthly magazine which is designed to be a two-way street for ideas and information between business and government. It is especially aimed at the second and third tier of business who are not as well informed as the big companies who have easy access to the corridors of power. It has a 'people' section which includes biographies of senior civil servants with photographs.

What is likely to be relevant to business?

Almost anything can be relevant to business at different times. What is absolutely certain is that up-to-date intelligence relating to new governmental legislation, hints of government intentions indicated in a ministerial reply, a few hitherto unpublished statistics languishing in a written answer, a full report of a ministerial speech outside the House and available via a press release; all these can be essential sources of business information.

Debates

That up-to-date account of what a Minister said is often difficult to locate if it happened in the last few days. As *Hansard* indexes appear slowly it may mean leafing through the debates for the previous two or three weeks. If the Minister's department will add your library to their mailing list for press releases, this may ease the problem. Departmental press offices are becoming more cost-conscious, however. Whereas, at one time, most departments and quangos were only too happy to add libraries to their mailing lists, now many only supply press releases to the press. If you do not receive the relevant press releases and have difficulty in tracing the speech in *Hansard*, perhaps because it only took place earlier that week and so the relevant issue has not yet arrived, *The Times* still provides the best coverage of debates of all the major newspapers. Since the *Times Index* is also slow to appear, glancing through the paper copies may well be the only answer. In these circumstances, online is the swiftest and most efficient method of tracing the speech. TEXTLINE is excellent for this type of query and NEWSLINE is ideal for locating recent material. Some libraries may also have access to the House of Commons' own database POLIS and it should also be remembered that a telephone call to the House of Commons Public Information Office may provide the answer to your question. Not only do they provide very helpful information very swiftly, they also produce a *Weekly Information Bulletin* which documents everything that has happened the previous week and what is scheduled for the current week. If you get a regular flow of enquiries relating to parliamentary topics a subscription is essential.

While on the subject of *Hansard*, it is worth remembering that it contains not only debates but also written answers. Written answers occur when a Minister is asked a question to which he/she cannot provide an immediate answer. The Minister goes away and asks a researcher to find the relevant data, and it is later published in *Hansard* as a written answer. Often very important information, including valuable statistics, can be found only in written answers.

Command papers frequently address subjects of importance to the business community. I have already mentioned that these may be reports emanating from the labours of Royal Commissions or from a Select Committee, but command numbers are also given to other categories of material, including white papers. A white paper is usually a firm statement of government policy, whereas a green paper is a tentative statement of government proposals, a testing of the water, suggestions published to stimulate discussion. A recent example which is fresh in the minds of most librarians was the green paper on public libraries[1].

Acts

Acts of Parliament may be essential reading in the industrial context, for example, legislation relating to health and safety at work. An Act starts life as a bill. There are two main types of bill: public bills and private bills. Private bills are now very rare and should not be confused with private members' bills which are, in fact, public bills! There is a great deal in the way our legislature works that seems very strange and archaic to the layperson.

All bills have a long gestation period before they see the light of day as publications. Before a bill is drafted, a committee may well have discussed it and the relevant department will have undertaken lengthy research. The bill will then be drafted by a Parliamentary Counsel in the Office of Parliamentary Counsel. It is this counsel's job to ensure that the bill is unassailably good law. Counsels are very highly paid and extensively-trained lawyers who study precedents with the aid of LEXIS (the legal database), *Statutes in force* and other sources including the 'old boy' network.

Bills are usually printed on pale green paper and are published after the first or second reading. After the second reading, which usually involves a lengthy debate, the bill is sent to a committee. During discussions in committee, amendments may be tabled. The next stage is the report stage when amendments can be discussed in detail. Finally, as far as the House of Commons is concerned, there is a third reading before the bill is passed to the House of Lords. Eventually, if the bill passes successfully through both Houses, it becomes a Public General Act.

It will be the business information specialist's task to select those acts which the organisation may need to refer to regularly. It may be a matter of scanning newspapers or the *Daily List* for crucial legislation or it may be worth subscribing to *Statutes in force*.

HMSO's selected subscription service is a helpful way of ensuring that one obtains all the relevant material within a specified subject area. Such a subscription can save a lot of searching time if official publications are frequently used. Acts are sometimes not crystal clear to the layperson, and here also it is useful to note that HMSO frequently produces useful elucidatory material; for example, an explanatory book on the *Companies Act, 1985*.

Publications of specific departments and quangos

Certain government departments and quangos produce material of special relevance to the business information specialist.

Department of Trade and Industry

The publications of the DTI are likely to figure largely in the stock of most business libraries. The DTI produces a mass of statistics, but also a quantity of informational material.

In a recently published paper in *Aslib Proceedings*, Karen Johnson and myself scrutinised the role of press releases and, since the DTI is one of the largest departmental producers of press releases, their output was a particularly useful one to examine.[3] The DTI issues two types of news bulletins; first, facts and figures and secondly, pro-active information, that is, details of ministerial visits and speeches. The department attaches especial importance to their informational press releases on subjects including government policy relating to industry, consumer legislation and the safety aspects of industry. They are exceedingly conscious of the value of a high profile in the media and of the importance of style and colour. The DTI press office is staffed mainly by ex-journalists who appreciate that a good house style sells content. The librarian may also find it helpful to know that the DTI keeps back issues and also holds the material on a database. Recent stringent cut-backs have led to greater caution on the part of government departments in adding new names to their mailing lists and some departments and quangos are now charging organisations other than the press. For those who do not wish to receive all press releases many are reported efficiently in *The Times*, the *Financial Times*, the *Guardian*, the *Daily Telegraph* and the *Independent* and the full text of most news bulletins is usually available in *British Business*.

British Overseas Trade Board

The BOTB was set up in 1972 to take over export promotion work from the DTI, of which it remains a part. They provide information and advice to exporters and collect and disseminate overseas market information. They also provide advice and help to individual firms and organise trade promotions. The advice given by the BOTB is free and can include information on market prospects, status reports on potential overseas contacts and technical information relating to standards and regulations overseas.

A regularly revised leaflet lists BOTB services, the *Annual Report* is available free of charge and BOTB activities and publications are well reported in *British Business*. Other BOTB leaflets explain specific services, for example, the *Export Marketing Research Scheme* and *Trade Fairs Overseas*.

The BOTB has a range of Area Advisory Boards, for example, the Japan Trade Advisory Group, the Sino-British Trade Advisory Group, the Committee for Middle East Trade and the South East Asia Trade Advisory Group. The last mentioned of these groups is especially active and produces a bulletin, the *Seatag Bulletin*, which appears quarterly.

There is a special desk for most of the major countries with which Britain does business. The staff who man such a desk have access to a wealth of information and have considerable expertise. These desks are responsible for producing detailed and lengthy country profiles, which look at the economy, trade market opportunities, marketing methods, economic conditions and the investment situation of the countries concerned and also provide a mass of information for visitors to the country, including details of currency, hours of business, entry regulations, etc. A literally pocket-sized series which gives the businessman or woman all the essential facts about a country is the *Hints to Exporters* series. These booklets provide an immensely useful service and are updated regularly.

The business information specialists should not only know about BOTB publications but should get to know the location and staff of the nearest BOTB office and refer enquiries onwards to that office when this seems appropriate. The DTI is currently trying to increase the awareness of the business community as to the services that the DTI and the BOTB can offer and are especially concerned to reach the small businessperson.

In addition, the DTI are currently disseminating a great deal of data relating to 1992 and the *Single European Market* and, in conjunction with this, they have mounted an energetic advertising campaign. A 'phone call to 081-200 1992 will enable the library to receive a newsletter, a range of SEM orientated publicity and news bulletin and information about the DTI's European database, SPEARHEAD, which is hosted by PROFILE (for more information on this aspect of the DTI's work, see Chapter 5 by Mike Hopkins).

No other government department is as central to the work of the business librarian as is the DTI but, depending on the industry in which the business information specialist works, or the geographical and industrial area in which the public business library is located, various departments and their publications may play an essential part in the enquiry work that is received. It is quite likely that the publications of the Departments of Energy, Agriculture, Fisheries and Food, Health, Social Security, Employment, Transport and Defence, will be of value.

Quangos

The hideous word, quango, means quasi-autonomous national government organisation. Such organisations are government-funded but have a degree of independence as to the way in which they run their operation and the information which they disseminate. Many of these organisations are of great relevance to the business community. Their addresses and brief information as to their activities can be located via the invaluable CBD directory, *Councils, Committees and Boards*.

Three quangos which provide information and services vital to the business community are the *Equal Opportunities Commission* (EOC), the *Manpower Services Commission* (MSC) and the *Advisory Conciliation and Arbitration Service* (ACAS). The *Equal Opportunities Commission* is a good example of a quango which provides material which is of great importance to business and industry. They produce many explanatory leaflets and booklets; some of which are free and some of which are priced, for example, the *Equal Opportunities Commission Code of Practice*, 1985, £1.50. They also produce press releases at the rate of about one a week and all their formal investigations have to be publicised in this way.

Local government publications

Local government publications have proliferated in the last 10 years and, regrettably, there is no adequate bibliographical control at present. Many local government publications never appear in the *British National Bibliography* (BNB) and, therefore, are difficult for the business information specialist to obtain. They are often of especial relevance to public library business librarians who must contact their local authority and try to obtain copies of all that is new and of use. When the local authority has a library, the process is made easier since a relationship can be developed between the local government librarian and the staff of the public library business information service. Mutual help and co-operation can solve problems of information and acquisition. Likewise, a company may well be radically affected by changes in local government practices and may also need to obtain some local government publications. The business librarian must be a social being as contacts are often the best source of both information and documents.

A helpful publication is *Local authority information sources, a guide to publications, databases and services* which emanates from SCOOP, the Standing Committee on Official Publications. This group is part of the *Library Association Information Services Group* and has an active publishing policy in the official publications area and is, therefore, a group to which it is helpful to belong, as the *Government Libraries Group* may be also if your work involves a great deal of enquiries relating to government data.

UK official publications online

Government statistics are available online via a wide range of hosts but non-statistical UK governmental material is mainly available on POLIS. POLIS began life as the House of Commons' own in-house database but is now marketed commercially. It includes parliamentary information and EC data and draws material from parliamentary questions, proceedings of the House and official publications. It would be the obvious database to interrogate for material from recent debates. There is a thesaurus and a user manual and training courses are available. The system is moderately sophisticated and, initially, rather difficult to use, but like many sophisticated systems, it can be used very swiftly and efficiently by the regular user.

SPEARHEAD has already been noted as a source of European data, and up-to-date information relating to government decisions and ministerial statements can also be retrieved by interrogating TEXTLINE and/or PROFILE.

Bibliographical details about HMSO publications are available via BLAISE-LINE, DIALOG and now also on CD-ROM from Chadwyck-Healey.

Sources of business statistics

Learning to find and use statistics effectively is one of the more daunting but ultimately satisfying tasks that falls to the information scientist. There is some truth in the old adage, 'lies, damned lies and statistics', since some statistics are certainly more authoritative than others and the selective use of statistics in the House of Commons frequently demonstrates that both sides of the House can marshall perfectly accurate sets of figures to tell very different stories.

As regards the authority and reliability of statistics, it is helpful to make the time to read the introductions to the collections in order to ascertain how the statistics were collected; for example, a more or less comprehensive survey like the *Census* is obviously reliable, whereas a sample survey can produce misleading findings; for example, *Household food consumption and expenditure: national food survey* is compiled from a sample survey of 7,000 interviews. It is not surprising, therefore, that if, for example, you want to discover what percentage of the population buys books regularly you can find two or three different answers in UK government sources, all compiled in different ways.

The Government Statistical Service

The GSS comprises the statistical divisions of all the major departments and the Business Statistics Office, the Office of Population Censuses and Surveys and the Central Statistical Office, which co-ordinates the system. The government is by far the largest provider of statistics in the country. Although the GSS's primary role is to serve the needs of Parliament, the material is also of inestimable value to the business world and especially to the marketing sector. Social statistics reveal consumer trends, export figures reveal gaps in markets, while import figures provide warnings regarding the strength of foreign competition.

The GSS produces a small but useful free annual booklet, *Government statistics; a brief guide to sources*, which lists the major sources with annotations and also provides the addresses and telephone numbers of government departments with contact points for specific pieces of information; for example, analysis of company accounts; material on this subject is available at the DTI's Business Statistics Office, 071-215 5000 extension 2580.

The Central Statistical Office

In the UK, we have a decentralised system: that is, all government departments have their own statistical departments and the CSO has a co-ordinating role, only producing the overall national statistics in annual compilations, for example, *Annual abstract of statistics* and the guides; for example, *Guide to official statistics*.

Guides to UK statistics

The CSO is striving to make UK government statistics both more user-friendly and more commercial, and the first step in this direction came in 1976 when the *Guide to official statistics* was first published. Since then, it has appeared irregularly and at one point it was even rumoured that it might be discontinued but, to sighs of relief from all its devoted fans, it has continued to appear. If you are asked to find any statistics which are likely to emanate from the government and you are uncertain as to the best place in which to start your search, the very best place is undoubtedly the *Guide to official statistics*. It aims to help people who need statistical information but do not know where to start looking – a frequent dilemma! It covers all official and some important non-official sources of statistics for the UK and the Isle of Man. It is divided into chapters with headings such as Employment, and lists both regular and irregular sources of statistics. Although by no means foolproof or entirely comprehensive, the *Guide* is a godsend and, undoubtedly, the best starting-point for a statistical search. Useful special features include a bibliography and a list of government department contact points for use if additional information is required.

Statistical News, to some extent, provides a quarterly supplement to the *Guide* as it is a journal which offers a quarterly summary of current developments in statistics, both national and international.

A new small guide to statistics is *Key data* which is an annual research guide aimed at students. It first appeared in 1986 and is modestly priced. It is an attempt to marshall the 'key' statistics for students and might also be a helpful short compilation to keep on the shelves of a small public library reference collection or in a small company information centre. Among other topics, it features economic, social and industrial life, manufacturing production, transport, communications and finance.

General digests of statistics

The business librarian may spend a lot of time searching among the specifically business orientated statistical publications but he/she may also often either find an adequate answer in one of the major general statistical publications or start the search there and then pass on to more specialised sources.

The *Annual abstract of statistics* is published by the CSO and contains over 400 tables giving annual statistics usually for a run of 10 years. This is what is called a *time series*. Statistics are contributed by all the major government departments and the *Annual abstract* can, therefore, be used as a starting-point for a search since one is always given the name of the department from which the data originated.

Monthly digest of statistics

This is a source of more up-to-date figures but is only a collection of the main series from all government departments. It thus contains far fewer statistical series than does the *Annual abstract*. For the statistically-illiterate, that is, most of us, the *Monthly digest* produces an invaluable annual notes and definitions supplement which is well worth reading

Social Trends

Social Trends is both entertaining and easy to use. It is produced by the Government Statistical Service of the CSO and first appeared in 1970. It brings together some of the key social and demographic series and illustrates their findings via colour charts and tables. Material on health, education, housing, the environment, household expenditure and leisure activities is presented in a graphic and entertaining way. Although other government publications provide consumer statistics in greater detail or from a different point of view, *Social Trends* may present your marketing department with just the crisp, clear view of current trends that they need. The 1989 *Social Trends*, for example, pinpoints a drop in fat consumption; butter consumption especially has fallen sharply. The consumption of eggs has fallen by a third in the last 25 years regardless of the salmonella controversy, white bread has been supplanted by wholemeal and we are eating far less red meat and more chicken – invaluable information for the food industry.

Publishers, booksellers and librarians would be interested to find that women read more books than men. The statistics relating to sport and leisure given in *Social Trends* could also be vital to a company in the leisure business wondering at which age groups to target its advertising campaign. Often *Social Trends* may lead the enquirer on to the original source of the statistics; for example, to the *Family Expenditure Survey*. Another feature of *Social Trends* which can be valuable is the long articles at the beginning of each issue which elucidate perceived social trends; for example, the 1975 edition carried a valuable paper by Sally Holtermann on areas of urban deprivation in Great Britain.

Regional Trends

Regional Trends is another annual, this time displaying a selection of the main statistics that are available on a regional basis. It is, therefore, self-evidently, indispensible when decisions are taken as to which part of the country is most suitable for a specific product launch, new shopping complex, leisure centre or localised advertising campaign. *Regional Trends*, for example, is a good source from which to obtain a regional break-down of the recent sharp rises in house prices. The 1988 edition, number 23, reveals a substantial decline in cigarette smoking in every region, but the Scots still smoke the most while people in the southwest smoke least. *Regional Trends* repays attention since the information it supplies can be crucial to the planning strategy of a manufacturer and indispensible to the marketing division.

Scottish Abstract of Statistics

In addition to these general digests of UK Government statistics, the annual *Scottish Abstract of Statistics* should be noted if your company is located in Scotland, or has substantial business links North of the Border. This can be supplemented by the six-monthly *Scottish Economic Bulletin*.

Welsh Economic Trends

Welsh Economic Trends appears annually.

Major economic sources

Economic Trends

Economic Trends is a monthly journal which comprises a commentary and a selection of tables and charts which provide a background to trends in the UK economy; for example, trends in employment and unemployment. An *Annual Supplement* includes very long runs of quarterly figures for all the main series. Unless your business library deals with a good deal of economics-based queries, it is probable that *Economic Trends* might not be considered a valid subscription since the price of this publication has escalated alarmingly since it became Government policy to make official publications pay their way.

UK Balance of Payments

The two other major economic sources are known somewhat confusingly as the 'blue book' and the 'pink book'. The 'pink book' is really entitled, *UK Balance of Payments* and is, as the title suggests, the basic reference book for balance of payments statistics.

UK National Accounts

The business information officer will probably use the annual 'blue book' more frequently. The 'blue book' is, in fact, really entitled, *UK National Accounts* and used to be called, *National Income and Expenditure*. It is the place to look for detailed estimates of national product, income and expenditure for the United Kingdom. It provides the information in *time series*, that is, it provides comparative statistics over a number of years and so makes it possible to make comparisons; for example, how much was spent by UK consumers on bread and cereals at current prices in two different years? Has the amount spent on fire services by local authorities increased in the last five years?

Consumer statistics

Some consumer statistics are readily available in the *Annual abstract*, *Social Trends*, *Regional Trends*, and even in the 'blue book', which is invaluable for consumer expenditure trends; but the librarian servicing staff in a consumer industry would certainly subscribe to some or all of the official publications which are concerned solely with consumer statistics. The problem, however, is that while the specialised consumer publications are invaluable for the detail which they present, they appear very slowly. It is, therefore, essential to supplement data found in them with the more up-to-date, if less detailed, information to be found in *Social Trends* and the other more general statistics sources.

General Household Survey

The *General Household Survey* is based on a continuous sample survey of households relating to a wide range of social and socio-economic policy areas. It has been annual since 1971 but appears very slowly, usually two to three years after the year which has been surveyed. It is published by the Office of Population Censuses and Surveys. The detailed survey information which it offers complements the existing statistics and throws light on social situations in a way relevant to policy, as the reasoning behind the production of this particular survey was that it would provide politicians and planners with information which would enable them to plan the country's social policy more effectively. The *GHS*, however, has incidentally proved to be of great general interest since it includes survey data on population, housing, employment, leisure, education and health. It could be very useful to companies in the house building and home improvement areas since it contains a great deal of data on home ownership and house-related topics. It can answer questions such as what percentage of the population take part in active sports, what age group go to the cinema most and what percentage of owner-occupiers live in houses built before a certain date? It also provides data on the distribution of ethnic minority groups which could also have marketing significance.

Family Expenditure Survey

The *Family Expenditure Survey* is again annual but slow in appearing. The statistics that it offers should, therefore, be treated with some caution and supplemented from more current publications. It displays income and expenditure by type of household for the United Kingdom and it also provides some regional analyses.

Household Food Consumption and Expenditure: National Food Survey

Another source of useful information for both producers and retailers of food is *Household Food Consumption and Expenditure: National Food Survey*. This annual report analyses food consumption, expenditure and nutrition by type of household. It cannot be seen as an entirely reliable source since it is based on a sample survey of only 7,000 interviews. This can be compared with the *General Household Survey* which is compiled from a much larger continuous survey. Secondly, the *National Food Survey* appears very slowly, often four years after the year that is being described and, therefore, the data is usually out-of-date from the point of view of consumer trends. For example, the edition which appeared in 1985 showed a spectacular resurgence in the eating of red meat, but by the time these figures appeared, other statistics suggested that red meat eating was probably in decline. More recent unpublished data and analyses can also be purchased from the compilers, the Ministry of Agriculture, Fisheries and Food.

Business statistics

Although all the previously-mentioned sources of official statistics contain a mass of information relevant to business, there are, of course, some government publications specifically aimed at the business community and compiled from data collected from it.

Most business librarians will become familiar with the initially daunting *Business Monitors*, which are our major location for industrial production figures. They are variously published at monthly, quarterly or yearly intervals, or in a few cases, only occasionally, and emanate from the *Business Statistics Office* (BSO). The data is collected by sending out over 400,000 enquiry forms to businesses including the service and distributive industries as well as manufacturing, energy and mining. There are some drawbacks which the business librarian will discover after using the

Business Monitors for a while. First, they are not easy to use and it is best to take some time to familiarise oneself with their arrangement. Be careful of the provisional and revised figures that are given, and which must not be confused. Secondly, the flimsy format and odd shape makes them difficult to house and easy to misfile. Thirdly, since the BSO only sends its forms to firms employing more than 20 people, the figures tend to be misleading when they refer to the sort of industry which tends to contain a great many small units, for example, publishing. In such cases, it can be helpful to compare BSO figures with those compiled by the relevant trade association; in this case, the Publishers' Association. Small publishers, however, are the publishers who are also most likely not to join their trade association. Fourthly, any survey based on questionnaires is dependent on the good will of the people who have to fill them in. Many are not returned; some are returned late or incomplete; the BSO has no real control over the accuracy, currency and completeness of the material which they analyse.

All the same, *Business Monitors* are indispensible to the business world and, as the BSO's own leaflet on *Business Monitors* points out, the *Monitors* can help to monitor business trends, identify successful products, assess company efficiency (by comparing your own performance with the industry as a whole), identify new markets, pinpoint seasonal factors and market your products[4].

There are three main categories: Production Monitors (P series), Service and Distributive Monitors (SD series) and Miscellaneous Monitors (M series).

Business Monitors not only help a company to compare itself with its competitors but also to monitor trends in suppliers' and customers' industries and can help to identify new markets by revealing what products are selling well and what new retail outlets are being opened. In spite of its drawbacks, therefore, this service should not be disregarded. Some *Business Monitors* are now available online via *BSI Informat* and some industries can be purchased on floppy disc.

There are, of course, many other official statistical publications of relevance in the business context but this chapter aims to indicate a selection of the most relevant and heavily used items.

Non-official statistics

The statistics which emanate from non-governmental sources are always the most difficult to trace, and even those government publications that are not published by HMSO pose problems. As mentioned earlier, the *Catalogue of British official publications not published by HMSO* has made tracing non-HMSO items much easier, whether they are statistical publications or not. Non-official statistics still remain a largely unchartered sea. *The Guide to Official Statistics* does identify some non-official sources and, whenever possible, gives addresses and a very useful, but now rather out-of-date, book *Sources of unofficial UK statistics* can also be recommended[5].

Important sources of statistics which the business information specialist should not overlook are trade associations and banks. Trade associations frequently produce useful statistics relating to their industry while banks produce economic forecasting data and statistics relating to overseas markets. If you are having trouble locating some official statistical information, there are probably three obvious routes which you can take. You can contact one of the major libraries which specialise in statistics, you can contact the government department direct, using the contact numbers listed in the back of *Government statistics: a brief guide to sources* and in the *Guide to official publications*, or you can use online.

Library resources

The main UK library location for statistics is the Export Market Information Centre (EMIC) until recently entitled the Statistics and Market Intelligence Library (SMIL), Department of Trade and Industry, London; Warwick Business Information Service; the British Library and the House of Commons Library.

EMIC provides up-to-date trade statistics for all countries and holds general statistical publications from all over the world. They have an excellent collection of foreign directories, development plans and mail order catalogues, and they also hold a collection of foreign dictionaries in order to help users overcome the problem of foreign language publications. Statistical series are normally held for 10 years and, inevitably, some countries are better represented than others. The library is very strong in Western European, American and Canadian material and, obviously, less strong on smaller and more remote countries.

Development plans are a valuable resource and what these are and how they can be used was explained in an interview with Maria Collins, the then librarian of SMIL in *Business Information Review*.

> Development plans are produced by a number of countries. They outline the current economic state of a country and put forward its plans, usually for a five year period. The plans tend to concentrate on infrastructure projects for new roads, improving telecommunications, etc. However, used imaginatively they can be a great help in identifying markets. They give plenty of background data as well as specific market leads.[7]

The library is open to the public and brief enquiries are handled by telephone; otherwise users are expected to come to the library to undertake their own research.

The DTI has a second library the Business Statistics Office in Newport, Gwent, handles the production statistics end of the DTI's business which appears in its published form as *Business Monitors.*

Warwick Business Information Service was previously called Warwick Statistics Service and is located in the library at the University of Warwick. Warwick has a very large collection of international statistical publications in paper copies as well as UK official statistics, official statistics and unofficial statistics from all over the world, market research reports and company information. The service was established in 1972 and is available for an annual subscription or on a 'pay-as-you-go' basis. They produce a monthly bulletin of marketing information mainly of a statistical nature, and in 1984, they researched a *Survey of UK statistical sources and their role in business information* in which they located a huge range of official and non-official sources, many of which could very easily be overlooked.

The British Library, of course, handles official publications, both statistical and non-statistical, at several of its locations. The Official Publications Library in London is especially useful for older statistical material, while the Business Information Service at the Science Reference Information Service (SRIS) holds some basic core UK statistical series and a great many unofficial sources but, as far as extensive coverage of current and recent official statistics are concerned, does not seek to duplicate EMIC. Meanwhile, the main official statistical series are also available for loan from the British Library Document Supply Centre at Boston Spa, Yorks.

The House of Commons Library has been mentioned earlier as an information resource for MPs and for the public by telephone or letter. They do not, in fact, handle statistical queries from the public, only from MPs, and the information which they do supply to the public tends to be mainly about MPs. They do, however, house all the statistical series for the use of MPs and have a statistical section which undertakes statistical research projects.

Online resources

Statistics are obviously uniquely suited to online presentation and UK official statistics are now available on a number of hosts. There have been many mergers in the database industry in the last two to three years and numeric databases have been involved in some of these. Numeric databases tend to be aimed at the end-user rather than at the librarian/information intermediary and yet, rather surprisingly, most of them are comparatively difficult to interrogate since they are command-driven rather than menu-driven. This presents no problem to the regular user but many numeric databases are difficult to interrogate if they are used infrequently. In a recent paper in *Business Information Review*, Allan Foster points out that the divisions between bibliographic/textual databases and numeric ones is breaking down:

> Systems can no longer be simplistically defined as librarians' products or analysts'/planners' services (sometimes managed by 'information professionals' and sometimes not). They provide an important integrating function within the organisation and will co-ordinate and exploit data products of all kinds. This has led to a more intelligent response in terms of marketing and user support policies by the hosts/producers[9].

He argues that while information professionals have stayed aloof from numeric databases in the past, they must now integrate these sources of information into their overall information management strategy.

In the field of UK official statistics, it is obvious that the information scientist must not only know the way around the shelves of cumulated statistics but must also become at ease with some of the relevant databases in order to give a swift and efficient service. The major hosts in this area are DATASTREAM, the WEFA GROUP and I. P. SHARP (now owned by Reuters).

I. P. SHARP are a heavily used numeric database with a worldwide portfolio which embraces not only statistical data but company financial and equities data, energy and commodities. It includes a number of OECD databases and is valuable for economic forecasting. Like many numeric databases, I. P. SHARP is command-driven and is not initially very easy to use. It is, however, very popular with economists who find it flexible and efficient. It has recently been acquired by Reuters, who were especially interested in the 'historic' business databases covering the areas of finance, economics, energy and aviation. With I. P. SHARP, they also acquired the I. P. SHARP worldwide communications network. The new service is called REUTER FILE HISTORICAL INFORMATION PRODUCTS and is publishing a newsletter, entitled NEWS: FILE. From the official publications point of view, I. P. SHARP is chiefly of use as a mode of access to the CSO United Kingdom Macro-Economic and Financial Databank. The wide range of other countries covered and the extent of inter-governmental data available facilitates comparative exercises, while Superplot, the I. P. Sharp Associates plotting package, enables the user to produce coloured graphs and other presentational material.

CSO statistics are available via a number of hosts including DATASTREAM which claims to include approximately 10,000 series covering economic statistics from 25 countries. DATASTREAM also covers equities, stocks, company accounts, stock market indices, interest and exchange rates, commodities, financial futures and traded options. It is heavily used by the London Business School Information Service and is very popular with the world of finance. The sheer size of the manual is rather daunting although a small version is available. DATASTREAM also has a range of graphics services: DSPLOT – a package for use with colour plotters; DSLATER – for 300 dot per inch lasers and DSCOM – a 'paintbox' facility which permits the use of colour for lines, grids and shading.

The WHARTON ECONOMETRIC FORECASTING ASSOCIATES GROUP (WEFA) was created as the result of a merger between CISI-WHARTON and CHASE ECONOMETRICS to produce a major numeric host system. The group provides access to the CSO file which includes 14,000 time series on the UK economy. In addition to the main economic series, the database includes national accounts, balance of payments, index of production and cyclical indicators, production accounts, employment and earnings, prices and financial statistics. CISI-WHARTON was originally developed by economists and is relatively unusual among numeric databases in that it is quite easy to use and has 10 levels of prompts. The highest of these breaks down each command and guides the user through the enquiry step-by-step. This is very helpful for the infrequent user, but more experienced ones can take a faster route by which regularly used commands can be stored and re-run to save typing them again. Similar facilities are available on DATASTREAM and I. P. SHARP.

In conclusion, statistics are not as daunting as many people think. In order to use them efficiently try not to hurry or panic. Read the introduction at the beginning of the collection which you are interrogating. If you have not studied statistics, a few minutes reading the notes and definitions section provided in several of the publications is time well spent. When you find the relevant page, notice if the figures that are listed in the columns are hundreds, thousands or millions. It makes quite a difference! A useful paper by Doug Scott in *Business Information Review* also includes a very helpful list of statistical terms, and his paper can be thoroughly recommended as a piece of lively and informative further reading[10]. I shall close with a quotation from his paper:

> Statistics do not exist in a vacuum: they are a quantitative complement to qualitative investigation. Statistics alone will rarely be accepted as proof positive (and, indeed, should not be) but rather used as indicators in a discussion or argument. A blend of background subject knowledge and statistical awareness is the most useful background: statistics is not a pure science and common sense should be rigorously applied[11].

References

1. *Financing our public library service*, four subjects for debate: a consultative paper. HMSO, 1988, Cm 324.
2. PARROTT, T. and TAYLOR, P. Patents and the public library: a report of a survey in Liverpool. *Refer*, 4, 2, Autumn 1986, 12–13.

3. JOHNSON, K. and HAYTHORNTHWAITE, J. Press releases: a neglected source of information. *Aslib Proceedings*, March 1989, 99–107.
4. *Business Monitors*. HMSO for the BSO, 1987, *Publicity Leaflet*.
5. MORT, D. and SIDDALL, L. *Sources of unofficial UK statistics*, Gower Press, 1986.
6. COLLINS, M. The Statistics and Market Intelligence Library – face-to-face with Maria Collins, Librarian. *Business Information Review*, 3, 4, April 1987, 3–8.
7. *Ibid*, 4.
8. *Survey of UK statistical sources and their role in business information*, BLRDD, 1984.
9. FOSTER, A. Online numeric databases: four years later. *Business Information Review*, 5, 3, January 1989, 4.
10. SCOTT, D. Making the most of statistics. *Business Information Review*, 3, 3, January 1987, 14–23.
11. *Ibid*, 23.

Further reading

BUTCHER, D. *Official publication in Britain*. Bingley, 1983.
CHAPMAN, M. *Plain figures*. HMSO, 1986.
ENGLEFIELD, D. *Parliament and information*. Library Association, 1981.
HUFF, D. *How to lie with statistics*. Gollancz, 1964.
OLLE, J. G. Government publications. In: HIGGINS, G. (ed.) *Printed reference material*, 2nd ed. Library Association, 1984.
SCOTT, D. Making the most of statistics. *Business Information Review*, 3, 3, January 1987, 14–23.

Useful addresses

BLAISE Information Services, British Library, Bibliographical Services, 2 Sheraton Street, London W1V 4BH. Tel: 071-323 7074

Chadwyck-Healey Ltd, Cambridge Place, Cambridge CB2 1NR. Tel: 0223-311479 Fax: 0223-66440

Datastream International, 58-64 City Road, London EC1Y 2AL. Tel: 071-250 3000 Fax: 071-253 0171

Export Market Intelligence Library, DTI, 1–19 Victoria Street, London SW1H 0ET. Tel: 071-215 5444/5

HMSO Books, 51 Nine Elms Lane, London SW8 5DR. Tel: 071-873 8372

House of Commons Library, Public Information Service, Westminster, London SW1A 0AA. Tel: 071-219 4272
Key Facts, The Old Rectory, Northill, Near Biggleswade, Beds SG18 9AH.
Marketing Communications Group, Historical Information Products, Reuters Ltd, 85 Fleet Street, London EC4P 4AJ. Tel: 071-250 1122 Fax: 071-353 0745
SCOOP Publications, c/o Valerie J. Nurcombe, 8 Kingfisher Drive, Over, Winsford, Cheshire CW7 1PF.
WEFA Group, 23, Lower Belgrave Street, London SW1W 0NW. Tel: 071-730 8171

Chapter Five

1992 AND ALL THAT: BUSINESS INFORMATION FROM THE EC

Michael Hopkins

Introduction

In 1988, for the first time since the United Kingdom joined 15 years earlier, Her Majesty's Government (HMG) placed the full weight of its information machine behind British membership of the European Communities (EC). The occasion was the start of a massive campaign designed to alert British industry to the challenges and opportunities presented by the decision to dismantle the remaining technical, physical and fiscal barriers preventing the free movement of goods, services, people and capital between member countries and the creation of a genuine single market of 320 million consumers by the end of 1992. The 'Europe open for business' campaign included extensive television and media advertising, travelling exhibitions, business breakfasts, seminars, conferences, publications, videos and other promotional activities. By the end of 1988 the Department of Trade and Industry (DTI) could confidently claim that more than 90 per cent of companies had heard of 1992, even if many still had little appreciation of its actual implications[1].

The reality is, of course, that the European Communities have played an increasingly significant part in the business life of British industry ever since UK membership in 1973. The single market programme may have turned a welcome spotlight on Europe but it represents merely the culmination of a process set in motion in 1957 by the Treaty of Rome establishing the European Economic Community. Membership of the European Communities has introduced a new economic order in which Community institutions have authority to legislate in sectors of the economy previously determined at Westminster and on matters which directly affect business competitiveness and profitability.

The purpose of this chapter is to describe the nature of business information needs as they relate to the EC and to highlight the principal sources of information available to the business community. The chapter begins with a review of the ways in which the EC impinges upon business activity and concludes with brief comments upon some of the problems that business managers experience in their use of EC information. Observations on the information habits and needs of business managers are largely based upon the findings of a British Library research project published in 1987[2].

Impact of EC on business activity

The EC pursues policies and adopts legislation in many areas which affect both the economic climate within which industry operates and the conduct of specific business activities. The main thrust of its policies is to improve business efficiency and increase wealth by creating a domestic market of 320 million consumers in which economies of scale, increased competition and technological innovation provide an industrial base strong enough for Europe to compete successfully with the likes of Japan and the United States. A large number of legislative measures have been adopted in relation to the removal of technical, physical and fiscal barriers to trade, steps have been taken on the economic front to stimulate growth and curb inflation and policies which impact upon business activity have been developed in such fields as energy conservation, environmental protection and research and development.

The 1992 programme in particular has sparked an explosion of literature designed to inform and alert British business to the challenges and opportunities presented by the single internal market. Key documents prepared by the Commission of the European Communities, including the original white paper prepared by Lord Cockfield upon which the legislative programme is based and the subsequent progress reports charting the gradual implementation of its 300 or so specific measures, may be traced through *Documents*, the EC's monthly catalogue of public documents[3]. The numerous publications issued by the EC on 1992 issues, including, for instance, the multi-volume Cecchini report, which quantifies not only the immense cost of maintaining 12 separate national markets but also the opportunities which the completion of the internal market will open up, are listed in *Publications of the European Communities*, the monthly catalogue of EC publications issued by the Office for Official Publications[4]. Also listed in this catalogue are the highly informative introductory guides to various aspects of the single market programme which have been published by the EC in both the *European documentation* series and in the somewhat more condensed *European file* series[5]. Further information on EC documents and publications and also on the burgeoning volume of secondary literature on the subject may be obtained from standard bibliographies and specialist current awareness tools such as *European access* and the *SCAD bulletin*[6].

Demand for EC information

It would be naive to assume that every business manager is thirsting for information on the EC or that there is a constant and consistent demand for EC information across the whole of the business sector. The level of interest in and demand for EC information is largely determined by the extent to which the business activities of individual companies are affected by EC membership. Those companies whose products, processes, business practices and markets have been directly affected by the harmonisation programme, for instance, or by other legislative programmes are likely to be more aware of the Community dimension than those for whom the EC is nothing more than a remote and sometimes interfering bureaucracy.

Generally speaking, the larger the company the more its business operations are likely to be affected by EC membership and the more it is likely to have the inclination and resources to adopt a positive approach to the acquisition and use of EC information. Large companies conduct their operations across national boundaries and do business in markets which are international rather than domestic; they recognise the strategic importance of the EC to their future performance and profitability and are prepared to invest time and effort in intelligence-gathering activities. Small firms, on the other hand, often operate from a single location, do business in a limited geographical area and are frequently more concerned with short-term survival than with long-term, export-led expansion; their managers are not generally information-oriented and do not have the resources or inclination to monitor EC developments on a continuous basis.

Nature of demand

In broad terms, members of the business community require information on three main topics, a) the legal framework which governs the conduct of business activity in the EC, b) the economic and commercial conditions which affect company performance and profitability and c) the financial incentives and opportunities that are available to business enterprises.

Each is dealt with in turn in the following sections. Technical information, although mainly issued in the form of directives, is treated separately.

Legislative information

Business managers cannot afford to ignore the EC because the founding treaties invested in Community institutions the power to make law which can supersede existing national legislation in socio-economic and other areas which impinge directly upon the business sector. The legal instruments available to Community institutions include the *regulation*, which is binding and directly applicable in all member states, and the *directive*, which is also binding as to the result to be achieved but which leaves national governments to decide how best to give effect to its provisions. If British business is to comply with the many rules and regulations which govern industrial and commercial activity and to respond to the challenges and opportunities afforded by the enlarged domestic market, then it must be aware of the existence of EC legislation and take due note of its provisions[7].

For those members of the business community who require access to the authentic texts of Community legislation, the principal source of information is the *Official journal of the European Communities*. The 'C' or Information series contains among other things the texts of Commission proposals for legislation and the resolutions and opinions adopted by the European Parliament and Economic and Social Committee on those proposals. The 'L' or Legislation series contains the official texts of the several thousand separate regulations, directives and other legal instruments adopted each year by Community institutions.

The sheer size and complexity of the *Official journal* make it an intimidating and unwieldy publication to use, particularly when most business users have an interest only in a small proportion of its contents. For those business managers who wish to establish the exact state of EC legislation on a particular subject the *Directory of Community legislation in force*, published twice yearly by the Office for Official Publications, offers a welcome if general subject approach, providing bibliographic references to legislation currently in force arranged according to broad subject headings. The most important legislative texts are replicated in commercial publications such as the *Encyclopedia of European Community law*, published by Sweet & Maxwell, which although more user-friendly than the *Official journal* suffer to a greater or lesser extent from problems concerning the currency of their contents. Alternative sources of reference are the handbooks of EC law and practice tailored to the needs of the business sector. Typically, such handbooks appear in loose-leaf format and are intended to keep practitioners up-to-date on all the important legal developments likely to affect their business, particularly in relation to 1992 initiatives[8].

Online databases form an alternative source of legislative information. The EC's own legal database CELEX contains, among other things, the full text of secondary legislation back to 1 July 1979 in its English version. An alternative to CELEX, which has a reputation for complexity of use, is the JUSTIS database produced by Context Legal Systems Ltd, which provides access to CELEX via a much more user-friendly menu-driven interface. In response to the interest created by the 1992 programme several specialist databases have been devised primarily for business use. *Spearhead* is the DTI's own online database of single market information, providing full information on current and prospective measures relating to 1992. Others include *1992 – the internal market*, also produced by Context Legal Systems Ltd, whose object is also to monitor the progress of measures to introduce the single market, and the *EC 1992* database from Deloitte Haskins and Sells.

Many of the large companies that are eager to take full advantage of the opportunities afforded by the single domestic market and upon whose business activities the EC's regulatory actions have a significant impact, employ 'Euro-watchers' to monitor EC legislative activities on a continuous basis. Timely intelligence, not only on legislation currently in force but also upon proposals currently passing through the legislative pipeline, is vital if such enterprises wish to lobby for changes in legislative provisions or to prepare effectively for the consequences of impending legislation.

Although it is possible to obtain copies of the original COM documents in which the Commission makes its proposals for legislation to the Council, the EC makes no significant provision through its publications programme for keeping business concerns informed about the most recent decisions, proposals and legislation. Consequently, a wide range of international news agency and current awareness bulletins have emerged from the private sector, often in direct response to the increased demand created by the 1992 campaign. Two alerting services which have a long pedigree and substantial reputation are *Europe*, published by Agence Europe, and *European report*, issued by the European Information Service, both of which are published in Brussels and provide informed comment, analyses and reports on the most recent activities and actions of Community institutions. Such publications provide not only a comprehensive news service on the day-to-day business of Community officials and institutions but also advance warning of forthcoming events and Community business. Examples of more recently established current awareness services intended to provide business users with information on 1992 are *1992 European alert*, a weekly bulletin published by Infomat Ltd with summaries of the key developments in Europe leading up to

1992; *1992: single market news*, a monthly newsletter published by Blenheim Online Publications reporting on EC legislative changes affecting industry and commerce; *1992 single market monitor*, a monthly newsletter on 1992 published by Tolley Publishing Co. Ltd, and *Towards 1992*, published by the University of Warwick Business Information Service, which is more of a guide to the vast amount of information being published on 1992.

Intelligence on current EC legislative activities is also provided to business firms by representative organisations of various kinds and by the banks, accountancies, legal firms, consultants and other specialist advisory services that now exist to provide industry with management and financial support. Multinational accountancy firms are a particularly rich source of EC information. Many now have offices in Brussels for the purpose of gathering information for the use of their clients and customers. The information services they offer typically include regular bulletins on EC legislative activities, business guides on EC affairs, online databases and a range of personalised current awareness services designed to match the needs of individual clients[9].

Economic and commercial information

Many companies are interested in the EC only insofar as it affects their performance and profitability. They view the EC as a collection of national markets and are less interested in policy than in practical and operational information concerning such matters as differing customs procedures, import/export regulations and the technical standards that have to be observed if they are successfully to expand beyond their own domestic markets. Exporters and traders need access to up-to-date and detailed commercial information on market and economic conditions in individual member countries and on the legal provisions with which they have to comply if they wish to do business in those countries. Moreover, business and financial advisers, EC and management consultants all need access to large amounts of mainly quantitative data for the purpose of corporate planning, strategic decision-making, economic forecasting and so on.

The EC is not itself a significant source of specialist information on market conditions in member countries; it operates on a European level, while much of the data required for marketing and commercial purposes is necessarily national in character. However, the EC does produce a wide variety of publications on economic conditions and a large amount of statistical data on the performance of the European economy, mainly in the form of statistical bulletins and reports produced in both printed and online versions by the Statistical Office of the European Communities. The quantitative data made available in this way is of particular interest to the business community because its largely harmonised nature facilitates comparative analyses between member countries.

It is not possible in a chapter of this kind to describe specific publications. Suffice it is to say that it is the function of the Statistical Office to provide the European Commission with the quantitative data it requires for the purpose of policy-making and decision-taking and that the publications it produces in the form of statistical yearbooks, monthly bulletins, weekly rapid reports and one-off studies and analyses reflect the many socio-economic sectors in which the European Commission is active. In fact, the *Eurostat catalogue* published by the Office for Official Publications, lists and describes the principal titles published by the Statistical Office in eight broad subject categories or themes; general, economy and finance, population and social conditions, energy and industry, agriculture, forestry and fisheries, foreign trade, services and transport and miscellaneous. The catalogue also provides descriptive information on the various statistical databanks which are available for public use. These include CRONOS, the most comprehensive databank containing some 1.3 million macroeconomic time series divided into 23 separate domains, COMEXT, which contains data on external and intra-Community trade and REGIO, which provides statistical data on the regions of Europe. Further information on the work and both electronic and printed publications of the Statistical Office may be obtained from its quarterly publication *Eurostat news*.

It should also be noted that the EC is a supplier of commercial information in the sense that it can provide opportunities for companies to win new business in both other member states and in associated countries. There are EC rules, for instance, that require public purchasing authorities to give companies in all member states a chance to tender for public works and supply contracts. Substantial contracts can also be won in the African, Caribbean and Pacific (ACP) countries that are signatories to the Lome Convention through the operation of the European Development Fund. In both cases, invitations to tender for contracts are published in the 'S' series or *Supplement* to the *Official journal of the European Communities*, which is devoted specifically to tender information of this kind. The same information is also available through TENDERS ELECTRONIC DAILY (TED), the online version of the 'S' series available through ECHO, the EC host organisation.

Financial information

The EC is not only a source of business but also a source of finance for business. That is to say, grants are available from structural funds such as the European Social Fund and the European Regional Development Fund; cheap loans can be obtained from specialist Community institutions such as the European Investment Bank to finance investment and infrastructure projects, and generous financial support is given to industrial partners in collaborative research and development programmes initiated by the EC. Although guides for the use of practitioners do not make up a very significant proportion of the published output of EC institutions a number of useful examples are published for prospective applicants in relation to the various grants and loans schemes administered by Community institutions. These include *Finance from Europe*, a booklet published periodically by the London Office of the Commission which provides brief details of the principal grants, low-interest loans, and research monies available from Community institutions; *Operations of the European Community concerning small and medium-sized enterprises* (EC, 1988), a practical guide whose aim is to alert small and medium-sized enterprises (SMEs) to the various opportunities offered by the EC for financial assistance and support, and *Grants and loans from the European Community* (EC, 1985), an introductory booklet which provides both general information on the schemes available and practical guidance on how to apply and find out more about each programme. Publications which concentrate more on research and development activities include the *Vade-mecum of Community research promotion* (EC, 1987) and *Industrial innovation: a guide to Community action, services and funding* (EC, 1988).

Although some companies have their own contacts and sources of information on financial incentives and opportunities the majority depend upon information and advice provided by the trade and other representative organisations to which they belong. In particular, banks, accountancy firms, other financial advisers and business consultants make a speciality out of providing their clients with detailed guidance on how best to exploit the numerous opportunities that exist for business concerns to derive financial benefit from Community membership. Designed primarily for the benefit of customers and clients many such publications nevertheless have a wider applicability and, although perhaps not publicised to the same degree as commercial publications, are generally publicly available. Typical of such publications are guides to the full range of grants and investment incentives available to UK businesses from both private and public sector initiatives, including the EC[10].

Technical information

Differences in national standards and specifications constitute one of the most serious non-tariff barriers to trade between member countries. In order to allow manufacturers to benefit from the economies of scale promised by the 'common market', the European Commission has made considerable efforts over many years to harmonise national standards.

Nearly 200 detailed directives relating to the elimination of technical barriers in such sectors as motor vehicles and electrical equipment have been adopted. More recently, arrangements have been adopted for EC directives to establish the essential requirements for health, safety, consumer protection and the environment, leaving European standards bodies to work out the technical detail.

The technical documentation generated by EC institutions is legislative in character. New technical requirements, norms and standards take the form of directives which appear, along with the several hundred other directives adopted each year, in the *Official journal of the European Communities*. As such they may be traced in the same way as other EC legislation through the indexes to the *Official journal* and the various alternative sources mentioned earlier in this chapter. Additionally, reference may also be made to the *Catalogue of Community legal acts and other texts relating to the elimination of technical barriers to trade for industrial products* (EC, 1988), a periodically updated publication from the Office for Official Publications which collates references to the appropriate legal texts. Commercial publications whose purpose is to keep members of the business community regularly informed of legislative developments on technical subjects include *Eurodoc*, a microfilm service from Technical Indexes Ltd.

It should also be noted that the appropriate government departments, specialist bodies such as the British Standards Institution and Technical Help to Exporters, and trade associations are an additional source of information on EC technical standards. EC directives are binding as to the result to be achieved by an agreed date but leave the method of implementation to national governments. Consequently, as with other EC legislation concerning British business, the provisions of EC law have to be translated into national legislation by means of new Acts of Parliament, amendments to enacted legislation or the use of existing powers by means of statutory regulations. Whatever the means the result is that information becomes available in the form of government publications, ranging from the consultative documents that are often issued by the Department of Trade and Industry asking for advice on how specific directives might be implemented, to Parliamentary bills and subsequent Acts of Parliament[11].

Intermediary organisations

Many companies, particularly those in the small and medium-sized enterprises (SME) sector, are not information-oriented and do not have the resources or need to monitor EC developments on a continuous basis. They express only occasional demand for EC information, usually when confronted by practical problems that need immediate attention. In this respect the representative, professional and trade organisations to which business managers belong constitute an important source of EC information. They provide a quick reference enquiry service on matters which fall within their purview, including those of a European nature; they provide representative services in respect of EC legislative developments as appropriate and the trade and house journals usually produced by such organisations as trade associations, chambers of commerce, employers' organisations, etc. form part of an established network of communication which is one of the most effective means of reaching the grass roots membership of the business community.

For those business concerns that wish to monitor EC developments on a continuous basis and to have information services designed to meet their own specifications the monitoring and lobbying services offered by private consultants, accountancy firms, legal practices and financial advisers provide an additional source of expertise. Representative organisations of the kind referred to in the previous paragraph tailor their services to the collective needs of a broad membership; professional and private consultants offer services which are much more client-oriented, which are more specifically targetted on the EC and whose object is to anticipate events and to provide clients with early warning of impending actions. Of course, there is a price to pay for customised services; the services offered by such organisations as trade associations and chambers of commerce are determined by what their budgets can afford; the services offered by professional and private consultants are determined by what their clients' budgets can afford.

EC information services

For many practitioners the demand for EC information is triggered only occasionally by a need to solve a particular problem. The EC provides a quick reference service for this purpose through the Press and Information Offices (PIOs) which have been established in each member country. The London Office of the Commission has a small but well-stocked library of EC documentation and associated literature which is open to the public each weekday morning. Members of the Information Unit provide a telephone and general enquiry service which is heavily used by members of the business community. Smaller sub-offices in Belfast, Cardiff and Edinburgh offer a similar if more limited service. The London offices of the European Parliament and the European Investment Bank are also able to answer enquiries and to provide information relating to their own activities.

The European Commission is anxious to establish a decentralised network of relay organisations which are able to provide information services on Europe to their own particular target audiences and thereby take some of the pressure off the already over-burdened resources of the PIOs. The business community has already been targetted for special attention insofar as a Community-wide network of specialist Centres for European Business Information has been established. So far four have been set up in the United Kingdom, although more are planned[12]. Intended mainly for the purpose of providing specialist information and advice to SMEs the EC provides such centres with relevant documentation, online access to EC databases, contact points in Brussels and other training and support services.

Availability

The information centres mentioned above are not only sources of information but also places where texts, documents and publications may be consulted and sometimes acquired. EC offices usually have stocks of the numerous free publications which are available and also provide public photocopying facilities. It should be noted, however, that the EC offices are not sales offices for official publications. Priced publications issued by the Office for Official Publications of the European Communities must be ordered from HMSO, the official sales agent, or from Alan Armstrong Associates, the official sub-agent for EC publications.

Outside London the most substantial collections of EC publications and documents are likely to be found in the 45 European Documentation Centres (EDCs) established by the EC in institutions of higher education for the purpose of promoting teaching and research into European integration. Although the university and polytechnic libraries in which such collections are housed are not always able to provide sophisticated information services, most are happy to receive visitors from the local business community who might wish to consult or browse the collection. Although most public libraries have no more than a selection of basic texts, the inter-library lending network benefits from the fact that the British Library enjoys the status of Depository Library for EC publications and documents[13].

Conclusions

It is abundantly clear that there is no shortage of EC information available to members of the business community. EC institutions, government departments, intermediary organisations of many kinds, professional and private organisations are all involved in keeping the business world informed about developments which affect their business and commercial operations. Moreover, the large-scale publicity campaigns associated with the 1992 programme have provoked a deluge of literature and information services, some of which are merely opportunistic, others of which have inherent value.

Paradoxically, despite the sheer volume of material available, there remains a distinct feeling among some business users that they are deprived of information or that they are unable to obtain it in the form or at the time when required. Many of the problems that arise may be explained by the still disappointingly low levels of familiarity with EC affairs exhibited by members of the business and general public. Other explanations relate to the complexity of some of the documentation, the inadequacy of its means of bibliographical control and the lack of co-ordination between the various sources of expertise that exist in abundance in the United Kingdom. Whatever the circumstances, it is likely that those whose task it is to service the information needs of the business community will increasingly be expected to display a familiarity with the EC and with the sources of information and expertise that are available on EC affairs. It is hoped that this brief review will make the task a little less daunting for those who are faced with the challenge of exploiting this sometimes intimidating but important material.

References

1. The principal publications prepared by the Department of Trade and Industry on the 1992 programme consist of *The single market: the facts*, a series of informative fact sheets on the most important aspects of the programme, and *The single market: an action checklist for business*, which highlights the main issues which British business must confront if it is to flourish within this new business environment. Both publications are available free of charge from the DTI and have already entered their third editions. The Department also publishes a quarterly newsletter called *Single market news*. Further information services available from the DTI include a quick reference information hotline (081-200 1992) and *Spearhead*, an online database of single market information.
2. HOPKINS, M. and BINGHAM, G. *The business use of European Communities information in the United Kingdom,* British Library, 1987. (Library and information research report, 59).
3. Legislative proposals and policy documents prepared by the European Commission are usually referred to as COM documents. Lord Cockfield's white paper, *Completing the internal market: white paper from the Commission to the European Council (Milan, 28–29 June 1985)*, (COM(85)310 final. 14 June 1985) and the subsequent progress reports on implementation prepared in 1986 (COM(86)300. 26 May 1986), 1987 (COM(87)203. 11 May 1987) and 1988 (COM(88)134 final. 21 March 1988) may be traced through *Documents*, the monthly catalogue issued by the Office for Official Publications of the European

Communities, in which COM documents, the reports of the European Parliament and the reports and opinions of the Economic and Social Committee are listed by broad subject. COM documents may also be purchased through HMSO or Alan Armstrong Associates.

4. *Publications of the European Communities* is issued quarterly with annual cumulations by the Office for Official Publications in Luxembourg. The Cecchini report, *Research on the "cost of non-Europe": basic findings*, was published in 16 volumes in 1988.
5. The numerous introductory booklets published in the European documentation series include, for instance, *Europe without frontiers – completing the internal market* (European documentation 4/1987). The brief leaflets on the internal market published by the Commission in the European file series include *The social policy of the European Community: looking ahead to 1992* (European file 13/88), *Towards a big internal market in financial services* (European file, 17/88) and *The removal of technical barriers to trade* (European file 18/88).
6. *European Access* is a bi-monthly current awareness bulletin published by Chadwyck-Healey Ltd, which provides authoritative guidance on the latest news, developments, documents, articles and publications relating to the EC. The first issue, published in February 1989, contains an excellent bibliographical review on the Single European Market. The *SCAD bulletin*, published weekly by the Office for Official Publications, is a bibliographical review of Community legislative acts, documents and publications together with articles abstracted from periodicals received in the Central Library of the Commission. It is also available in an online version from Eurobases.
7. Although outside the scope of a chapter of this kind it is important that those who seek to exploit EC information have a basic familiarity with the Community legislative process and with the role of the main institutions. *Working together: the institutions of the European Community*, by Emile Noel (EC, 1988), constitutes an excellent introduction to the way in which each of the main Community institutions contributes to the decision-making process.
8. Examples include *Croner's Europe*, published by Croner Publications and *EEC Brief*, published by Locksley Press Ltd.
9. Examples of newsletters include the *EC bulletin* issued by Price Waterhouse, the *EEC newsletter*, published by Peat Marwick and *Econews*, issued by Ernst & Whinney.
10. Good examples of these include *Finance for new projects in the UK: a guide to private and public sector initiatives and grants*, published by Peat Marwick, Mitchell & Co., *Financial incentives and assistance for industry*, published by Arthur Young and *Official sources of finance and aid for industry in the UK*, published by the National Westminster Bank. An established source from the private sector is *A guide to European Community grants and loans*, published by the specialist consultancy group Eurofi (UK) Ltd.
11. See ENGLEFIELD, D. *Parliament and the European Communities, in* HOPKINS, M. (ed.) *European Communities information: its use and users*, (Mansell, 1985), for a discussion of the impact of EC membership on parliamentary practice and publications.
12. The Scottish Development Agency; Birmingham Chamber of Commerce; the

Northern Development Company; the Department of Employment, Small Firms Service.

13. For further information on European Documentation Centres and Depository Libraries contact Mr Ian Thomson, Secretary, Association of EDC Librarians, Arts and Social Studies Library, University of Wales, College of Cardiff, PO Box 430, Cardiff.

Further reading

HOPKINS, M. and BINGHAM, G. *The business use of European Communities information*, British Library, 1987. (Library and information research report, 59).

HOPKINS, M. (ed.) *European Communities information: its use and users*, Mansell, 1985.

NOEL, E. *Working together: the institutions of the European Communities*, Office for Official Publications, 1988.

THOMSON, I. *The documentation of the European Communities: a guide*, Mansell, 1989.

Useful addresses

United Kingdom Offices of the European Commission

8 Storey's Gate, London SWIP 3AT. Tel: 071-222 8122
4 Cathedral Road, Cardiff CF1 9SG. Tel: 0222 371631
Windsor House, 9/15 Bedford Street, Belfast BT2 7EG. Tel: 0232 240708
7 Alva Street, Edinburgh EH2 4PH. Tel: 031-225 2058

European Parliament Information Office

2 Queen Anne's Gate, London SW1H 9AA. Tel: 071-222 0411

European Investment Bank

68 Pall Mall, London SW1Y 5ES. Tel: 071-839 3351

Statistical Office of the European Communities

Information Office, L-2920 Luxembourg. Tel: 010 352 4301 4567

European Commission Host Organisation

Customer Services, BP 2373, L-1023 Luxembourg. Tel: 010 352 488041

Department of Trade and Industry

1 Victoria Street, London SW1H 0ET. Tel: 071-215 7877. 1992 Hotline: 081-200 1992

Office for Official Publications of the European Communities

2 rue Mercier, L-2985 Luxembourg. Tel: 010 352 499281

HMSO Books

HMSO Publications Centre, 51 Nine Elms Lane, London SW8 5DR. Tel: 071-873 8372

Alan Armstrong

Arkwright Road, Reading RG2 0SG. Tel: 0734 751769

Chapter Six

MANAGEMENT INFORMATION

Bob Norton and **Sharon Barker**©

It is a sad thing that nowadays there is so little useless information.
(*Oscar Wilde*)

Introduction

Marketing, company and financial information, it can be argued, lend themselves to clear, distinct definitions of content. What then of management information? If information is defined as published source data turned into useable intelligence, for the purposes of creativity or decision-making, by adding value, by monitoring, judgement, analysis and interpretation, then we begin to approach a definition for the purposes of this text. At the risk of pre-empting much debate, perhaps we can define management as the art, or science, of getting things done through the effective exploitation of people and resources.

Increasingly more and more literature, and thus information, is available to help managers manage. Not all of it is new, but most of it has to be monitored, assessed and analysed to see if it is of any value. If we knew which bits were going to be valuable before we catalogue, classify, analyse, process, index and abstract, then we could probably write out the formula and retire. However, life is not like that.

Nonetheless, experience, reputation, judgement and most importantly, direct contact with demand, enable some anticipation of what is going to be of value. Rapid change and development create new difficulties which have to be constantly mastered. For example, transactional analysis, entrepreneurship, management by objectives, quality circles and just-in-time production management were or are all buzzwords or 'hot' topics, just as new terms, trends, techniques and theories rise, develop, become established or fall, anticipating which, how and when poses increasing problems in times of accelerating change. On the job learning is no longer once and for all, but a lifetime of learning and re-learning and re-training to keep pace with change and avoid obsolescence. Hence the need for more, better and more palatable management information.

How do we describe management information?

At its simplest, management information is information on, or about, the function of management. Within this context therefore it is not facts and figures. It is not data. It is not, as such, verifiable. It is not an annual report, nor is it statistical, market or industrial data. It is not how many shoes were sold in Scotland last year, nor is it how many tractors were exported to Saudi Arabia. It is not the most recent share price of Company X, nor whether it has just acquired, or merged with Company Y. It is not a mailing list of all companies manufacturing widgets in Wessex, nor is it the profit and loss ratios of Company Z.

It is *how* to manage the sale of shoes in Scotland, *how* to market and sell tractors to Saudi Arabia, *how* to assess and implement the most effective way of manufacturing widgets in Wessex, or anywhere else for that matter. It is how to understand and interpret the important factors of a balance sheet, and how to activate a merger, acquisition or take-over having assessed the how, what and why of its pros and cons. In short, management information is information on how to manage. It is information on the theory and practice, on the techniques and experience, on the skills and expertise of those who have already tried, succeeded or failed. It is learning from the experience of others, especially in an age which is notable, regrettably, for its duplication, overlap and waste. It is arguably more important than facts and figures, because it is information which helps the individual to learn and assess whether or not he or she can improve their own personal or organisational performance. It enhances effectiveness because it strikes at the core of successful enterprise by capitalising on that single most valuable asset: human performance.

The purpose of this pre-amble is to attempt to illustrate that there could well be a world of difference between that which managers perceive as information and that perceived by publishers or librarians. In the search for information, managers have a number of doors open, or a number of possible sources to tap:

1. The organisation's processes (internal information): brainstorming, creativity, memoranda, analysis, judgement – reports for decision-making.
2. Published data and sources available through disciplined research (external information): available from outside the four walls of the

organisation, data from the world of competition, wider experience and the environment in which the organisation operates.

3. Random recovery: serendipity: a friend, chance, stumbling on one item when looking for another.

To be realistic, 3 is wonderful when it happens but it is, perhaps unfortunately, no substitute for constructing a scientific method for information access, recovery and redissemination. Experience and intuition tell us that management information, as understood by managers, falls largely in the domain of category 1. Personal files and indices, reports, memos, minutes and notes of meetings, statistics – whether of sales, marketing, forecasting, accounting, purchasing or customer all appear to be largely the foundation on which managers work to base their decisions. It is not unnatural that managers look to the organisation's internal processes for what they think they need to know. After all, it is – or should be – accessible, tangible and finite in a world which appears increasingly intangible, complex and infinite. Habit, together with ready and easy availability, makes it even more natural. The traditional low value and low profile of library and information services in business and management tends to reinforce this view. This becomes all the more entrenched with difficulties imposed by ever increasing numbers of sources, services and systems, by an apparent lack of delivery exacerbated by naive anticipation of immediate receipt, by expectations of 'tailor-made' answers whatever the question, and by attitudes of 'I know better' and 'don't confuse me with the facts...I've made up my mind...'.

For managers, information must be useful , meaningful, and applicable. It must be delivered by an appropriate channel: fax, online, e-mail, telex or in person. It must be appropriately selected or tailored: masses of unsorted references may only serve to confuse or delay. It must be accurate, pertinent, reliable and up-to-date. It involves choices and trade-offs in time and money.

Information sources – on the inside

At the risk of over-simplification, it is arguable that:

— the librarian's position in the corporate hierarchy has been reactive, low profile and the first to shoulder cuts when austerity impinges
— the library is not the only, and arguably not the first, place a manager would seek out when in need of information
— the manager may not be an inveterate information user, may believe implicitly that the answer should be provided at the touch of a button, whatever the question, and may not be used to asking questions appropriate to information channels.

In this case there is a very strong argument for starting with what the manager is used to. Any first port of call must begin by getting to know contacts close at hand and the operating departments in which they function. It is essential to give knowledgeable, first-hand support to know who's who, what they do, where they do it, what their place is in the corporate hierarchy, and, as much as possible, how they operate. It is the first weapon in building a picture of user-needs before the second stage of establishing:

— what information is needed
— what it is needed for and what is going to be done with it
— how it is going to be obtained.

It is important to discover what internal systems exist, if any, for gathering, accessing and re-disseminating data and information generated by the organisation itself. Re-inventing the wheel seems to be among the most enduring of human qualities, but it wastes time and money. Therefore, it is vital to discover what there is in terms of reports and departmental documentation to gain an insight into a company's thinking. Many companies will have produced their own policy statements or codes of practice on, for example, health and safety policy, performance appraisal, long-service awards, negotiation procedures, and these, along with the Chief Executive Officer's statement in the annual report, can provide primary sources which will probably never reach the world of hard copy or electronic bibliographies, except perhaps on an internal basis.

Books – classification

Ascertaining the extent of an organisation's own internal information systems will provide one element in any potential response to a manager's information need. External sources remain critical, however, as a vital source of new ideas, competitor intelligence or emerging theories which must be integrated with the results of internal processes to arrive at a realistic view of the organisation's position in the marketplace. Despite the proliferation of electronic information sources, printed documents remain the most familiar and hence the most habitually used sources. For the manager, however, it is essential that the values of speed, accuracy and topicality are maintained. The information centre which is geared up to respond 'Chapter 6 or pages 105–134 contain the required information' is more likely to be meeting the manager's need than document overload or a number of books broadly covering the subject. Classification remains the key to adequate exploitation of printed material but the purpose must be clearly defined – not at the information worker's convenience, but by the swiftest method of locating information relevant to the enquiry. Time spent on (i) analysing user needs and patterns and (ii) devising, adapting and utilising an appropriate classification to reflect these, is amply repaid by the speed and greater precision of retrieval. The information worker, in the role of intermediary, must be able to acquire and control the mass of data received and to organise it in such a way as to provide retrieval relevant to the manager's needs. Guidance and signposting are critical whether using an accepted scheme such as Bliss or Dewey or an adapted version of UDC or appropriate subject headings. To take a working hypothesis the discipline of management may be broadly divided into the major functional areas of:

— general management
— management techniques
— financial management
— marketing management
— production management
— personnel management
— office management
— physical distribution, or logistics management.

Each of these areas in turn generate numbers of more specific terms so that an approximation can be made at locating and thus fixing, in terms of subject relationships, the content of the document in hand. Given the notoriously 'soft' nature of the language of management, the certainties of scientific definition do not apply.

The literature of management follows the same general pattern as in other subjects, from encyclopaedias and reference tools such as the *International dictionary of management* (Kogan Page, 1986, 3rd ed.) to texts like Rosemary Stewart's *The reality of management*[1] to practical guides such as the BIM series of *Essential guides*[2]. Management is not a subject which remains static and concepts and theories rise and fall in popularity. This may, for example, be illustrated by the recent interest in defining managerial competences as a critical aspect of the Management Charter Initiative, referring to work first reported by Boyatzis[3] and the American Management Association in the 1970s. A perceptible trend is the recent increase in popularising books on management such as the genre typified by Lee Iaccoca's autobiography[4] and the Peters and Waterman[5] works on the identification of excellence. In addition to the growth of books on management theory, practice and principle, there has been an increase in the 'checklist' type of publication which fulfills the key criteria of brevity and relevance as well as supporting the desire of managers to have access to the hard experience of others in what is still viewed as a very practical based profession.

If a manager's use of printed material is regarded as reflecting the particular information needs of the moment, the information worker, in attempting to meet that need, must be prepared to respond to an erratic, non-specific, intensive, sudden demand and must, in consequence, develop a sophisticated, detailed retrieval system which is able to pull together the disparate elements of the subject to respond with speed, with accuracy and with relevance.

Publishers

Just as the information industry as a whole has expanded in the last 10–15 years then so too has the growth of specialist publishers. Until the 1950s, the number of books on management available in English could be counted in the hundreds. By the 1960s, this quantity was published each year and by the 1980s, hundreds were being published each month. To be fair, not all that is published is new knowledge. Indeed only a tiny fraction could probably be accurately described in this way. But each addition to the information available constitutes a potential resource, and only when it has become known and examined can its relevance be evaluated. So, it is only recently that specialist management publishers have emerged. While the international giants, such as McGraw Hill, Prentice Hall, Addison Wesley, Jossey Bass and Wiley must be monitored for their output, it is worth being on the mailing-list of:

— Croners
— Gower
— Macmillan
— Kogan Page
— Hodder & Stoughton

to name a selective few.

Journals

While *Current serials* (BLDSC) lists journals in their thousands, the following list has been collated as those core journals most used in responding to management information enquiries from BIM's Management Information Centre. It is not exhaustive. It is highly selective.

Accountancy
Accountant
Business Horizons
Director
Employment Gazette
European Journal of Marketing
Harvard Business Review
HR Magazine, formerly called *Personnel Administrator*
Human Resource Management
IDS Study

Industrial and Commercial Training
Industrial Engineering
Industrial Management & Data Systems
Industrial Marketing Digest
Industrial Relations Journal
Industrial Relations Review and Report
Information and Software Technology, formerly called *Data Processing*
Internal Auditing
International Management
Journal of European Industrial Training
Journal of General Management
Journal of Management Development
Journal of Systems Management
Leadership and Organisation Development Journal
Long Range Planning
Management Accounting UK
Management Decision
Management Review USA
Management Services
Management Solutions
Management Today
Management World
Managerial Planning
Marketing
Marketing Week
McKinsey Quarterly
Multinational Business
Office and Information Management
Personnel Journal
Personnel Management
Personnel Review
Planning Review, formerly called *Management World*
Public Finance and Accountancy
Purchasing and Supply Management
Sales and Marketing Management
Sloan Management Review
Supervisory Management, formerly called *Management Services*
Taxation
Training and Development Journal
Training Officer

Abstracting, indexing and online services

There is no shortage of management abstracting and indexing services.

The growth of online databases has been contemporaneous with continued demand for hard copy sources although industry commentators maintain that there is still enormous potential for qualitative, evaluative and selective online services. However, the evolving importance of management education has probably done much to influence the maintenance and development of those information services whose overall goal is to support and enhance management performance.

The services covered in this section are not exhaustive but they do point to the major players:

Business Periodicals Index
H.W. Wilson Co. Bibliographic.
Coverage Over 300 English-language business journals, with emphasis on US trade journals. Includes some book reviews and excludes newspapers. Journals are generally indexed cover to cover. Published 11 times p.a. with quarterly and annual cumulations, the price of subscription is based on the extent of the subscriber's journal holdings.
Indexing An A – Z arrangement of subject and company headings. A typical entry includes title and source, but no abstract. Indexing is very specific and each subject area is divided into further sub-headings.
Online through WILSONLINE. Adds some 70,000 records p.a. with updating twice a week. Payment is by connect-hour rates; offline prints are available at a nominal fee, there is no charge for online records.
Summary A highly specific index to principally American business, company, industry and some management information. Document delivery can prove difficult for some of the American sources.

ANBAR
Anbar Management Publications.
Coverage There are five separate abstracting services: Personnel and Training, Work Study and OM, Marketing and Distribution, Accounting and Data Processing and Top Management. Anbar covers some 250 general management journals of which about 10 per cent are foreign language. For inclusion the article must be on a subject relevant to one of the five services and clear a subjective quality barrier imposed by the editors. Anbar started in 1961 and is produced eight times p.a. There is a joint annual index for all five services and an annual cumulated volume called the Compleat Anbar.
Indexing Anbar employs its own controlled-language 'classification framework'. To locate a record, the user consults a Keyword Register – an A-Z subject index which allocates a unique number which is then checked against the Instant Index under which relevant abstracts are listed. Each abstract is located by its own individual alpha-numeric code.
Online There is no online service. Anbar was recently bought by MCB University Press. At the time of writing it was understood that there is a

proposal to create a 'Floppy Anbar' which will consist of the Anbar database in machine-readable format to be sold on floppy disc.

Summary The business of finding an appropriate abstract can be time-consuming and not particularly easy. Anbar's strength lies in its hard copy current awareness service and not so much as a retrospective searching tool. Circulated on arrival to managers, it has been used for years as an alerting bulletin whose effectiveness is not reliant on its classification or arrangement. This could well remain the case for some time to come if practising managers' resistance to using online services stays unchanged. Anbar remains, justifiably, one of the best known UK management abstracting services, drawing further strength from its evaluative approach to its abstracts and its full back-up document delivery service.

Management & Marketing Abstracts (MMA)

PIRA (The UK Technical Centre for the Paper, Board, Printing and Packaging Industries) in association with the British Institute of Management. A monthly abstracting journal is published. Bibliographic.

Coverage Some 260 journals are scanned 'to keep readers abreast of developments and new techniques in all aspects of management. Case studies relating to specific companies, products and industries are included. Business conditions in Western Europe, the United States and other countries are covered extensively.' 180 of the titles are UK, 50 US, and the rest foreign-language and newspapers.

Indexing Access to PIRA's informative abstracts is through a simple controlled subject index. The hard copy journal also has an author-index, with the abstracts arranged under some 26 main subject headings.

Online through PERGAMON FINANCIAL DATA SERVICES. The database comprises some 30,000 records with about 6,000 added p.a. Charging is mainly by connect-hour rates with online and offline hit charges.

Summary Despite claims as to coverage, MMA offers a highly selective approach to management and marketing literature. The service is supported by document-delivery.

British Institute of Management (BIM)

Management Information Centre, British Institute of Management. Bibliographic.

Coverage BIM produces seven databases in support of its mission to improve management performance. Constructed as a means of servicing enquiries from BIM's member managers, the databases cover the whole spectrum of management theories, techniques, training, principles and practice. Entries are selected for their contribution to and coverage of management practice, education and development:

(i) Short Courses: full details on specific training in management skills and techniques provided by some 60 commercial and non-commercial organisations.

(ii) Audio-Visual: full details of films and videos on management skills and techniques for staff training at all levels.

(iii) Training simulations: details of computer packages, business games and training exercises.

(iv) Journals: references from 1980 onwards selected from over 400 English language journals covering all aspects of management. (Indicative abstracts from 1987.)

(v) Books: bibliographic details from BIM's management literature collection, initially from 1986, with ongoing retrospective conversion.

(vi) BIM file: a companion to (v) above – BIM publications: books, reports, series and seminars.

(vii) Company practices: examples of company policies and practice mainly in the fields of employment and personnel, donated by corporate members of BIM.

Indexing There is no hard copy indexing or abstracting journal. Access to online records is achieved primarily through BIM's management thesaurus, a controlled vocabulary, which includes subject, geographical and organisation entries.

Online via the BIM HELPLINE, direct to BIM. Both menu-driven and command language approaches are available. There are currently some 30,000 records online, of which 20,000 are in the journals database. All databases are updated continuously. There is a sign-on fee and usage is charged by connect-hour. Document delivery is available from the printed materials databases with some restrictions on book loans.

Summary BIM is a new entry to the online market. Its strength lies in its management specialisation and the quality and range of its information sourcing.

SCIMP

European Business Schools Librarians' Group. Bibliographic.

Coverage A European index of management periodicals, which was developed as a co-operative venture between major European business school libraries. SCIMP covers some 170 worldwide management journals with a mix of US, European and UK titles. Entries are selected for their contribution to and coverage of management education and development.

Indexing Access to the index, whether hard copy or online, is via SCIMP's controlled thesaurus of subject terms, which at the time of writing is in its seventh edition. The hard copy journal is published 10 times p.a. with index cumulations in April, July and December. Records are entered in original language, although the subject terms are in English. There is a

proposal to make the thesaurus available in French and German. There are no abstracts in the service.
Online from London Business School on direct dial, or from the Helsinki School of Economics, via PSS and IPSS. Currently there are some 60,000 records with about 6,000 added p.a. Charging is by connect or annual subscription.
Summary SCIMP provides a good low-cost, first search on management theory. The database was developed as a result of student and academic needs in European Business Schools, and perhaps errs to a business-academic bias. Despite its lack of abstracts, it is currently Europe's largest English language management database. As a co-operative venture across language and borders it is unrivalled. Its scope and potential for the 'European 1990s' will not remain unrivalled but makes it a strong contender.

ABI/INFORM (ABI)
UMI / Data Courier. Bibliographic.
Coverage Contains references and abstracts on business and management from over 800 journals.
Online from BRS, DATA-STAR, DIALOG, ESA-IRS and others. The database carries over 400,000 records with informative abstracts and is updated weekly with about 1,000 new records.
Indexing There is no hard copy abstracting or indexing journal. Like the other providers in this section, ABI's indexing is based on its controlled term thesaurus which includes subjects, company names, organisation names and geographic terms.
Summary Arguably the market-leader in online provision of management information. The first major American entry into the bibliographic management sector in 1971, ABI has, naturally enough, American origins and American leanings which is something of a weakness in Europe. Nonetheless, it is a proven source on techniques and trends in management and business which benefits from host-based document delivery services as on DIALOG. ABI is also available on CD-ROM.

Management Contents (MC)
Information Access Company. Bibliographic.
Coverage While there is some overlap with ABI/INFORM, emphasis in Management Contents seems to be on theory and decision making, as opposed to application and experience in ABI. MC covers mainly US journals, as well as newsletters, books, proceedings, and research reports.
Indexing Similar approach to ABI and, as with other producers mentioned, it has its own controlled subject approach. Currently some 220,000 records in the database.
Online via BRS, DATA-STAR, DIALOG.
Summary American bias. Apparently dwarfed by ABI.

DELPHES

Surprising though it may seem, entry of at least one foreign-language service (as opposed to SCIMP which is international and therefore English-based) is more than appropriate in view of the rush of services gearing for 1992.

Paris Chamber of Commerce and Industry in assocation with other French Chambers. Bibliographic.

Coverage DELPHES (formerly ISIS) covers administration and management, business and industry, computer science, economics, insurance and law. Its sources include some 1,000 periodicals and an input from books and reports, the vast majority of which are French in origin. DELPHES also takes English language source material and indexes and abstracts into French. Started 1975.

Indexing As with ABI, Management Contents and BIM there is no serial hard copy equivalent. Access is through standard controlled terms with the usual additional online searchable elements.

Online Via G-CAM which has the same BRS-based search lanaguage as DATA-STAR. Currently holds some 300,000 records – with indicative abstracts – adding some 500 per week.

Summary Included in this section as an indication that if we wish to tap foreign markets then perhaps we ought to tap foreign sources. DELPHES' closest equivalent would be as a French version to Business Periodicals Index, but with abstracts. It is clearly the most used French management-business bibliographic database.

The news: the management – business overlap

Of course, not all that appears on company management will come from an abstracting or indexing service. Although established theory and practice provide the backbone to understanding the core of the management process, news services are also essential to keep abreast not only of changing development but also of evolving management structures as well as trends in the market. The practice of buy-outs, the implementation of negotiating practices, the effects of personnel policies, the process of merger and the actuality of acquisition can be monitored in the press as they occur. Such reporting services complement the abstracting and indexing services above, in printed format these are the Reports Index and the Research Index which are also available online and the Monthly Index to the *Financial Times*.

Meanwhile, the online services are TEXTLINE, MCCARTHYLINE, PREDICASTS PROMT and FT COMPANY INFORMATION DATABASE. (See also Chapter Three on Newspapers.)

Organisations and libraries

In addition to business school libraries and their information services (such as those of London, Manchester, Warwick University, Cranfield and Ashridge) government department libraries and their associated bodies also offer specialist management information as in the case of the Department of Employment and ACAS (the Arbitration, Conciliation and Advisory Service).

For practising managers, however, a common route to information problem solving is via the major organisations some of which have specialised library and information services:

British Institute of Management (BIM)
BIM is the largest management organisation in the UK with over 70,000 members. BIM's Management Information Centre (MIC) has the largest collection of management literature in western Europe. 70,000 books, 400 journal title holdings, 1,000 topical information files, and smaller collections of company practices, policies and reports form the basis for responding to a wide range of enquiries on all aspects of management theory and practice, principles and techniques, education and development. (See the Abstracting, Indexing and Online section above.) Of particular interest are the monthly journal *Management Today* and the range of books and reports published by BIM on management practice.

Institute of Personnel Management (IPM)
The IPM is the leading UK institute dealing with personnel matters. The IPM has a large library of books, pamphlets, company reports and material pertinent to personnel management, industrial relations, employment, law, discrimination and equal opportunities. IPM publishes the monthly *Personnel Management* together with an extensive range of publications on personnel.

Institute of Directors (IoD)
The IoD offers library and information services to member directors, and an online information brokerage service. Publishes the journal *The Director*.

The following management bodies also run library and information services in support of their specific mission, and for their members:

Institute of Management Services
Institute of Sales & Marketing Management
The Institute of Administrative Management
Chartered Institute of Marketing Management.

Management training opportunities: databases and directories

Since the publication of the Constable/McCormack and Handy reports which fuelled subsequent drives towards management education such as the Management Charter Initiative, information sources on training opportunities for managers have taken on an increased importance. With government support, the position promises to change and evolve rapidly in the next few years. At the time of writing, the following services are available in the marketplace.

Databases

TAP (Training Access Points)
Launched in July 1986 and funded by the MSC in co-operation with the DES, TAP is directed at the needs of individuals and employers, and provides information on education and training opportunities direct to the public through online terminals sited in publicly accessible areas. Local Information is collated by TAP agents who develop local databases of local opportunities offered by both public and private providers. At the end of 1988 there were some 100,000 such opportunities, courses or programmes in total. National Information is provided by three national databases – ECCTIS, MARIS-NET and PICKUP which, between them, hold details on some 75,000 learning opportunities. TAP has a wide target market such as the employed, unemployed, women returning to work, ethnic minorities, inner city residents, and the business community and training providers.

ECCTIS (Education Counselling and Credit Transfer Information Service)
Launched in 1983, ECCTIS holds information about UK-wide advanced level courses leading to formal qualifications, including postgraduate, first degree, HND and certificate courses. Only courses of more than six weeks full-time, or equivalent part-time, duration are covered. ECCTIS targets students, whether school-leavers or adults returning to study.

MARIS-NET (Materials and Resources Information Network)
Established in 1983, MARIS provides details of open-learning and self-study materials, organisations, training films and videos, training and education services, articles and books. MARIS targets trainers and providers especially those concerned with Open Learning and self-study materials.

PICKUP (Professional and Industrial Commercial Updating Training Directory)
PICKUP provides information on work-related short courses, seminars and workshops in the UK. It includes adult training courses and those run by colleges, polytechnics, colleges and universities. PICKUP targets adults wanting to retrain or update their skills using short courses.

TAP is a conglomeration of online databases available via PSS. ECCTIS, MARIS-NET and PICKUP are also available on PRESTEL.

BIM (British Institute of Management)
BIM's Short Courses database contains approximately 2,000 records of short management courses offered by major UK providers. (See also section on Indexing, Abstracting and Online.) BIM's database targets managers' needs to update and develop their knowledge and awareness of management techniques and skills. Available online via PSS and PRESTEL through ECCTIS.

Directories

National Training Index
Management training opportunities are listed by subject and by provider. It includes courses, management games, multi-media packages, films and videos, management associations and management training organisations.

Directory of Management Training (Directory of Training Ltd. ISBN 0-947586-113)
Holds information on 2,700 UK classroom-based courses on general management and supervisory training, 1,000 training packages covering management/business games, multi-media packages, films and videos, development schemes, initiatives and associations.

Management Training Directory.
A guide to post-experience courses offered by the major training organisations. (TFPL Pub., 9th ed. 1988/9) 2,092 courses and information on 170 course providers.

Service

Information must be applicable to its recipient. Data – raw material – becomes information when it is retrieved and used. Processing and adding value to data turns it into intelligence, the critical ingredient of decision-making. Information is thus at the mid-point of the cycle. Data can only become useful information if its access, retrieval and re-dissemination meet certain criteria. Information must be:

— Delivered by an appropriate channel or medium: a parcel of books, delivered by post may be more thorough and less expensive than an electronically mailed database search ... but it may not be more appropriate for the user.
— Appropriately selected: masses of unsorted data can be worse than useless, serving only to confuse and delay.

- — Delivered at the right time: information about the strength of the enemy's forces will not help if it arrives after the battle.
- — Accurate and reliable: misinformation may be the stock-in-trade of the spy, but is never of help to the manager.

Packaging, tailoring and customising information to specific needs becomes more essential as sources, systems and services continue to multiply. In trying to transmit the awareness that criteria such as those listed above are, in today's information market, choices which involve commercial decisions, it would appear that we are perhaps as much in the education as in the information business.

References

1. JOHANSSEN, H. and PAGE, G. T. *International dictionary of management*, 3rd ed. Nichols Pub, 1986.
2. SCOTT, J. and ROCHESTER, A. *What is a manager? Managing people, Managing work, Managing money.* Essential guides series, BIM.
3. BOYATZIS, R. E. *The competent manager: a model for effective performance*, Wiley, 1982.
4. IACOCCA, L. *Iacocca*, Sidgwick & Jackson, 1985.
5. PETERS, T. J. and WATERMAN, R. J. Jr. *In search of excellence: lessons from America's best run companies*, Harper & Row, 1982.

Further reading

BLAGDEN, J. *Management information retrieval: a new indexing language*, Management Publications (for BIM), 1971.

FOSTER, P. Business management indexing services: a buyer's guide, *Business Information Review*, 2(1) 29–38.

HADDON, A. *Management and marketing databases*, 2nd ed. Aslib, 1989.

NORTON, B and HADDON, A. Online information: the question for management, *Management Education and Development*, 19(2), 1988, 109–115.

WITHEY, R. How managers use online information, *Business Information Review*, 3(1), 12–19.

Useful addresses

Anbar Management Publications, MCB Publications, 62 Toller Lane, Bradford BD8 9BY.
British Institute of Management, Cottingham Rd, Corby NN17 1TT.
ECCTIS, PO Box 88, Walton Hall, Milton Keynes MK7 6DB.
European Business Schools Librarians' Group, c/o The Librarian at either London Business School, Regents Park, Sussex Place, London W1, or Manchester Business School, Booth St. West, Manchester M15 6PB.
Institute of Personnel Management, 35 Camp Rd, London SW19 4UW.
Institute of Directors, 116 Pall Mall, London SW1Y 5ED.
MARIS-NET, Bank House, 1 St. Mary's St, Ely, Cambs CB7 4ER.
National Training Index, 1st. floor, 25–26 Poland St, London W1V 3DB.
Pergamon Press Ltd, Headington Hill Hall, Oxford OX3 0BN.
PICKUP, DES, Elizabeth House, York Rd, London SE1 7PH.
Training Access Points, The Training Agency Training Branch, St. Mary's House, c/o Moorfoot, Sheffield S1 4SQ.

Chapter Seven

COMPANY INFORMATION

Diana Edmonds

Company information is often regarded as the central element in the practice of business information, as the business community revolves around company activity. Companies constantly require information about other companies, perhaps because they want to monitor the activities of their competitors, because they wish to market their products to them, or because they wish to buy goods from them. Indeed, company acquisitions and mergers have proliferated in recent years, and the would-be purchaser may wish to buy not merely the company's products, but the company itself. As a result of this high level of interest in companies, business librarians receive many diverse requests for company information, ranging from enquiries about a company address to requests for a detailed financial history. This chapter is concerned primarily with the sources of information on UK companies, although details of some European sources are also provided.

Business organisation and company structure

It is easy to assume that every enquiry received about a business must relate to a company. There are, however, a number of forms of business structure. An individual working on a self-employed basis can operate as a sole trader, and is not obliged to register this status other than with tax authorities; when the individual decides that the work has expanded too much for one person to cope with, he or she may move into a partnership, which is usually regulated by a legal contract between the partners.

Both the sole trader and the partnership are subject to unlimited liability: if the business encountered financial difficulties, the individual businessman or woman could also experience personal financial hardship, as there is no formal separation between the individual's assets and the assets of the business. Many sole traders and partnerships take the decision to form a limited company in order to reduce their personal liability. A limited company, unlike the sole trader and the partnership, has a legal entity of its own. In the event of liquiditation, creditors' claims are restricted to the assets of the company. The shareholders are not liable as individuals for business debts beyond the paid-up value of their shares.

In return for this limited liability, a company has to register formally with Companies Registration Office, providing a Memorandum and Articles of Association (documents which are often referred to as the Mem. and Arts.) The Memorandum of Association gives the company's name and the address of its registered office. It then sets out the main objects for which the company is formed and what it is allowed to do. In addition, the Memorandum states the company's nominal or authorised share capital and the par value per share. In this context, the value of share capital is a purely nominal figure – what counts more is the issued share capital which represents what the shareholders have actually put into the business, or have pledged to do. In his book on *Working for Yourself*[1], Godfrey Golzen comments that it is quite possible to have a company with a nominal capital of £1,000, but with only two shares of £1 each, issued to the two shareholders that are required by law. The Articles of Association establish the rules under which the company is operated. They govern matters such as the issue of the share capital, the appointment and powers of directors and the proceedings at general meetings.

In addition to providing this initial documentation, the company has a number of ongoing responsibilities. Companies are required to hold an Annual General Meeting within 18 months of incorporation and then once in every calendar year. Within six weeks of the Annual General Meeting, the company must send an Annual Return to Companies Registration Office, providing particulars of the directors of the company and giving details of indebtedness, including all mortgages and charges.

Whether or not the company is actively trading, the company must also submit annual accounts. The accounts should cover a period not exceeding 18 months, starting from the date of incorporation or the day immediately following the end of the previous accounting period. The accounting period covered should end on the Accounting Reference Date (ARD) or a date up to seven days either side of the ARD. Under recent company legislation, small and medium-sized companies are allowed to submit abbreviated accounts. Small companies (with a turnover under £2 million, less than 50 employees or a balance sheet total not exceeding £0.975 million) may submit simply an abbreviated balance sheet with notes. A medium-sized company (with a turnover under £8 million, less than 250 employees or a balance sheet total not exceeding £3.9 million) must submit a directors' report, a balance sheet and a profit and loss account, although this may be abbreviated and need not disclose the turnover.

It may be useful at this point to clarify the difference between the various sections within the annual accounts: the profit and loss account identifies whether the company has made a profit or a loss on trading and covers income and expenditure over a given period of time. The balance sheet, on the other hand, is a snapshot of what the firm owes and what it owns: it is a statement of the share capital and reserves (the shareholders' investment in the business), the liabilities or debts and the assets.

The vast majority of companies (and there are now over 900,000 registered in the UK) are private companies, denoted by the abbreviation 'Ltd' after the company name: the shares of a private limited company cannot be traded. In order to develop the business, however, some companies chose to raise money by selling their shares to the general public: most of the funds raised in this way are used for long-term capital investment such as plant and machinery. Raising money by selling shares is a comparatively low cost method of acquiring these long-term funds. When a company comes to the International Stock Exchange to raise capital, it must, however, fulfill certain stringent minimum requirements. It must have a market capitalisation of at least £700,000, although in practice this is usually several million pounds. At least 25 per cent of the company's issued shares must be in the hands of the public and the company has to show a trading record for five years. An application for listing commits the issuer to ensure the continuing obligations covering disclosure of information, the directors' code of dealing and compliance with the City Code on Take-Overs and Mergers and other matters. Currently in the region of 7,000 securities of some 3,000 companies are bought and sold on the International Stock Exchange of the United Kingdom and the Republic of Ireland. Public limited companies whose shares are traded on the International Stock Exchange are denoted by the initials 'plc' after the company name.

In 1980, the Exchange introduced the Unlisted Securities Market (USM) allowing growing companies to come to the stock market to raise new capital without having to meet the more stringent requirements applied to listing. At present these companies need only place 10 per cent of their share capital on the market, and they need have only a three year trading record. There is no minimum size of company on the Unlisted Securities Market, and since its beginning more than 600 companies have had their shares traded on the USM.

The success of the USM encouraged the International Stock Exchange to introduce the Third Market at the beginning of 1987, to fulfill the needs of companies which may not meet the requirements for entry to the USM or a Full Listing. It is intended for companies which are young (no trading record is required) and which therefore may have good prospects for growth.

It is also worth mentioning the Over-The-Counter Market, which is usually known as the OTC. This operates outside the Stock Exchange marketplaces and is operated by licensed dealers in securities; there are no requirements for companies to meet before their shares are traded on this market, so the companies involved may be even smaller, younger and riskier than those on the Third Market.

Wherever is it? Tracing the address of a company

At the most basic level, requests for company information concern the company's whereabouts: the enquirer will require the company's trading address, the telephone number and perhaps a telex or fax number. Sometimes the enquirer knows the name of the company or a partial version of the name; on other occasions, the enquirer is trying to locate the manufacturer of a particular product or companies in a particular geographical location. Business librarians should beware the deceptively simple request for a business address; it can often take considerable time to find a current trading address, particularly if the enquirer's information is incomplete or the enquirer's memory is flawed.

All British and foreign companies registered in Great Britain (ie England, Scotland and Wales) are included in the *CRO Directory of Companies*, which often provides a useful starting point for tracing a company. The entry for each company includes the following:

1. *Company name*. Companies registered in Scotland are identified by the prefix SC; foreign companies registered in Scotland are prefixed by SF, while foreign companies registered in England/Wales are prefixed by FC.
2. *Company Registration Number*. The letter I after the number denotes that a full search of the company's records is recommended before any correspondence is instigated.
3. *Date of incorporation*.
4. *Accounting Reference Date*. The day and month is provided and denoted by the abbreviation ARD.
5. *Annual Return Date*. The made up date of the annual return is denoted by AR; 'none' beside AR indicates that no annual return has been supplied. Foreign companies are not in fact required to provide an annual return, except for Isle of Man and Channel Island companies.
6. *Accounts*. The made up date of the latest set of annual accounts is denoted by AC; 'none' beside AC indicates that no accounts have

been filed since July 1976, although the company file may contain accounts received before that date.

The *CRO Directory* is completely revised every three months. In addition, cumulative weekly supplements are issued, listing in alphabetical order the name and address of each company which has been newly registered or has changed its address; a cumulative supplement in numerical order is also available, indicating annual accounts and returns which have been received since the Main Directory was produced. The *CRO Directory* is available on microfiche, roll film or on magnetic tape. Information from the directory is incorporated in a number of online databases, including KOMPASS UK, the company databases produced by Jordans and ICC as well as a number of real-time information services.

Although the *CRO Directory* is a useful source for establishing the existence of a company, the directory provides only the registered office of a company rather than the trading address which is often required. Many companies prefer to use the address of their solicitor or accountant as their registered office; this is likely to be a more permanent address than their trading offices which may change frequently as the company's business expands.

The quickest way to trace a company's trading address is to use a directory. Company directories usually provide an alphabetic list of the companies included, together with an index to the products they manufacture or sell. Directories have traditionally been the staple stock of a business library; because they are used so often, many libraries still buy the hard copy versions although a number of the major company directories are now available online.

Of all the directories covering the UK, *Kelly's Business Directory* published annually by Reed Information Services, is probably the best known and the most used. The publicity material for the directory claims that 75 per cent of users refer to it each week: many business librarians certainly use it much more frequently! The 1989 volume of *Kelly's* is the 102nd. edition, and includes details of some 84,000 companies. These are all listed in alphabetic order in the Company Information Section (the blue pages) which provides address and telecommunication details, together with a trade description. The Classified Section gives details of manufacturers, merchants, wholesalers and firms offering an industrial service listed under an appropriate trade or professional heading, while the Brand and Trade Names section of the directory provides an alphabetic list of brand and trade names and shows the name of the manufacturer or, in the case of products manufactured abroad, the name of the UK distributors.

Details of 60,000 companies are included in *Sell's Directory: products and services* which is issued annually by Sells Publications. The directory provides an alphabetic listing of the companies included. Some 25,000 products and services are listed under alphabetic headings which include fascinating items such as 'football club pennants and banners' and 'footpath snow ploughs'; in addition, *Sell's Directory* includes 10,000 trade names with appropriate company details.

Some directories provide rather more information on the company than the simple name and address; this additional information takes up extra space, however, and tends to reduce the number of companies covered by the directory. The *UK Kompass Register*, published annually by Kompass Publishers in association with the Confederation of British Industry, is a multi-volume set which includes separate volumes for Products and Services, Company Information and Financial Information. The 1989 edition provides address and telecommunications data for 41,500 companies: additional information given on each company includes the name of its bank, share capital and turnover figures, the company registration number and the number of employees, details of its product range and a list of trade names used. For 30,000 of these companies, more detailed financial information is provided: an analysis of three years' accounts is used to show trends in turnover, profit, assets, liabilities, shareowners' funds and capital employed. Performance ratio data is also provided, as are details of holding companies and UK subsidiaries.

The online version of Kompass UK (File 591 on Dialog) is a merged file which incorporates data from a number of directories including *Kompass UK*, *Kelly's Directories*, *Dial Industry Directories*, *British Exports*, *UK Trade Names* and the *Directory of Directors*, together with some CRO data. This combined file provides information on some 110,000 UK companies, giving a single entry for each company covered.

Key British Enterprises is available both in hard copy and as an online file. The hard copy version is published annually by Dun and Bradstreet, with twice-yearly updates, and covers 25,000 'top UK manufacturers, distributors and service companies'. Information is classified under three complementary sections, the alphabetical sequence, an industry-sector listing by Standard Industrial Classification (SIC) and a location listing by geographical area. A standard entry is included for each company, giving details such as directors' names and job functions, associate companies, sales turnover in the UK and overseas, markets in the UK and overseas, the number of employees and the SIC code. *Key British Enterprises* is available as the online file KBE on PERGAMON FINANCIAL DATA SERVICES (PFDS). Using the online file extends the search capabilities offered by the hard copy version: range searching, for companies within specific parameters, can also be extremely useful.

Dun and Bradstreet's DUNS MARKET IDENTIFIERS is an online database (File DMI on PFDS) which provides information on a large number of UK companies: 150,000 companies are covered in this extensive file which gives details such as the address, telephone and telex numbers, directors, parent company, annual sales turnover, export sales, number of employees and SIC code. There is no single hard copy equivalent of the DUNS MARKET database which is compiled by Dun and Bradstreet's business analysts by means of telephone surveys.

As there are over 900,000 companies registered in Great Britain, it is clear that the major national directories cannot list all of them. There are, fortunately, many specialist directories which cover specific industry sectors: these can be useful for tracing the manufacturers and suppliers of those obscure products which lighten the business librarian's day. Manufacturers of teddy bears, for instance, are included in the *Teddy Bear Guide* published by Hugglets, while Punch and Judy acts, another of childhood's delights, are listed in the *Directory of Professional Puppeteers*, issued by the Puppet Centre Trust. Details of these and many more fascinating directories are included in *Current British Directories* produced by CBD Research Ltd and now in its 11th edition. *Current British Directories* is an excellent source of information on directories of all sorts: no business library should be without it!

In addition to the many specialist directories, there seem to be an ever-increasing number of directories and databases which cover local firms, produced by organisations such Chambers of Commerce, Small Business Clubs, local authority Planning Departments and libraries. As these local directories are produced by such a variety of organisations, the standard of production is not uniform throughout the country, and alphabetisation can sometimes be a problem! Nonetheless, these local directories are often a useful source of addresses as they include sole traders and partnerships as well as the companies which are included in the larger, nationwide directories.

The value of telephone directories as a source of company information is often under-estimated. No business can afford to be without a telephone! Certainly, it would be time-consuming to look through all UK telephone directories to find that elusive firm – but a company's trading address is often in the same area as its registered office, and can be traced using the local telephone directory. Particularly useful is the London Postal Area Business and Services Directory which includes all business subscribers in the London Postal Area. As the use of newer technology has increased, *The Telex Directory* and *The Fax Book: the UK Facsimile Directory* have become more important sources of company locations. The *Telex Directory*, for instance, currently has some 110,000 listings.

Who owns it? Tracing company ownership

Business librarians are often asked for details of company ownership, and the directory *Who owns whom: United Kingdom and Republic of Ireland* can often provide the answer. The UK edition lists more than 100,000 subsidiaries owned by over 6,500 parent organisations. Volume 1 lists parent companies, providing details of addresses, telephone numbers, the line of business and all subsidiaries and associates; also included are the names of consortia with their member organisations. Volume 2 lists all companies in alphabetical order, linking each company with its immediate parent. *Who owns whom: United Kingdom and Republic of Ireland* is available as an annual hard copy publication, which is updated by four quarterly supplements. As the WOW file on PFDS, it is also available as an online multi-national file, merged to give worldwide coverage with the three other regional directories in the *Who owns whom* series.

More details, please ... finding financial data

The primary source of information on a company's financial performance is its annual accounts, and all limited companies, whether public or private, trading or non-trading, are required to submit accounts each year to Companies Registration Office. In addition, public companies also publish their accounts in an annual report which is issued to all shareholders and to other interested parties. The annual report is an important public relations exercise for public companies which are concerned to publicise their activities (or an optimistic picture of their activities, at least) among their shareholders and those who might wish to become shareholders. Private companies, on the other hand, are not normally so concerned with publicity as their shares are not available for public purchase. Consequently, while it is relatively easy to obtain financial data on public companies, it is often deceptively difficult to research the financial affairs of private companies.

The annual reports of public companies are usually produced in a glossy format and are available (normally free of charge) from the company's registrar. A notice of company meetings to be held during the following week is included in *The Week's Financial Diary* published each Monday in the *Financial Times*: the company meetings included in this diary signal the announcement of companies' interim and final results. When the Annual Report and Accounts is published, it is then summarised in the newspaper. The Annual Report usually includes the Chairman's statement which describes major developments during the year and plans for the future, together with the Report of the Directors which includes detailed accounts. There may also be additional notes on the accounts produced by the auditors.

Although many libraries collect annual reports in hard copy, they are bulky and occupy considerable space on the shelves. The Report and

Accounts of 3,000 major UK companies are reproduced on microfiche by the MIRAC service marketed by McCarthy Information Services: subscribers may take the full service or restrict their purchases to a selective list. MIRAC can also provide a back issue service, for older reports. Online coverage of these reports is provided by the ICC INTERNATIONAL BUSINESS RESEARCH database (File 563 on DIALOG) which provides the full text of all annual reports and accounts issued by British companies listed on the London Stock Exchange.

The annual accounts of all registered companies, whether public or private, are available from Companies Registration Office. Company files, including the annual accounts, may be inspected at the Companies Registration Office in Cardiff or London (or in Edinburgh for Scottish companies). Not everyone can visit one of the CRO search rooms in person, however, and a number of commercial search agents will obtain copies of company data, for a fee, on behalf of a client. Companies House will also provide microfiche or paper copies of company files for enquirers who apply in writing for information on a particular company. Companies House is now actively marketing their search service and attempting to make the service more attractive: the results of a search can be supplied by post, by fax or by courier, and clients can even pay by credit card.

If the annual report is the primary source of financial data, the *Extel* card is often regarded as the most important secondary source. The *Extel* card service is produced by *Extel Financial Ltd*, and over the years has become an institution. For each company, *Extel* provides an annual card and, when appropriate, a news card. The annual card contains basic facts concerning the company's formation, its capital history, main activities and subsidiaries. It also shows how the board of directors is composed and summarises the latest annual statement by the chairman. The annual card, which is prepared shortly after its annual report and accounts have been published, also gives figures, in tabulated form, covering five years profit and loss accounts, analyses of turnover and profit, source and application of funds and the latest balance sheets; details of share prices and dividends are also provided, when appropriate.

Whenever the company has news to report, *Extel* issues a news card: the facts contained on the card may include details of an acquisition or merger, a change of directors, or any other relevant information about the company's activities. The figures provided always include tables of interim financial results (quarterly or half-yearly) as well as the preliminary announcements of the annual figures; details of recent dividends may also be provided. The news card may be updated several times each year until the next annual card replaces it.

Extel's UK card services cover a number of different sectors: the *UK Listed Service* contains information on approximately 3,000 companies whose stocks and shares are listed on the British and Irish Stock

Exchanges. 1,200 of these companies are reviewed in more depth in *The Analyst's Service* which provides a 10 year record of capital changes, share prices, dividends, yields and selected profit and loss and balance sheet ratios.

Information on all companies traded on the Stock Exchange's Unlisted Securities Market are included in *Extel*'s *Unlisted Securities Market Service* which currently covers some 400 companies; the *Third Market Service* provides a parallel service for those companies traded on the Stock Exchange's Third Market, while information on some 100 leading companies traded on the OTC Market is given in the *Over The Counter Service*. *Extel* also produces the *Unquoted Companies Service*; some 1,900 unquoted companies are covered on these cards.

In addition to its traditional card services, *Extel* also provides a range of electronic information services. MicroEXSTAT provides a database of company financial information which includes up to six years' detailed balance sheet and profit and loss account data, together with supplementary information: included on the database are companies listed on the UK Stock Exchange, USM-traded companies, the largest unquoted companies and selected companies from Europe, Japan and Australia. The data can be manipulated, using in-house computer facilities, to produce customised reports and tailored searches.

The company accounts and returns filed at Companies House provide the base information for several online databases. The JORDANWATCH database which is available direct from JORDANS and on PFDS, is derived from records held at Companies Registration Office and supplemented with information taken daily from the *London* and *Edinburgh Gazettes* and listings of charges and receiverships. In addition to the basic details available for all UK registered companies, full financial information is available on over 70,000 companies, including the larger companies, which have a turnover figure greater than £1 million or a pre-tax profit greater than £50,000 or shareholder funds greater than £1 million. The JORDANWATCH database is updated weekly and may be searched using a menu system as well as using standard commands. It is now also available as the FAME database on CD-ROM.

ICC also uses the source data from annual reports and accounts filed at Companies Registration Office in the compilation of its database of British companies: the ICC database contains information on 100,000 British companies, including the majority of quoted and Unlisted Securities Market companies. The database appears in a number of forms on a variety of host systems including DIALOG (File 562: ICC BRITISH COMPANY FINANCIAL DATASHEETS), DATA-STAR, DATASTREAM and ICC's own viewdata system.

Despite the range of online services now available, it can still be extremely difficult to trace financial information on private companies;

even if the annual accounts are obtained from Companies House, the enquirer may find it difficult to compare the results with others in the sector. It is therefore still useful to consider using one of the directories listing unquoted companies. *Macmillan's Unquoted Companies*, an annual volume published by ICC Information Group Ltd, provides financial profiles of 'Britain's top 10,000 unquoted companies'. Financial information included in the volume includes data for three years on items such as sales, pre-tax profit, the number of employees and their remuneration, capital employed, net worth and stocks, together with return on capital employed and pre-tax profits as a percentage of sales. Information on private companies is also provided in a series of directories produced by Jordans: *Britain's Privately Owned Companies: The Top 4000* is issued in two volumes, with Volume 1 covering *The Top 2000* and Volume 2 giving details of *The Second 2000*; an additional volume on *Britain's Third 2000 Privately Owned Companies* has also been published. In these volumes, companies are listed in order of sales turnover and in alphabetic order of company name. The directories also provide 12 comparison tables which rank the companies by criteria such as pre-tax profits, profitability and liquidity. The financial data included in the directories includes the year-end date, sales figures, net tangible assets, pre-tax profits, the total number of borrowers and details of shareholders' funds.

Can I trust them? Credit rating data

Companies often wish to know how much credit they can extend to other companies, without excessive risk of financial loss. Credit-rating services are usually aimed at the end-user company, rather than the information provider. These services should be used with care; an article in the *Financial Times* in 1986 compared several credit rating sources and found that the credit limits suggested for the same company varied from £10,000 to £90,000[2]. One of the most easily accessible credit status databases is INFOCHECK on PFDS. The database covers some 210,000 UK companies, and is apparently increasing at a rate of 3,000 companies per week. For each, a range of information is provided including a credit rating and data derived from up to four years' annual accounts; an expert summary of company performance and future expectations is also given.

Requests for share price data

After the Second World War, the number of individuals owning shares decreased steadily, due to the post-war tax structure and the increase in indirect investment through financial institutions such as pension funds and insurance companies. In the 1980s, however, this trend began to reverse, and it is estimated that the number of people owning stocks and shares rose from about three million in 1979 to more than nine million in 1987. So business librarians who deal with the general public are now more likely to receive enquiries about share prices than ever before. Business librarians working in commerce and industry will also receive requests for share price data as the value of a company's shares is an important element in the calculation of its market capitalisation and the appraisal of its performance.

When answering queries relating to share prices, it is essential to understand the precise requirements of the enquirer. While the professional investor will need the real-time price, as it is at this point in time, others will be quite satisfied with the latest close-of-trade price, while some will require historical share price data to monitor the company's performance over a period of time.

Again, it is also important to obtain precise information about where the share is traded, whether on the London Exchange itself (formally titled the International Stock Exchange of the United Kingdom and the Republic of Ireland), on the Unlisted Securities Market (the USM) or on the Third Market. Some shares are also traded outside the formal Stock Exchange markets; these are sold 'Over the Counter' (OTC) by licensed dealers in securities.

At the centre of the International Stock Exchange trading network is a screen-based electronic price information system known as SEAQ (Stock Exchange Automated Quotations) which was introduced in 1986 initially as a means to allow trading to take place off the floor of the Exchange. All member firms of the International Stock Exchange are broker/dealers who are able to act both in the capacity of an agent (broker) buying and selling shares on behalf of a client, or as a dealer, dealing in shares on their own account and earning money by making a profit on buying and selling shares. At the heart of the trading system are the market-makers, a group of broker/dealers who specialise in the dealing function. Market-makers actively make markets rather than just matching orders, and they compete with one another for business in the stocks in which they deal. The competing market-makers are obliged to enter into SEAQ their bid and ask prices (the prices at which they are prepared to buy and sell shares) together with details of the numbers of shares they are prepared to buy or sell at this rate. Through SEAQ, this information is transmitted to brokers' offices in the City and throughout the country as well as throughout the world. When a deal is done, the market-maker is obliged to enter details of the deal – the time, the price and the number of shares involved – into the computer system within five minutes of the time of execution.

Thus SEAQ provides price information on thousands of equities and fixed interest securities; these are divided into three categories, namely the Alpha's which are the most actively traded securities, the Beta's which are actively traded and the Gamma's which are relatively inactive securities. Over the past few years, foreign equities, securities which are listed on overseas exchanges but not in London, have become increasingly important business for securities firms based in London, whether or not those firms were members of the Exchange. In 1985, the Exchange set up SEAQ International to provide a marketplace for those equities which were previously traded in London on an informal basis. Open to firms which were not Stock Exchange members, SEAQ International has grown rapidly: it now has more than 40 market-makers quoting prices for more than 600 foreign stocks from 17 countries.

SEAQ and SEAQ International are trading systems which are used only by professional dealers. The data which they contain, however, forms the basis of many other commercial information systems and is fed into them, often on a continuous basis. The majority of the systems relating to share price data are produced and delivered to the user electronically; in this area of business information, hard copy is rare.

TOPIC is perhaps the best-known screen-based system covering the London market. A videotex system produced by the International Stock Exchange, it includes the SEAQ Market Maker competing quote service and the SEAQ International competing quote service together with a variety of information taken from a wide range of sources, including real-time feeds from other financial markets throughout the world. Company announcements are displayed as they are issued and foreign exchange prices are provided live from the major banks. A mid-price trend service covers over 2,000 UK equities and gilt-edged securities and dealing prices from the London Traded Options market. Also included on *TOPIC* are a number of closed user group services provided by market-makers and stockbrokers which are available only to their own clients.

TOPIC is a professional service aimed at the professional investor and at those who depend upon a wide range of financial information. For those who are interested in real-time information but cannot justify the high costs of the traditional real-time services, the International Stock Exchange has developed MARKET EYE which includes some of the information available on the more comprehensive TOPIC system. The information available on MARKET EYE covers best bid and ask prices and mid-price trends for all UK equities listed on the main market, the USM and the Third Market; it also covers fixed interest securities, such as debentures and loan stocks, and gilts, together with all London traded international securities. The FTSE 100 shares are reviewed in depth. There is, however, no foreign market data. MARKET EYE is accessed via the broadcast network, like the teletext systems, rather than via telephone connections. MARKET EYE users can also access CEEFAX data and can move from MARKET EYE to CEEFAX – and back again – with ease.

A similar information system, CITISERVICE is available via PRESTEL; CITISERVICE covers FTSE and USM – but not foreign securities. Three levels of service are available on CITISERVICE, namely the Closing Price Service, the Real Time Service and the Regular Update Service which provides five updates each day of the price of FTSE 100 shares and of the FTSE index.

A number of services now provide a range of data on individual companies, making available share price data together with annual account information. ANALYSIS is an online system which covers all companies quoted or traded in the United Kingdom. Each Analysis Report includes closing share price and full share information, key ratios, the balance sheet and profit and loss accounts for five years, plus notes and interim results, lists of major shareholders and details of the company's financial advisers. ANALYSIS is updated overnight; a direct feed from SEAQ is used to provide the latest close-of-trade prices.

Trading in shares is an international business, and a number of real-time share price information systems provide access to share price data from a wide range of sources. REUTERS EQUITIES 2000 claims that it provides 'the most comprehensive real-time equities database in the world'. It covers 'every major stock exchange in the world and every stock, bond and option quoted on each exchange'. In addition to the real-time information, there is some historic data, designed to show short-term trends. EQUITIES 2000 provides a range of facilities, including a user-defined quotes list for 50 shares on each terminal. The data can be manipulated using a graphics package to allow, for instance, a share price history for an individual equity to be overlain on the sector trend covering the same period.

ESPRIT produced by Extel Financial Services is also a real-time database which provides continuous feeds of pricing data and intra day prices. A wide range of securities are covered including FTSE and USM securities, together with over 20,000 European securities traded in Denmark, Sweden, Germany, France, the Netherlands, Belgium, Spain, Italy, Portugal, Austria and Switzerland. US data is not available in real-time at present – but Extel have just acquired an American subsidiary – which will enable them to provide real-time US data in future.

Analysts often require access to historical share price data in order to study the progress of an individual company or a particular industrial sector over time. DATASTREAM is an extensive information system which includes a number of databases: the EQUITIES DATABASE is particularly relevant as it provides extensive price data on shares traded in London and on foreign exchanges. Research data is stored on approximately 20,000 equities traded in the UK, Europe, the United States, the Far East and South Africa. Within each series, the user can select the level of detail required – which can range from a simple share price, yield and market value, for instance, to complete share price performance and growth rates. The historical database is particularly extensive: for most of the top 1,000 UK quoted equities, records are held back to 1965, while data available on international stocks dates back to 1973. Real-time information is also available on DATASTREAM: the London, Amsterdam, Brussels, Paris, Frankfurt and Zurich Stock Exchanges provide continuously updated stock prices for these markets. Datastream is accessed online; results can be manipulated using DATASTREAM's specialist software – and increasingly can be downloaded and integrated into in-house computer facilities, using standard packages such as Lotus 1-2-3.

Many business librarians do not have the resources to access the real-time information services on behalf of their users, and indeed their users would never require the level of detail available within those services. Often enquiries can be answered with the latest close-of-trade prices: the *Financial Times* is probably used most frequently to answer these questions. The coverage of share price data differs on some days. Each Monday's edition provides Friday's closing prices, together with the market capitalisation figures, based on market prices of the company's shares; it also gives the last date the share is quoted ex-dividend and the dates (in months) when the dividends are usually paid. The newspaper's coverage of share prices is, however, limited to those of general interest, and includes only those which are heavily traded. It does include some USM and Third Market shares, however, which are simply listed within the appropriate industry sector. The *Stock Exchange Daily Official List* provides more comprehensive coverage although foreign data is limited to the more interesting securities.

These hard copy sources can be supplemented by telephone services which provide real-time price data at the end of the telephone line. Both FT CITYLINE and SHARECALL offer share price data on 4,000 securities, including London-traded and SEAQ International shares.

Share ownership data

In addition to knowing what the shares cost, some enquirers need to know who owns them. Annual returns, containing a complete list of 'members of the company' (i.e. shareholders) must be filed each year within 48 days of the company's Annual General Meeting. Once the document has been lodged, CRO microfilm the shareholder listings (which for quoted companies are usually extensive) and make the microfilm available for public inspection. The ICC SHAREWATCH database provides details of share holdings of 0.25 per cent of issued share capital and above in British companies quoted on the UK Stock Exchange. ICC obtain the information from the Annual Returns; details are also provided directly by a number of companies, which allows the listings to be updated on a quarterly rather than an annual basis. Each ICC SHAREWATCH record contains details of the company's issued share capital, nominal share capital, par value of shares, the date of the shareholder listing, a statement of how many shareholders own over 0.25 per cent of the equity and what proportion of the total that represents – plus the name, address and size of holding for each of those shareholders. The ICC SHAREWATCH database is available on a variety of host systems including DATA-STAR, ICC VIEWDATA and TOPIC.

JORDANS also provide a database of share holdings. The JORDANS SHAREHOLDER SERVICE has been produced for many years in hard copy and is now also available in machine readable form, for use on an in-house computer: the service is updated on a monthly basis. The JORDANS database reveals shareholders with a holding equal to or above 0.15 per cent in publicly quoted and USM companies; in addition, the database holds information on beneficial owners who invest through nominee accounts.

What the media says

Against this wealth of financial and share price information, it is also crucial in the area of company information to know what the media has said about a particular company. The range of newspaper indexes available are discussed in depth in Chapter Three, 'Newspapers: a negelected resource'.

Increasingly, press and trade coverage is derived from online sources which allow the user to access not only the title and bibliographic reference of a relevant article but which also provide a summary of that article, or in some cases, the full text. Company information, like most business information, is required here and now; online sources provide up-to-date information and that immediacy can often be essential. There really is no substitute for online information; published indexes simply take too long to produce to be of relevance. Of all the online systems, TEXTLINE has probably played the greatest role in developing a dependence upon online searching of media coverage. In addition to its coverage of the national press, TEXTLINE provides a coast-to-coast coverage of the daily UK provincial newspapers, ranging from the *Aberdeen Press and Journal* to the *Plymouth News*, from the *East Anglian Daily Times* to the *Belfast Telegraph*. TEXTLINE's coverage of trade literature is also extensive, and is expanding.

PROFILE, a more recently established online service, also provides easy access to a wide range of publications; its simple command language is a great incentive to the end-user to try an online search, while the range of newspapers and journals covered is now extensive. In addition to a range of full-text sources, Profile also provides online access to the MCCARTHY Database, which provides information on individual companies together with data on a wide range of industry sectors. The information contained within the MCCARTHY database is derived from company annual reports and accounts, together with extracted trade and commodity statistics and articles from a range of journals.

While newspapers usually provide coverage of a company's financial performance, detailed technical information is more often found in trade journals. *Research Index* indexes a wide range of these specialist publications; many of the more significant trade and technical publications are now also available online in full text.

Sources of information on European companies

With 1992 and the Single European Market now appearing just around the corner, there is an increasing awareness of the business advantages which Europe has to offer and an increased demand for information on European companies. It is not intended to discuss European sources in detail in this chapter (indeed we would require another book to do that thoroughly) but rather to indicate some of the major sources which are more widely available. Initially, it may be helpful to mention an excellent source of information on those information sources which is produced by the London Business School Information Service. *European Country Information: EEC countries*[3] provides a thorough guide to company formation within individual European countries, together with an annotated listing of country-specific information sources. Also useful is Kogan Page's guide to *Setting up a company in the European community*[4] which provides information on the legal and financial requirements for companies registered in each of the 12 member states.

Before providing details to the enquirer of a European firm, the librarian has to locate the company. This can be a real problem; for instance, Is the French name registered in France or Belgium? Could the Dutch name really be Flemish? Is the Spanish company possibly Portuguese? One clue in this business Babel is the initials after the company name. All European countries have some form of public and private company system, similar to that operated in the UK, and most use distinctive abbreviations after the company name to indicate the company's status. Table 1 provides a list of the abbreviations used by EC countries, for ready reference in moments of panic!

Country	Public	Private
Belgium	SA (Société Anonyme) or NV (Naamloze Vennootschap)	SPRL (Société de Personnes à Responsabilité Limitée) or PVBA (Personenvennootschap met beperkte aansprakelijkheid)
Denmark	A/S (Aktieselskab)	ApS (Anpartsselskab)
France	SA (Société Anonyme)	SARL (Société à Responsabilité Limitée)
Germany	AG (Aktiengesellschaft)	GmbH (Gesellschaft mit beschrankter Haftung)
Greece	AE (Anonymous Eteria)	EPE (Eteria Periorismenis Efthinis)
Italy	SpA (Società per Azioni)	SRL (Società a Responsibilita Limitata)
Luxembourg	SA (Societé Anonyme)	SARL (Société à Responsibilité Limitée)
Netherlands	NV (Naamloze Vennootschap)	BV (Besloten Vennootschap met beperkte Aansprakelijkheid)
Portugal	SARL or SA (Sociedade Anonima de Responsabilidade Limitada)	LDA (Sociedade por Quotas de Responabilidade Limitada)
Spain	SA (Sociedad Anónima)	SA (Sociedad de Responsabilidad Limitada)
UK	Plc (Public Limited Company)	Ltd (Private Limited Company)

Table 1. European company abbreviations

A number of directories include address and telecommunications details for companies throughout Europe, and these directories provide an excellent start point for tracing a European company. Graham and Trotman produce a three-volume publication on *Major companies of Europe*; volume 1 covers the EC countries other than the UK, while volume 2 covers UK companies and volume 3 covers the non-EC countries of Austria, Finland, Liechtenstein, Norway, Sweden and Switzerland. A total of 7,000 companies are included, and the directory includes data on the companies, operations, finances and executive staff, in addition to details of location. *Europe's 15,000 largest companies* are listed in a directory published annually by ELC International. In addition to an alphabetic listing of the companies, the directory provides a number of ranked tables: these tables include lists of the top 100 companies in each country ranked by the sales value as well as the 100 greatest loss-makers in Europe. The directory is also available as an online file (under the title *Europe's Largest Companies*) on PFDS; the online version covers more companies (25,000 in December 1988) and includes both UK and continental European companies. Data provided for each company includes the address and telecommunications details, names of chief personnel, number of employees, financial data and International Standard Industrial Classification code. *Principal International Businesses* produced by Dun and Bradstreet, provides international coverage of company activity, listing some 50,000 companies in 133 countries. In addition to the full alphabetical listing, the directory also provides a geographical list, by country, together with a product index. *Principal International Businesses* is also available online, as INTERNATIONAL DUN'S MARKET IDENTIFIERS on DIALOG.

Individual European countries are usually covered by one of the Kompass directories which provide valuable company listings and product indexes. Several of the individual volumes have been merged to form a single online file covering France, West Germany, Italy, Denmark, Norway, Sweden, Belgium, Switzerland, the Netherlands, Luxembourg and Spain. This single *EUROPEAN KOMPASS* database is available via KOMPASS ONLINE.

Many libraries have a surprisingly extensive range of telephone directories covering European countries, and these can often prove useful when tracking an elusive company. Similarly, the international telex directory and, increasingly, the international fax directories can often prove helpful.

Who owns whom: Continental Europe lists over 8,000 European parent companies and provides details of their domestic and foreign subsidiaries. Parent companies registered outside Europe, but with subsidiaries or associates within those countries are also included in the directory. The publication is available online in the merged *Who owns whom* file on PFDS.

The Extel card system extends to Europe too; some 700 'leading European companies' from 15 countries are included in the series. For each company, the information provided includes the company name, address and telephone number, names of board members and subsidiary companies, details of principal activities and summaries of the consolidated profit and loss accounts, consolidated balance sheets and the chairman's statement.

The full annual reports of European companies are available on microfiche from the CIFAR International Annual Reports Collection; 12 European countries are currently covered by the CIFAR service.

European media coverage is provided by a number of sources. The *McCarthy European card service* provides the full text of relevant articles relating to a large number of European companies; this service is available in hard copy, on microfiche or online via PROFILE. TEXTLINE's Database 1 includes both UK and Western European sources: the newspapers covered range from *le Journal de Genève* to the *Helsingin Sanomat* and from the *Norges Handels og* to the *Frankfurter Allegemeine Zeitung*. The INFOMAT file which is available on a number of hosts including DIALOG, DATA-STAR and PFDS, provides coverage of business news articles taken from over 400 business newspapers and journals, and translated into English from the language of publication. The database provides useful coverage of European company activity. The coverage provided on PTS PROMT on DIALOG and DATA-STAR is also extensive and covers 'thousands of newspapers, business magazines, government magazines, trade journals, bank newsletters and special reports throughout the world'. The information on the PROMT database includes acquisitions, capacities, international trade, market data, new products, production, regulations and technology.

Due to the keen interest in European sources, it seems likely that the 1990s will see a rapid expansion in the number of information services covering European companies and a standardisation of the sources available on individual countries. There is at present a desperate need for improvement in some of the company directories covering the newer EC members such as Portugal and Greece.

Further reading

1. GOLZEN, G. *Working for yourself*, *Daily Telegraph* guide to self-employment. 7th ed., 1984.
2. Consumer test of credit checking and company information agencies, *Financial Times*, 8 April 1986, 16.
3. London Business School. Information Service, *European company information: EEC countries*, 3rd ed., 1989.
4. Brebner and Co. *Setting up a company in the European community*, 1989.

Chapter Eight

MARKETING INFORMATION

Jo Haythornthwaite and **Diana Edmonds**

Collins concise English dictionary defines marketing as 'the business of selling goods, including advertising, packaging, etc...'. The process of marketing a product may be seen as dividing into three stages: planning, advertising and selling. During each of these stages, the information service available to the company's marketing department will have a valuable role to play.

General reference books

Some basic background books deserve a mention. The Advertising Association produce the *Marketing pocket book* which is a small annual compilation of invaluable statistical information on consumers, distribution, advertising and the media which also includes a wealth of demographic and economic data. *The marketing directory* is a handbook for the UK marketing industry which is published by Professional Books and appears twice yearly. It is basically a slim volume of useful addresses, telephone numbers and contacts, relating to audio-visual equipment, conference services, direct marketing journals, market research, the media, public relations companies and trade associations. It is a helpful current source of addresses for the busy information professional.

The librarian in search of definitions of terms used in marketing and advertising can turn to the *Macmillan dictionary of marketing and advertising*, edited by Michael Baker and compiled by the staff of the Marketing Department of the University of Strathclyde.

Marketing: sources of information

Sources of information about marketing are currently well documented in three books which cover the same ground in different ways. First the *Market research sourcebook* by Tricia Walters, Headland Press, 1985. This publication comes in a ring binder to allow for updating. Chapters include 'What is market research?' 'Market research techniques explained.' 'How to do-it-yourself.' 'How to buy research off-the-shelf.' 'How to commission market research.' Appendices include lists of books, key magazines, libraries, associations and courses.

Euromonitor are, at the time of writing, just about to publish the 1989 edition of their *Compendium of marketing information sources* which they claim covers 1,500 sources. It lists libraries, market research agencies, associations, databases and databanks, journals, company information services. They also publish a smaller and cheaper *A-Z of UK marketing information sources.*

Key Note have also produced a *Guide to marketing research* which looks at much the same subject areas: how to obtain research, the different types of data available and the sources in which to find it. The first section describes the role of marketing research and how to use it. It also describes the functions of desk research, field research and syndicated research. Finally, it explains how and where to obtain marketing research. The second section is a guide to sources and includes company directories, company financial information, market information, market research companies, advertising data, trade associations, periodicals, official sources of information, libraries and information brokers and online information.

Planning

Consumer research

Planning the marketing of a new product involves collecting background material and looking at any available market research and consumer research. The essential background material is frequently to be found in the statistical series published by HMSO for the UK Government. These are particularly rich sources of marketing data which can provide a sound demographic and sociological basis for a marketing strategy. Many of the statistics published in these government series are not 'dry' figures or 'head-counts' but are an evaluation of the lifestyle and mood of the country, based on personal interviews with representative samples of the population. These statistical series can be traced via the *Guide to official statistics* and the *Catalogue of British official publications not published by HMSO.*

Social Trends and *Key Facts* are annual publications which summarise the statistical data published in a wide range of government statistical series. Both are intended to make statistics more 'user friendly' and make extensive use of charts, diagrams and informative commentary to present a snapshot of the nation. They are a good starting point for anyone approaching such statistics for the first time and include demographic and other data alongside the results of surveys; for example, on the amount of disposable income spent on leisure pursuits.

The 10-yearly *Census* remains the most authoritative source of demographic information as it is the only complete survey of the whole UK population. However, as the time lapse between censuses is unacceptable to most users, the importance of other sources has grown. *Population projections*, based on the *Census*, forecasts the future population levels of the UK well into the next century and so is a key source of predicting future market size.

Business Monitors and *British Business* are invaluable sources of information on UK industry which are dealt with elsewhere in this book. They provide useful information on production, sales and export levels of manufactured and other goods and so can help in the planning of the marketing campaign by indicating sales levels of existing products.

The Employment Gazette, published by the Department of Employment, is a monthly journal containing readable and informative articles and a statistical section which gives information on the RPI, earnings and employment/unemployment levels on a monthly basis.

Valuable information can be gained from the surveys conducted by the OPCS, the CSO and individual government departments, most of which are based on randomly selected samples of the population.

The Family Expenditure Survey has been taken annually by the Department of Employment since 1957. It is based on a representative sample of private households (selected by postcode) and it contains information on household structure, income, and expenditure on a variety of products and service groups, both at national and regional level. Its prime purpose is to show how expenditure patterns of different households vary according to the characteristics of the household, e.g. the number of persons or the number of breadwinners. Over 12,000 households annually are invited to take part in the survey and usually over two-thirds agree to keep records of their expenditure and to participate in regular personal interviews. *The Household Food Consumption and Expenditure – National Food Survey* is conducted on a similar basis.

The General Household Survey is produced by the OPCS Social Survey Division as a continuous survey of households, based on a postcode selected sample of private addresses. It has operated since 1971 and its prime role is to act as a policy-making tool for central government. It is based on over 12,000 interviews, conducted through the year by OPCS staff. Information is presented in a variety of tables, pie charts and bar charts alongside highly readable textual commentary. Subjects covered include family structure, ethnic groups, marital status, owner-occupier versus tenant, educational background, etc. Of particular interest to market researchers is its analysis of ownership of consumer durables, for example white goods, analysed by the type of household. It includes opinion as well as hard fact and a recent survey question asked for public opinion on the perceived pros and cons of home ownership.

Unpublished, additional data is often available on request from the originating department for many government sponsored surveys and this data can be tailored to suit the user's exact needs. Most survey results are also available electronically, either as an online service or by the purchase of the survey and other results on disc.

Market research

When the marketing director requests to see what market research is available relating to a specific product or group of products, the first thing to do is to check the various indexes and bibliographies of published market research reports. The *International directory of published market research* is an authoritative source produced by the BOTB and is often a fruitful starting point for such a search. However, as this is published irregularly, other sources must be checked to ensure a thorough search for relevant reports has been made.

Marketsearch, the international directory of published market research is published annually with a mid-year supplement and, in addition, the publishers also provide a round-the-year telephone hotline service to subscribers of the hard copy publication to provide information about reports published since the directory went to press. It covers approximately 18,000 reports issued over the previous five years by nearly 700 authors (mainly market research firms and consultancies), and is international in coverage. It is comprehensive and useful for retrospective searching as well as for tracing current reports. Its indexes are based on the UK SIC codes and references can also be retrieved by subject or by publisher. For each report, the title and sub-title, number of pages, geographic coverage, date, source and price are given. The publications covered are from mainstream business information publishers, e.g. Key Note, market research companies, institutes and government bodies, manufacturers' organisations and commercial companies.

Both of these directories are useful for retrospective searching and allow the researcher to find out what has already been published on a given product or service, but to trace newly published reports indexes and abstracts must be checked. A number which cover market research reports are available, in hard copy and online.

Marketing Surveys Index is published by the Institute of Marketing, the Business Information Service of the Science Reference Library and Marketing Surveys for Industry. It is an A4, loose-leaf publication which is updated monthly and indexes market research reports from a wide variety of publishers. There is a cumulative subject directory and a section containing publishers' details. The entries indicate subject, country or countries covered, the number of pages, the report title and a brief note on report content. The index is also available online via PROFILE.

Since no indexing service can be entirely comprehensive, it is essential, however, to check in a few other places. Another regularly published index is the *Reports Index* which is published every two months and includes reports from mainstream business information publishers (e.g. Frost & Sullivan), academic and research institutions, government bodies, finance houses and market research companies throughout the world. Each issue includes reports published in the previous three to four months. The reports are indexed by subject, industry sectors, product groups, business or general topics and the subject index is cumulated throughout the year. For each report, the title, author, corporate author, date, price, number of pages and availability are given, along with a brief abstract or contents listing.

Whereas both *MIS* and *Reports Index* help you to find market research reports published as complete, priced reports, it is important to remember that many valuable market reports appear in trade journals and the national press.

Statistics and market research: a guide to current periodical articles is published by the Birmingham Public Libraries and includes references to articles selected from over 50 journals including general business titles such as *British Business* and specific trade journals, e.g. *Brewing Review*. Some government statistics and some international titles are included. The references are listed in product or subject groupings and for each entry the title, journal code and date and page reference is given. This is a very useful title as it indexes British journals which are likely to be in the stock of most public business libraries. Published monthly, each issue indexes articles which have appeared in journals published in the previous two months and so it is useful for tracing recent articles.

Two indexes which cover US marketing reports are available on DIALOG. *Findex: the directory of market research reports, studies and surveys* covers 1977 to date and is updated quarterly. It indexes and abstracts all industry and market research reports commercially available from US and international publishers. INDUSTRY DATA SOURCES covers from 1979 and is updated monthly (also available via DATA-STAR). It provides bibliographic references to published market research reports, statistics and special issues of journals on 65 major industries.

Remember that all the major market research organisations publish catalogues of their publications, for example *Euromonitor*, and it is therefore well worth scanning these regularly. An index to the Frost and Sullivan current market research reports is available via DATA-STAR, with a brief abstract for each report.

Other useful indexes include *Research Index*, available in hard copy or online via PFDS, which covers 125 trade journals and papers. *Marketing and Management Abstracts*, produced by PIRA and available from several online hosts, abstracts articles from journals, books, reports and statistics on marketing, PR and forecasting. *Market Research Abstracts*, available via TEXTLINE, also covers market research and marketing journals and is good for techniques, methodology and general marketing issues.

Another key online source of information in this field is the *Marketing and Advertising Reference Service* (MARS) produced by PREDICASTS and available via DIALOG, DATA-STAR and TEXTLINE. Although this still retains a US bias in its coverage, it indexes and abstracts over 100 publications (journals, newsletters and trade publications) in addition to the advertising columns in major newspapers. It concentrates on the advertising and marketing of consumer goods.

The INFOMAT database available via several online hosts contains more than 350,000 references. Its main strength is in consumer market information, and its international coverage has a definite European bias as 60 per cent of its records are references to UK and western European publications. It offers English summaries of all foreign language titles and is good for sales leads, business trends, competitors' activities and economic forecasts.

PROFILE's online service claims to offer 'instant access to market sizes, brand shares, consumer research, media spending, press comment and social and economic forecasts on virtually every consumer goods product and market in the UK'. In reality it offers access to the full text of a number of trade journals and market research and marketing journals, including *Campaign*, *Marketing*, *Media Week* and the *Mintel Daily Digest*.

TEXTLINE offers the largest number of full text journals online including several specialist marketing titles, e.g. *Marketing*, *Journal of Consumer Research*, within the Marketing and Media database. It also offers access to specific trade journals in other databases, e.g. *The Grocer* in the retailing database.

NEXIS (within the Advertising and Public Relations Library) offers full text access to advertising, PR and marketing journals which may be searched individually or in groups. NEWSNET provides full text access to 300+ business newsletters but retains a strong US bias.

When you have located what sounds like a relevant market research report, your troubles may be just beginning. Many market research reports are very expensive and some are very poor value for money since they consist of desk research which the trained information specialist could do just as well or better, given the time in which to do it. If it is decided that you cannot afford to buy the report but you would still like to see it, this may be possible. BL Document Supply Centre does have some of the cheaper ones which are available for loan and BL SRIS also has a good collection of the cheaper titles. These are, of course, not available for loan so the SRIS collection is only of use if Holborn, London is accessible for you or the staff of the marketing section. *Market research: a guide to British Library holdings*, sixth ed. 1989/90 has recently appeared and is available from the Publications Sales Unit at BL, Boston Spa.

Some business libraries buy the occasional market research report on request but many now feel that purchasing such expensive data which is very soon out of date is a doubtful use of public funds. The information manager can only be guided by past experience when deciding whether or not to buy. The name of the publisher usually indicates the reliability or otherwise of the product.

Many online databases, however, now offer the full text of reports and so this can be a way of accessing either the whole or part of a report without purchasing the hard copy publication. PERGAMON FINANCIAL DATA SERVICES offers access to the MAID database which provides full text retrieval of market research reports, market size information, advertising expenditure data, financial surveys and company profiles. Sources include key publishers such as Jordans, Key Note and MEAL. MAID sees itself as the premium product in the advertising and marketing field. Originally aimed at advertising agencies and management consultancies, it has now widened its client base to include banks and industrial companies. However, its annual fee of approximately £4,500, in addition to online time costs, will make it too expensive for many clients.

PROFILE offers access to some market research reports in full text as part of its 'normal' online service, including Euromonitor Market Direction (added to the service in 1988 and providing detailed reports on 58 consumer markets in five countries) and Market Research Reports produced by Marketing Strategies for Industry. On payment of an additional fee, PROFILE also provides access to the publications of the Henley Centre (Leisure Futures and Planning Consumer Markets); MINTEL publications (including Leisure Intelligence, Market Research Reports, Marketing Intelligence, Personal Finance Intelligence and Retail Intelligence); and the MEAL Quarterly Digest. Many of these titles are also available in full text on the TEXTLINE Service.

Advertising information

Advertising a product has to be carefully planned. There is considerable market research involved long before the decisions as to how, when and where the product will be advertised. Companies, in general, do not handle the advertising of their products, it is handled by an appropriate advertising agency. Information scientists may work in the information centres of advertising agencies or in companies where the marketing department is trying to decide on the choice of an agency or is co-operating with the chosen agency in planning the advertising campaign.

There are three stages in the advertising process at which the information scientist may be involved: first, in evaluating market size; secondly, finding out what competitors spend on advertising and how they spend it; and, finally, ascertaining what agencies handle which brand names.

Evaluating market size

An enquiry as to market size will draw on the market research reports described earlier in the chapter and also on a number of less substantial reports published either as slight monographs or as part of journals. There are a number of these journals including *Market Intelligence*, *Leisure Intelligence*, *Retail Intelligence* and *Personal Finance Intelligence*, which are all *Mintel* publications. Other important titles include *Market Research Great Britain*, *Market Assessment*, *Food Growth Markets*, *Non-Food Growth Markets* and *Retail Business*.

The first four titles mentioned are part of Mintel's market information service. Mintel is a London-based company which was founded in 1972. In addition to publishing journals, Mintel markets its information service which is based on a substantial library which has a large press cuttings collection on microfilm and long back runs of relevant government publications; for example, the *General Household Survey*. They also provide a desk research service for a fee.

Mintel produces four journals of which the best known is the monthly *Market Intelligence*. Each issue analyses five or six consumer goods markets or services. Consumer research is carried out into purchasing and usage habits for each study using a sample of over 1,000 respondents. Each report goes out to the trade for comments prior to publication.

A typical recent issue looked at prepared salads, dark spirits, heat conservation, kitchen wraps, TV sets and ethnic foods. The report on prepared salads defined the product carefully and cited examples. Prepared salads were then divided into chilled salads, dried salads (new to me) and canned salads. Next, the distribution of the product was analysed and a consumer profile was provided. This consumer profile section is obviously invaluable to those planning an advertising and marketing strategy. Finally, the report provided a section on the future prospects of the product. All the reports included in *Market Intelligence* follow roughly this pattern. The reports are, of necessity, brief and based on a relatively small sample. They provide a starting point for further research and have the advantage of being up-to-date.

Retail Intelligence is quarterly and looks at both different types of retailers and at general aspects of retailing. *Leisure Intelligence* is also quarterly and contains studies relating to leisure products and activities. A further quarterly research journal looks at the world of *Personal Finance Intelligence*. Mintel reports are available online via PROFILE.

Euromonitor is a major publisher in the market intelligence field and publishes books, journals and reports. One of their handbooks of special interest to marketing departments is the *A-Z of UK Brand Leaders* which identifies over 500 companies in the UK which have brand leadership in a significant sector of the consumer market. In addition, they offer a consultancy service which will produce reports on specific products or companies. They also provide a conventional fee-based information service called DIAL, which stands for Direct Information Access Line. A service called Market Direction updates market information on consumer products in five major world markets: France, Italy, West Germany, the US and the UK. This file and two other Euromonitor files of European data are available via MAID on PERGAMON FINANCIAL DATA SERVICES.

The major journal which Euromonitor produces is *Market Research Great Britain*. It appears monthly and is similar to *Market Intelligence* in that it presents the reader with a collection of market reports each month. A recent issue features hi-fi, wine, catering for children, shavers and garden supplies.

Euromonitor also publishes some more weighty market surveys, such as surveys of *The World Book Industry* and *The World Petroleum Industry*. They also produce, as the company name might suggest, a number of reference books with a European slant and some ranging even further afield. *Retail Business* is a monthly journal which concentrates on trends in retailing. It is an EIU Economist publication and has existed since 1958.

Market Assessment is a bi-monthly journal published by BLA Publications which has been disseminating short market research reports since 1979.

Market Assessment Publications describe themselves as business and market information specialists. Their publication *Market Forecasts* is annual and appears in two volumes. It covers 250 UK consumer and office markets in one-page summaries. The emphasis, as the title suggests, is on forecasting and the data is based on extensive trade interviews. In addition, Market Assessment produce market sector reports, two quarterly publications – *Food Growth Markets* and *Non-Food Growth Markets* and an annual publication entitled *Top 400 UK Markets*. Like most of their competitors they also provide consultancy and research services.

In addition to these journals and annual publications, there are several other publishers who produce market surveys. One of these is Key Note Publishers Ltd who produce a wide range of *Key Note Reports* which provide up-to-date market information on industry sectors. Each report explains the industry structure, notes major manufacturers, analyses market size and provides a consumer profile, together with an overview of trends in UK sales and, where relevant, import and export activities. The reports also provide information on market and brand shares, recent developments within the market, future prospects, the financial state of the market, further sources of information for those who wish to pursue their research further and, finally, a 'what the papers say' section, which lists recent press items relating to the industry sector. Recent reports have included *The Business Press*, *Baby Products* and *On-line Databases*. Key Note undertake to supply all reports by return of post and also have a substantial reference section which can be used by those requiring an even more specific knowledge of the market. They also publish some books, including *A guide to market research* (mentioned earlier). They are now an ICC Group Company. ICC Financial Ratios and Jordans also produce reports but their reports have a stronger emphasis on financial data. ICC KEY NOTES database is a separate database which is available on DATA-STAR. It is a full text database which provides information on more than 100 sectors of the UK economy. In addition to the full text, the database provides well-written abstracts which make it possible for the user to decide whether the full text is worth consulting for their particular query. Another helpful feature is the provision for searching under SIC codes. A series of over 200 market research studies from ICC Key Note reports are now also available on PROFILE.

FINDEX is an annual reference guide produced by Euromonitor which provides an index to over 11,000 market and business research reports from 450 international market research organisations and, thus, provides the researcher with a key to all these varied sources of market surveys.

Advertising queries: agencies, advertising rates, etc.

Once the market size has been established and all the market research has been completed, the advertising team will have to decide where, how and when to advertise. They will need to find out the relevant advertising rates of the various media which they hope to use and they may decide where to advertise on the basis of information as to what their competitors spend and where they spend it. Do they use newspapers, journals, TV, cinema commercials, billboards, etc? They will also be interested to discover what agencies handle what brand names. If the company plans to ask a well-known agency to handle the advertising, it should be one that does not already have a brand leader in that specific product range.

There are a number of useful reference books of which the most useful is undoubtedly the *Advertisers annual*, which is published by British Media Publications. It is now in three volumes:

Vol I: Advertising
Vol II: UK media, newspapers, TV and radio, outdoor advertising, overseas media
Vol III: Services

The overseas media section has been greatly expanded in the last few years and is invaluable. It divides down into Europe, the Middle East and North Africa, Africa (excluding North Africa), the Americas, Asia and the Far East and Australia and the Pacific. In addition, it includes an index to countries, a list of UK representatives in the various countries, a list of consultants for overseas media and a section on in-flight media (the captive audience should make this a good place to advertise!).

The *Advertisers Annual* is very good for information on local and free newspapers and contains so much information that it could be seen as the *Whitaker*'s of the advertising world.

BRAD (British Rate and Data) is a monthly publication which provides information about the cost of advertising in newspapers, periodicals, radio, TV and via other advertising media. A more detailed account of its coverage can be found in the chapter *Newspapers: an undervalued resource*. *BRAD* is available online on PROFILE which is now part of the *Financial Times Business Information Service*. MEAL (Media Expenditure Analysis Ltd) is the service which provides data on what companies spend on advertising via television, newspapers and magazines. The data is broken down by product. MEAL is also available on MAID which is hosted by PERGAMON FINANCIAL DATA SERVICES.

Tracing the advertisements

It is possible to find out what is being spent on advertising in the press via the *Press Register*. The *Register* logs advertisements on the day they appear and can provide expenditure data and copies of the actual advertisements. This service avoids the necessity of looking in two or more places to obtain expenditure statistics and copies of the advertisements. The *Television Register*, which is part of the same organisation and is at the same address, maintains a video tape research library of all the commercials used on UK television. They also now monitor some overseas television advertising and the satellite channels. They will supply a copy of a specific commercial or a review tape covering, for example, a year's commercials. They also supply cinema commercials, product specific review tapes, a tape updating service and a subscribers service, under which subscribers receive a monthly tape of the newest and most interesting commercials. Commercials can be supplied as video tapes or as high-definition graphic storyboards with the text printed beneath the relevant still photographs, which are available in black and white or in colour.

Telepictorials provide a similar service. They have a library of television commercials which they claim is the biggest in the UK and possibly in the world. They also have a library of radio commercials. The advertising industry can order their material as a storyboard, in colour or black and white, as a verbatim script or as a video. Radio material can be supplied as a script of a tape. Free delivery is available in Central London.

Advertising journals

Many advertising queries can be answered by scanning the main advertising journals: *Campaign*, *Marketing Week* and *Marketing*. Many libraries in the marketing and advertising field still scan, clip and file extensively from these journals and a range of other journals and newspapers. This is now less and less the case since all three journals are available on MAID, MARS and TEXTLINE. *Campaign* and *Marketing* are available on PROFILE and all three journals are also indexed in the *Research Index* which is now also available online via PERGAMON FINANCIAL DATA SERVICES. All of these journals are invaluable for information on market shares, brand shares, references to marketing reports which can be followed up, details of new product launches and accounts of advertising campaigns. They provide the most convenient channel through which the marketing department can help keep abreast of what competitors are doing.

Campaign is weekly, glossy, well-illustrated and concentrates on news, reports of events, interviews, accounts of advertising campaigns and material relating to the media. Its target audience is really anyone concerned with marketing and advertising.

Marketing is also weekly and concentrates on marketing and media news and the analysis of news.

Marketing Week is aimed at a rather different market from the other two journals; senior management in marketing, advertising and the media. It includes news, articles, surveys of all aspects of marketing and advertising, company news, new products, and information on campaigns, conferences and exhibitions.

There are many other journals of relevance to people working in marketing and advertising but these are the three essential titles to which every library working in this area would subscribe.

Abstracting journals should be mentioned here although the two relevant titles have been described in some detail in the *Management information* chapter.

Anbar appears eight times per year in five sections, one of which is

Marketing and Distribution Abstracts. There is a joint annual index and a cumulated volume. Anbar is not available online but has recently been purchased by MCB University Press who are considering the potential of a floppy disc edition.

Management and Marketing Abstracts (MMA) are produced by PIRA in conjunction with BIM. They appear monthly and are available online on PERGAMON FINANCIAL DATA SERVICES.

Market Research Abstracts are published by the Market Research Society and appear twice yearly. They are also available on microfilm from UMI. Many of the databases mentioned in the earlier section on market research are also those which contain advertising data and material of relevance to marketing in general. Here, however, it is necessary to mention their advertising content.

Advertising data online

PROFILE and MAID are very strong in the market reserach field and have a UK bias. MARS, which is part of PREDICASTS, has a strong American bias although it does abstract material from the three main UK journals. As it provides only short abstracts, not full text, it has limitations but it is a quick way to look at advertising trends in the UK and the US. The coding and indexing provided are very efficient so that it is easy to retrieve material in a swift and very exact way. Searchers in consumer products can use a set of codes to track down competitors' test marketing, product launches, advertising campaigns and other activities. It also has a searchable trade name field.

HARVEST contains both full text and bibliographic material and differs from the other services available in that it compiles all its own market reports. HARVEST is aimed at the marketing, advertising and PR industry and is menu-driven and on viewdata. It also has an updating service called NEWSFILE which contains abstracts based on items from newspapers and journals. Each bulletin details the company brand and agency. An advertising factfile gives details of agencies and their clients, citing company name and brand name including account gains and losses. A product news section provides details of product launches, relaunches, withdrawn products and new product forecasts.

Statistical data on HARVEST includes a UK and regional evaluation to assist in target market identification and, finally, there is a consumer research section. The strength of HARVEST is that, since their own staff produce their market overviews, they have more control over their currency and accuracy. In certain cases, it might be possible for a marketing executive to locate all the necessary information needed for the planning of a product launch from HARVEST alone.

Other sources of advertising information

Associations

Associations are an invaluable source of information in the marketing field. Most associations have libraries and are very helpful but many will, of course, only supply information if you are a member. The associations which are likely to be the most useful are the *Institute of Practitioners in Advertising*, the *Advertising Association*, the *Institute of Marketing* and the *Market Research Society.*

The Institute of Practitioners in Advertising serves advertising agencies and both corporate and individual membership is available. It is concerned with the image of the advertising agency business and seeks to help members to become more efficient, profitable and respected. It has a library and information service and also runs conferences, meetings and courses.

The Advertising Association is the trade association for the advertising industry. It publishes the journal, *Advertising* and has a library and information service.

The Institute of Marketing is the professional association for senior people in marketing. The objects of the institute are to improve knowledge of marketing, to provide services for members and to make the principles of good marketing more widely known and effectively used throughout industry. The institute has a library and an information service. Quick enquiries are answered free but the information service also undertakes in-depth research for a fee.

Libraries of journals and newspapers

Like newspapers, journals often have their own libraries and the libraries of both journals and newspapers are often very helpful. Many newspapers now offer a fee-based service; for example, the *Financial Times Business Information Service* and the *Daily Telegraph*.

Journals usually have libraries and these are not only very helpful but seldom charge. Two very helpful libraries are the *Campaign* library and the *Grocer* library.

Some examples of the available commercial marketing information services have already been mentioned and, in addition to these, there are, of course, the more general business information services, such as the *Financial Times Business Information Service* and a range of organisations who specialise in undertaking consumer research for clients, including the Target Group Index and British Market Research Bureau.

Advertising plays a crucial part in the marketing process and the information scientist can fulfil a key role in providing the information necessary to facilitate a successful product launch.

Information for the sales drive

The process of selling can be divided into sales and distribution within the UK and sales and distribution overseas, that is, exports.

Sales and distribution within the UK

A successful sales drive in the UK requires back-up material. It requires consumer research, which will normally be bought in by commissioning a market research company to undertake it, a thorough overview of any published market surveys and information about the different areas of the UK where the product is to be launched. This information will include statistical data, general background and travel information, material abstracted from some specialist reference books and data retrieved from databases.

The statistical data that can prove invaluable includes population statistics (for example, the *Census*), *Regional Statistics*, all the compilations of consumer statistics mentioned earlier in this chapter, and statistics relating to the social class and financial status of the population. The *Abstract of Scottish Statistics* would also be helpful if it was planned to sell the product in Scotland, as would the statistics emanating from Wales and Northern Ireland if sales drives in these areas were planned.

General background and travel information would include any directories of the area, any up-to-date guide books, guides to hotels and restaurants, local newspapers, any glossy local interest journals; for example, *Warwickshire and Worcestershire*, any printed material; in fact, any publication that could help to give the sales force a clearer picture of the area.

There are some specialist reference books which could be of great assistance in planning a sales drive in a specific place. One of these is *Kompass Regional Sales Guide* which appears biennially in seven volumes:

1. North and North East England and Scotland
2. North West England and Northern Ireland
3. Midlands and North Wales
4. Eastern England
5. South West England and South Wales
6. South East England
7. Greater London

ICC also produce *Regional Company Surveys*. These form a valuable addition to their *Industry Sector Reports*. They set out to monitor all companies of substance trading in individual regions. The surveys assess the financial status and standing of the companies monitored and include data on trading activities, contact addresses and directors. The aim of this series is to help sales forces to target their sales efforts more precisely, to produce direct mail campaigns accurately, co-ordinate telesales operations and facilitate the choice of the right region in which to test a new product or launch an advertising campaign. A regional survey of Leicestershire has just been published. The material in the survey is based on data derived from ICC's database of UK companies and from additional research.

Sales and Marketing Information Ltd (SAMI) is an organisation which produces a range of marketing services, one of which is the FRS database on finance and banking. Their SHOPS database is available on PERGAMON FINANCIAL DATA SERVICES. This database holds data on Britain's busiest shopping areas and gives trading names of retail outlets, addresses, activities, size of chain, square footage of actual shops and TV area for each entry. The hard copy service includes good plans and claims to cover 260,000 retail outlets. It is updated monthly by qualified surveyors and provides an excellent tool for the identification of sales prospects. They also produce a small but glossy magazine, *Target*.

Euromonitor have produced a handbook entitled *A-Z of UK retailing* which analyses the top 50 retailing groups in depth and gives some information about all retailers with more than 20 outlets. It is also a useful source of retailing information including addresses and telephone numbers.

Industrial Market Locations identifies 140,000 UK manufacturing and warehousing businesses. It is compiled on a site basis and, therefore, gives very different information to that given by the online databases. Since it is bi-monthly it provides an up-to-date source of information. It can be used to identify sales prospects and identify samples for market research, as it provides company addresses, the names of senior executives, chief buyers, a description of the trade involved and the number of employees.

Direct mail shots and selective marketing campaigns are now a very important part of most marketing strategies. Another growth area is mail order selling and a useful reference book in this sector is David B. Hanlon's *Guide to business mailing lists*. This is a small annual publication which enables the user to pinpoint business categories and geographical areas. The book is backed up by a Marketing Support Service which will actually handle the mail-shot, if required.

Jordan Information Services provide lists of company addresses which are invaluable when direct marketing is contemplated.

An organisation which is active in the field of retail planning information is the Unit for Retail Planning Information Ltd (URPI). A membership fee entitles the individual or corporate members to the use of an enquiry service, an advice service, the library, newsletters, information briefs, discounts on URPI publications, and discounts on conferences, workshops and commissioned surveys. URPI produce *Shopping Centre Trade Area Reports*. They will provide advice on how to carry out shopping surveys or undertake the full survey themselves.

There are many other organisations and publications of relevance to the planning of a sales drive or product launch but it is possible only to cite a representative selection. In addition to these services and books, the researcher would, of course, also consult the specialist directories and journals relating to the specific product area, for example, the *Shop Equipment Display and Shopfitting Directory*.

Databases are becoming more and more useful in planning a sales drive. DUNS MARKETING ONLINE and Dun and Bradstreet's KEY BRITISH ENTERPRISES (KBE), both of which are available via PERGAMON FINANCIAL DATA SERVICES, provide UK company information in a format which facilitates direct mail shots and selective marketing campaigns. KOMPASS ONLINE can also be used in this way. HARVEST contains a UK and regional evaluation to assisting target market identification.

Certain organisations specialise in marketing and market research information including both the provision of client-specific desk and market research and of published reports and data. These include:

British Market Research Bureau
Mintel Information Services
Frost Phillips Russell
Unit for Retail Planning Information Limited
BBC Data Enquiry Service
London Business School Information Service
Market Assessment.

The use of such services may be cost-effective if the information team does not have either the necessary skills, time or access to the information requested.

These, then, are a selection of the sources available to information specialists concerned with marketing in the UK. This is a field in which relevant reference books and databases seem to proliferate almost daily, therefore, the field is so wide that it is almost impossible to give more than an overview while the subject of selling overseas is so immense that it requires a separate chapter.

Further reading

BAKER, M., (ed.) *Macmillan Dictionary of Marketing and Advertising*, Macmillan, 1985.

HADDON, A. *Online management and marketing databases*. Aslib, 1989.

WALTERS, T. *Market Research Sourcebook*. Headland, Cleveland: Headland Press, 1985.

WELSH, B., BUTCHER, H. and FREUND, A. *On-line information: a comprehensive users guide*. Basil Blackwell in association with the Institute of Chartered Accountants in England and Wales, 1987. Chapter 8: On-line databases: management and marketing services, 137–157.

Some useful addresses

BLAISE Information Services, British Library, Bibliographical Services, 2 Sheraton Street, London W1V 4BH. Tel: 071-323 7074

Chadwyck-Healey Ltd, Cambridge Place, Cambridge CB2 1NR. Tel: 0223 311479. Fax: 0223 66440

Datastream International, 58–64 City Road, London EC1Y 2AL. Tel: 071-250 3000. Fax: 071-253 0171

Euromonitor Publications Ltd, 87–88 Turnmill Street, London EC1M 5QU. Tel: 071-251 8024

Export Market Intelligence Library, DTI, 1–19 Victoria Street, London SW1H 0ET. Tel: 071-215 5444/5

HMSO Books, 51 Nine Elms Lane, London SW8 5DR. Tel: 071-873 8372

Harvest Information Services Ltd, The Mall, 359 Upper Street, London N1 0PD. Tel: 071-226 6414 or 071-226 1553

House of Commons Library, Public Information Service, Westminster, London SW1A 0AA. Tel: 071-219 4272

Jordan and Sons Ltd, 21 St Thomas St, Bristol BS1 6JS. Tel: 0272 230600

Key Facts, The Old Rectory, Northill, near Biggleswade, Beds SG18 9AH.

Key Note Publications Ltd, Field House, 72 Oldfield Road, Hampton, Middlesex TW12 1BR. Tel: 081-783 0755. Fax: 081-783 1940

MAID Systems Ltd, Maid House, 26 Baker Street, London W1M 1DF. Tel: 071-935 6460. Fax: 071-487 3768

Market Assessment Publications Ltd, 2 Duncan Terrace, London N1 8BZ. Tel: 071-278 9517. Fax: 071-278 6246

Market Research Society, 175 Oxford Street, London W1R 1TA. Tel: 071-287 3726

Marketing Communications Group, Historical Information Products, Reuters Ltd, 85 Fleet Street, London EC4P 4AJ. Tel: 071-250 1122. Fax: 071-353 0745

Mintel Publications Ltd, KAE House, 7 Arundel Street, London WC2R 3DR. Tel: 071-836 1814 or 071-379 3536. Fax: 071-836 1682

PROFILE, Financial Times Business Information, PO Box 12, Sunbury on Thames, Middlesex TW16 7UD. Tel: 0932 761444

SAMI, Sales and Marketing Information Ltd, 1 Warwick Street, Leamington Spa, Warwicks CV32 5LW. Tel: 0926 451199

SCOOP Publications, c/o Valerie J. Nurcombe, 8 Kingfisher Drive, Over, Winsford, Cheshire CW7 1PF.

Telepictorials Ltd, Pictorial House, 79 Bridge Road, Hampton Court, Surrey KT8 9HH. Tel: 081-941 6969

Television Register, 1-4 Langley Court, London WC2E 9JY. Tel: 071-240 3501
Unit for Retail Planning Information Ltd, 26 Queen Victoria Street, Reading RG1 1TG. Tel: 0734 588181
WEFA Group, 23 Lower Belgrave Street, London SW1W 0NW. Tel: 071-730 8171

Chapter Nine

WORLDWIDE MARKET RESOURCES

Jo Haythornthwaite

Accurate overseas business information is essential to any company which does business abroad, therefore, it is vital that the British information specialist should know how to track down up-to-date and accurate overseas information.

General sources of information to consult

There are some general sources of information that are worth consulting, including a new book by Sarah Ball entitled *The directory of international sources of business information*, Pitman, 1989. This directory covers sources for Europe, the United States, Australasia and Asia. It concentrates on companies, industries, finance and associations. Two chapters are helpfully devoted to the relevant online databases. This directory could provide a useful starting-point. From the point of view of advertising abroad, a good starting point is provided by the *Overseas media* section in Volume Two of the *Advertisers' annual* (which was described in the previous chapter). If your company would like to know who is exporting what to where, in order to find a gap in the market, or if they wish to place their product in the hands of a suitable import/export house, *British exports*, an annual publication from Kompass, will provide the answers. It comprises Volume I: A-R Products and Services, Volume II: S–Z Products and Services and Exporters. In fact, it lists more than 10,000 major UK exporters under a choice of 16,500 product and service classifications.

If finding a suitable export market is the problem to be solved, there is a relevant book by Keith Matthews, *Finding export markets: a guide to methods and information sources in the UK and worldwide*, Trade

Research Publications, 1986. Although now out of date, this book is a well arranged guide to the subject. it is in five sections:

1. An introductory chapter covering libraries, basic reference books, etc.
2. Information sources.
3. List of countries.
4. Countries in alphabetical order. Each entry provides the Embassy or High Commission address, the Chamber of Commerce address, trade information and a list of reference books.
5. List of publishers.

Euromonitor have now moved strongly into the international sources field with the *International directory of marketing information sources* which is a companion volume to their *European directory of marketing information sources*. Both publications cover the same ground, that is, official publications, libraries, market research companies, databases, abstracts and indexes, journals, associations, business contacts and socio-economic profiles.

Publishers to remember

Certain publishers specialise in the international field, among them Europa Publications, which produces directories such as *Africa, south of the Sahara*, *South America*, *Central America* and the *International Who's Who*. Graham and Trotman are invaluable to the librarian since they publish company directories for areas that are still poorly covered, for example, *Major companies of Latin America*.

A quick survey of the world

Information on the UK, the USA, Australasia and Canada is easy to find, therefore, I do not propose to spend any time discussing it. Information on European countries was surprisingly difficult to obtain until quite recently but is now a great deal easier as a result of pressure for more information emanating from the EC especially as a result of 1992 and the Single European Market. Another factor is the growth of online databases which has rendered company data and market information more readily available. The EC is itself responsible for disseminating a great deal of information relating to Europe and is facilitating UK access to this material by having set up, at present, three European Business Information Centres with the possibility of more to come.

In general, European company information and market surveys are now readily available both in hard copy and online. Some of the smaller European countries are still not as well covered as they might be but every week sees a new gap in the overall pattern of information being filled, for example, TEXTLINE recently announced an Italian language service which will provide an Italian news service. This service is the first step in their plans to introduce other European language databases.

Another significant publishing phenomenon is the growth of single country journals or newsletters aimed at people requiring current market information about a specific country. One of the latest of these is *Business Spain*, a monthly journal in English aimed at anyone with business interests in Spain. An expensive newsletter (£250 per annum) called *Glasnost*, published by Infoserv, looks at emerging commercial opportunities in Socialist Eastern Europe.

In the Middle East, some countries are well documented and some are not. Countries which are rich and with whom Britain has strong trade links, of course, tend to be better documented than small, poor, developing countries. It is, therefore, far easier to research Saudi Arabia than the Sudan. Saudi Arabia, for example, publishes a wide range of statistics, some of which are available both in English and in Arabic. Metra Consulting specialise in producing reference books on the Middle East and their series, *Business opportunities in...* includes Saudi Arabia and the Gulf States. These texts are regularly replaced by new editions. Euromonitor has produced a major report on *Consumer markets in the Middle East* which is arranged under country headings and contains brief but useful statistical data. This series also includes *Consumer markets in the Far East*, *Central America*, *Latin America*, *North Africa*, *West Africa*, *Central and Eastern Africa*, *Southern Africa*, *USA* and the *Indian sub-continent*. Euromonitor also publish a *Middle East economic handbook*. There is now a MID EAST database available on PERGAMON FINANCIAL DATA SERVICES and both TEXTLINE and PROFILE include a good deal of material relevant to the Middle East.

The situation as regards the Far East is, in many ways, similar to that pertaining to the Middle East. Some countries, for example, Japan produce a great deal of information which is efficiently disseminated and, therefore, easy to obtain. A great deal of information on Japan is available in English. It is much less easy to obtain material about some of the smaller and more backward countries in the Pacific basin. As in the case of the Middle East, coverage online has vastly improved in the last two years. DUNSPRINT now offers a service which provides direct access to information on businesses in Hong Kong, Macau, Japan and the People's Republic of China, ORBIT provides access to Chinese patents via CHINAPAT and TEXTLINE claims to offer a unique service by which investors can monitor the business opportunities offered by the Pacific rim via TEXTLINE and PRICELINK. PRICELINK offers numeric time-series data relating to equities, markets, futures, bonds, currency rates and corporate statistics for the countries of the Pacific rim including Australia and New Zealand.

DIALOG has recently loaded a new Asia and Pacific Rim database,

ASIA-PACIFIC, which concentrates on business and economics and draws its entries from newspapers, journals, government publications, newsletters, press releases and monographs.

Again, new journals and bulletins seem to be a growth industry! Infoserv produce *Japanese software alert* and *Korean fortune* both of which are very small, very expensive but packed with economic and trade data.

The picture is very different when the researcher turns to Latin America and Africa, both of which still present considerable difficulties from the point of view of the information gatherer. Latin American data is included in the new DUNSPRINT service and there is some material on Latin America and the Caribbean on TEXTLINE and PROFILE but, in general, this part of the world is still badly represented online.

Euromonitor has a series of handbooks which offer a *South American economic handbook* and the series also includes handbooks on the Middle East, Japan, Eastern Europe, Africa, China, the USSR, Asia, the Pacific Basin and the Caribbean. Europa's *South America, Central America and the Caribbean* and Graham and Trotman's *Major companies in Latin America* have already been mentioned and are very useful but neither are as up-to-date as one might wish. Africa is even less well-documented than Latin America. Numeric data relating to some of the less developed countries is often almost non-existent or, in other cases, late in appearing and unreliable. As in the case of Latin America, there are a number of good reference books but many of them have difficulty in obtaining current and reliable information. There are, of course, many more reference sources relating to the various parts of the world that I have mentioned. An exhaustive account of what is available would require a separate book. Here, I have sought only to provide an overview of general trends and a few examples of sources in order to give readers a feeling for the problems of tracing material relating to the less accessible parts of the world.

Having taken a brief whistle-stop tour around the world, I should like to discuss four types of information that might be necessary when researching a potential overseas market: company information; economic data; descriptive information and market reports. I shall also look at some alternative sources of information when books and databases fail.

Company information

Company information may be located in directories, card services, via online and in annual reports.

Directories

It is possible to find out if there is a directory for companies for a specific country via CBD Research Limited who publish *Current European directories*, *Current Asian and Australasian directories* and *Current African directories*. Some directories are what is called ranking directories, that is, they only describe the top so many thousand companies; for example, *Asia's 7,500 largest companies* published by ELC International. Tracing information about smaller companies overseas is frequently much more difficult. Dun and Bradstreet produce ranking directories which include *Italy's 2,000 largest companies* and *Austria's 10,000 largest companies*. There is also a ranking journal called *Business and Finance*. Although they do not have numbers in their titles as many ranking directories do, the Graham and Trotman directories are, in fact, ranking directories. Their *Major companies of Europe* includes, as the title suggests, only major companies and other titles include: *Major companies of the Far East*, *Major companies of the Arab World*, *Major companies of the USA*, *Major companies of Latin America*, *Major companies of Nigeria*. Among non-ranking directories, the huge Kompass range are invaluable and titles now include Indonesia, Israel, Malaysia, Morocco and Thailand. Graham and Trotman produce a *Guidebook on trading with the People's Republic of China* while the Longman Group publish a *Directory of Chinese foreign trade*. Japan produces several good directories of their own which are available in English including the *Standard trade index of Japan*, which is compiled and published by the Japan Chamber of Commerce and Industry. India provides two major directories, one published by Kothari and Sons and the other by the Times of India Press; *Kothari's Economic and industrial guide* to India and *Times of India directory and yearbook*. The latter has the more extensive coverage and also includes a who's who section.

Financial information about companies can be found in directories but is usually in too brief a form to be valuable to the business person who hopes to do business with that company. Often newspapers provide a fuller version of figures when they are first announced and such material can be retrieved using TEXTLINE, NEXIS and PROFILE, the major newspaper based online services. There are also online services which specialise in company financial data, for example, DISCLOSURE FINANCIALS for the USA, which is on DIALOG, and NIKAI ONLINE, a database of Japanese company accounts. A substantial number of German company accounts are also available online.

There is now an EC directive on filing accounts but adherence to this is somewhat uneven. Surprisingly, even Northern Ireland has begun to file accounts only relatively recently. In Germany, only companies over a certain size have to publish accounts while Denmark has a system similar to that in the UK and produces the information on microfiche. In Europe, generally speaking, it is relatively easy to obtain financial information from all public companies but not from private ones.

Outside Europe, with the exceptions of North America, Australasia and Japan, it is usually best to work through an agency who will search for financial information on your company's behalf; two well-known examples are Touche Ross International of New York and Hill House of London. ICC can obtain *status reports* for companies in some countries and often do so for Saudi companies. Since companies in Saudi Arabia are usually privately owned, they are not expected to disclose details of their financial status, so status reports are usually based on material gained via interviews and contain only limited financial details.

Card services

Extel cards are available for Europe, North America, Australia and New Zealand, Hong Kong, Japan, Singapore and Malaysia, Thailand and the Middle East. These services are updated weekly except the Middle Eastern one, which is updated twice monthly but they include only a small number of companies; for example, approximately 100 companies in Hong Kong and 100 in the Middle East.

Online company information

Company information relating to UK and the US is available on all sorts of databases almost to saturation point, while European coverage is much improved (and has been described in the chapter on company information).

Other parts of the world are rather less well served. The best service available in the UK is Dun and Bradstreet's DUNSPRINT which now offers access to company information from 74 countries. Meanwhile, KOMPASS ONLINE is expanding to cover more European countries and HOPPENSTEDT (Germany company information) is available on DATA-STAR and also on PROFILE who have loaded a German full text file and an English translation of the information. TEXTLINE and PROFILE have good international coverage of news about companies while PREDICASTS includes some international company data.

Annual reports

Annual reports are an excellent way of obtaining a great deal of company information both descriptive and financial. Obtaining UK and US annual reports is very straightforward since, in both cases, many are held in libraries, a great many are available online and when difficulty is experienced, a letter, telex or telephone call to the company usually results in the annual report being sent to the enquirer. The annual reports of other countries can be more difficult to obtain but various avenues are open.

First, Extel and ICC will provide some annual reports as a back-up to their services. Secondly, if it is possible to identify a UK subsidiary via *Who owns whom*, they can be contacted. In such cases, there may be a report in English. If the company has overseas subsidiaries, it may be feasible to ask them to obtain the annual report.

Libraries are always worth consulting. City Business Library has a good collection of overseas annual reports and so has the London Business School Library. The US Embassy has the annual reports of all the major American companies. The Department of Trade and Industry's Export Marketing Information Centre (EMIC) has a collection of status reports on overseas companies. Although these are not annual reports, they often contain comparable information. Finally, it is always worth contacting the company direct. If it is not possible to telephone, fax, telex or use electronic mail, a letter is, of course, a slow way to obtain the material but if speed is not essential, this may not be a problem.

Economic and statistical data

The business information specialist is likely to require three main types of statistics about a given country: general background statistics, for example, population, trade statistics and production figures. Background statistics are available from national governments and their statistical offices, for example, the Central Statistical Office (CSO) in the UK and the Central Bureau of Statistics in the Netherlands. A second source of such background statistics are international organisations. The United Nations publishes a *Demographic yearbook*, which is the standard collected source of population figures, and they also produce a *Statistical yearbook*. The problem about such official collections of statistics is that they are always slow to appear and, therefore, out of date. They also rely on the national statistics collecting bodies of the various countries to submit their figures to the UN promptly and this is often not the case. Some countries may also present inaccurate figures through inefficiency or may wish to give a more favourable view of their country as regards, for example, infant mortality. Many other international organisations compile helpful statistical reference works including OPEC and the ILO.

General statistics are available in a brief form in a wide range of general reference books including *Whitaker's almanack* and the *Statesman's yearbook*. Such sources, although very useful, must not be considered authoritative if a really current source of statistics is sought. Anything in book form must inevitably be out of date by the time it is in hardcovers. The official statistics of the country concerned will always provide the most authoritative and current source of statistical data. A useful guide to the statistics of one part of the world is the CBD research guide, *Statistics: Asia and Australasia*.

Trade statistics

Trade figures are usually cumulated once a year, in December, and in the weeks or months after December, the figures become available to researchers. Some countries disseminate their trade figures swiftly but others are exceedingly slow. France, for example, is remarkably quick, while Belgium is not. In general, most developing countries are understandably slow, so it is usually difficult to obtain current trade figures from them. More and more countries now produce trade figures on microfiche. France now produces no monthly hard copy and simply offers the choice of a fiche or a printout.

The OECD publishes the *Yearbook of international trade statistics* which is, inevitably, not very up to date. It is, however, supplemented by monthly issues and more detailed statistical data is available from the OECD on microfiche.

Eurostat publishes trade figures for the EC countries and the International Monetary Fund also publish collections of trade statistics.

Best of all, some trade statistics are now available online on TRADSTAT. TRADSTAT holds published government import/export information on all reported commodities and products from Europe, Japan, Canada and the USA. Statistics are acquired directly from the customs offices of the reporting countries on computer tape and the database is updated immediately they are received.

Production figures

Production figures are more difficult to obtain than are trade figures and they are in some ways far more useful since they provide a valuable barometer of the country's prosperity. In Britain, we are well served by the *Business Monitors Series* and, for the EC countries, *Eurostat* publishes *Industrial Short Term Trends*, which appears monthly.

Trade associations can be an excellent source of production statistics relating to the industry with which they are concerned, for example, the Publishers Association. Warwick Business Information Service have produced a useful list of *European Trade Associations Statistics* which was based on a survey they conducted in 1982.

Trade and production figures online can be accessed via I. P. SHARP (now owned by Reuters), DRI, the WEFA Group and DATASTREAM. (These databases are discussed in greater detail in Chapter Four on British Official Publications.)

Descriptive information

Before a marketing team is sent to another country, it is useful if they can have a reasonable idea as to the way of life of the country to which they are going. They will need to know about the climate, language, currency, religion and culture, health hazards, food, cost of living and myriads of other topics. The librarian may well make a start with a brief look through the reference books: *Whitaker's almanack*, the *Statesman's yearbook* and any others that are available on the library shelves. This type of book gives a few pages on each country and provides what amounts to a brief informative snapshot of the country. More detailed information can be obtained by consulting individual guides to the specific country to be visited, for example, World Trade Intelligence are now publishing a series of detailed guides to Euromarkets, such as *Exporting to Spain*. These guides are to be updated annually and are also available on floppy disc. The Economist Intelligence Unit also publishes good reports on a variety of countries.

The Government and official publications should never be overlooked as they supply an unequalled amount of authoritative data about overseas markets. The staff of the British Overseas Trade Board (BOTB) produce lengthy country profiles and also the small but superb *Hints to Exporters* (described in more detail in Chapter Four, British Official Publications). There is also a special desk for most of the major countries with whom Britain does business, from which additional information can be obtained. The DTI's little weekly journal *British Business* contains regular reports of overseas markets which frequently include invaluable trade and production statistics, and their library also houses some world development plans. Banks are a good source of both statistical and descriptive material.

Newspapers usually provide the most current source of material on a given section of the globe. *The Times* and the *Financial Times* are especially useful, particularly when they produce special supplements about specific countries which can be taken out and filed. The *Daily Telegraph*, the *Guardian* and the *Independent* also provide serious coverage of international affairs as do the more weighty Sunday papers. Newswire services should not be forgotten since they provide the raw data upon which the news features are based. The various indexes and online services through which newspaper articles can be traced was documented earlier in Chapter Three, Newspapers: An Undervalued Resource, so it suffices to reiterate that TEXTLINE, NEXIS and PROFILE provide access to a wide range of newspaper information and Reuters, in addition, make their Country Reports available online.

Journals are also a helpful source of information about other countries. Specific expensive and specialised journals which concentrate on one or more countries have already been mentioned but more general journals also play a useful role.

Business International is worth subscribing to if staff of the company travel a great deal and are sent to work abroad, as it monitors executive living costs in major cities worldwide.

The *Economist* remains a splendid and immensely readable weekly magazine which surveys world news in a masterly fashion. From time to time it contains supplements which look at various countries in some depth.

Commerce International is a monthly publication emanating from the London Chamber of Commerce and Industry and intended for Chamber membership. It includes market surveys and a good deal of international trade news.

Worldwide Marketing Opportunities Digest is produced by the International Commercial Network every month and includes business trends, economic data, company profiles and country reports. The material is tailored for the use of importers and exporters.

Exporters are well served by specialist periodicals since there are a further two titles, *Export* (from the Institute of Export) and *Export Direction* (published by Export House). Both of these appear every month and contain material with which it is worth becoming familiar. *Export* is intended for export directors and managers and, therefore, concentrates on the managerial aspects of exporting in that it covers general trends in exports, marketing and also focuses on law and finance. *Export Direction* is more general in its appeal and includes international trade reports, market and investment reports, and international freight news.

Travel information of a different kind is also essential for the man or woman journeying to a hitherto unknown part of the world. Here, guides to hotels are an essential part of a company information centre's stock and a useful recent addition to any small collection would be *Business traveller: guide to business cities of the world*, edited by Graham Boyhton and published by Simon and Schuster, 1989. This guide provides detailed reports on 40 key cities and recommends hotels in a selection of price ranges. It also includes where to eat and entertain, bargains to bring home and an overview of each city's political and business climate. *Owen's Africa business directory* is primarily a company directory but also provides details of hotels all over Africa.

Market reports

How to locate market reports was well documented earlier in Chapter Eight, Marketing Information. The *Marketing surveys index* is especially useful and *Market research: a guide to British Library holdings* – Edition 6, 1989–90 provides a recently published key to BL holdings. The information specialist will, however, soon become aware that while market research reports relating to the US and the UK proliferate and Europe is also fairly well covered, outside Europe market reports are few in number and those that exist are difficult to locate. As far as the UK and Europe are concerned, the various market orientated journals also provide a good source of information about, and reviews of, recent market reports.

As far as Europe is concerned, the journals which are most likely to be of use are the Economist Intelligence Unit's *Marketing in Europe*, Euromonitor's *Market Research Europe* and Mintel's *Market Intelligence Europe*. *Marketing in Europe* is monthly and covers specific topics in specific countries, for example, dishwashers in Germany. *Market Research Europe* is similar and might look at, for example, savoury snacks in France or consumer spending in Denmark. Mintel's *Market Intelligence Europe* is quarterly and examines specific markets in some depth, for example, the spirits market in France or dairy products in West Germany. In addition, Euromonitor and Mintel produce lengthy monograph market reports, some of which may look at a product in a European or a world perspective. If no market survey exists, one may be commissioned, usually from one of the marketing information companies who are familiar with what will be required. This is often necessary for non-European countries.

Interrogating online services would seem to be more and more the swiftest and probably most cost-effective way of obtaining access to what is often rather expensive data.

The files which used to be called MAGIC are now all part of PROFILE and include a range of marketing information services which are available for an additional annual subscription. These files include INTERNATIONAL RISK DATA, Henley Centre's LEISURE FUTURES and PLANNING CONSUMER MARKETS and the four main Mintel journals. Available without extra charges via PROFILE is the FTBR Business/Finance File in which there is a wide range of information on international trade and finance and analysis of markets in the Middle East, Latin America and eastern Europe. Other files which are available include EIS ONLINE (the online version of the BOTBS Export Intelligence Service), NATIONAL DEVELOPMENT PLANS, WORLD BANK INTERNATIONAL BUSINESS OPPORTUNITIES SERVICE and most of the major British marketing journals, such as *Campaign*.

PROFILE is also excellent for background information on other countries since it contains the BBC Summary of World Broadcasts, Keesing's Record of World Events, Asahi News Service (information on Japan and the Far East), the *Economist* and all the major UK daily newspapers.

MAID is a closed unit which is hosted by PERGAMON FINANCIAL DATA SERVICES (PFDS). It is a full text database which provides access to a large number of market sector reports emanating from sources including the Economist Intelligence Unit Key Note and Euromonitor.

The majority of the reports relate to the UK but some survey products in various parts of the EC; recent additions to the file have included three reports on television and video products in West Germany, in Italy and in France, respectively, and a review of the market for petrochemicals in Europe. Market reports from the USA are frequently included but areas other than the EC and the USA are sparsely represented as yet. MAID does feature, however, the *Business International – Country Forecasting Reports* series which has a Latin American Forecasting Service which has included reports on both Chile and Mexico this year. This service is an especially valuable one since a main report is produced on each country every six months with a concise update in between. Forty-six countries are featured and each report contains a summary, the political and social outlook, an economic forecast and a section on business environment trends. Significantly, no African countries are included and only the major countries in the Middle East and Latin America. *Marketing in Europe*, an Economist publication, is available on MAID. This is a monthly report on consumer goods markets, marketing and distribution in Europe. *International Tourism Reports* and *Travel and Tourism Analyst* (both from the Economist Intelligence Unit) provide an international perspective on travel and tourism markets, while the same publisher contributes *International Motor Business*, *European Motor Business* and *Japanese Motor Business*, all quarterly journals in full text. *Textline Outlook International* is yet another EIU publication which is offered.

Market direction reports from Euromonitor is quarterly and surveys 58 consumer markets, including fast-food, analgesics, pet foods and in-car entertainment in five countries: France, Italy, UK, US and West Germany. Other international Euromonitor publications available on MAID are *Market Research Europe* and *Retail Monitor* (which contains an international outlook section) as does *Food Monitor International Business Reports*, a new series of European business studies which look at 14 market sectors in France, Spain, Germany and Italy.

Key Note reports are featured on MAID but these also are purely European in coverage and concentrate mainly on the UK. Some United States market studies are included on MAID in the shape of *USA Monitor* which is made up of full text consumer and retail market reports.

FIND/SVP is a major US business and information research firm which produces market and competitor intelligence reports in full text and is available on MAID. Together with *USA Monitor*, this provides good coverage of American data. Finally, MAID features BIS INFORMAT NEWSLINE, a news information service which includes a long list of world newspapers and journals, including *Moscow News*, *Arab Banker*, *Singapore Business Times*, *China Daily*, *Caribbean Insight* and many other titles not featured elsewhere. BIS INFORMAT NEWSLINE is probably the widest ranging file of newspaper information available online.

Market forecasts are available online via PREDICASTS, FORECASTS and WORLDCASTS. Worldcasts appears on paper eight times a year and summarises over 75,000 published projections for products and markets in 50 countries. It is available online via DIALOG and DATA-STAR. Thus, market reports are, in general, only readily available online or in any other form for the UK, the EC and the United States.

Non-traditional sources of information

Often overseas information of an obscure sort can be best obtained via non-traditional routes. First, it may be possible to contact a person within the organisation who has visited the country in question and who may even know something about the market for bottled beer in that country. Secondly, if the company has overseas branches, the expertise of employees in these locations can be drawn up cheaply via telex, fax or electronic mail.

A third possibility, which was mentioned earlier, are banks (see also Chapter Ten, Banking Information). Banks can be traced easily via the yellow pages, the *Bankers' almanac* or any of several other banking directories. Most banks, especially those with strong overseas links, publish a range of helpful publications including economic surveys of countries, statistical publications and industry reviews. Barclays, Lloyds and the Midland Bank, in particular, produce profiles of countries and some banks also produce booklets on special topics. Most of these publications are given away free, but the changing economic climate in recent years has led some banks to make a small charge for publications. In addition to British banks, it is worth remembering that there are many foreign banks in London and, indeed, in other cities in Britain. Such banks are usually very happy to supply leaflets about their country of origin. Japanese banks often produce excellent reports, as do French, German and Dutch banks. There are also *financial institutions*, other than banks, who produce publications which they supply free. A good example is Peat Marwick McLintock, a leading firm of accountants and consultants, who even print a small annual catalogue of their publications. This catalogue lists a wide range of free publications including two exceedingly relevant series, the *Banking in ... series* and the *Investment in ... series*. Currently, the Banking series covers only 17 countries, but the Investment series is much more wide-ranging and goes as far afield as Fiji, Macau, Oman, Papua New Guinea and Brunei Darussalam.

Embassies vary widely from the very efficient to the totally useless. Most have commercial sections but some have not. When there is a commercial section, it will usually deal with trade and tourism in a general way. Some embassies also have excellent libraries; for example, the American Embassy in London.

Chambers of Commerce frequently produce directories and newsletters which may be worth obtaining and some also have libraries. The London Chamber of Commerce has a library which is worth joining for the London-based librarian since it runs meetings which feature speakers from all over the world. Chambers of Commerce can be valuable places in which to make contacts.

Trade Associations can be exceedingly valuable since many have libraries and almost all produce some publications. Some publish a yearbook, others annual statistics and many have a journal or a newsletter. Some will supply information free but many insist on membership.

Library and information centres are invaluable sources of overseas marketing information. The Export Market Intelligence Centre (EMIC) has already been mentioned both in this chapter and in Chapter Four on British Official Publications, and is, of course, incomparable. Other libraries have excellent facilities including City Business Library and Warwick Business Information Service, which is especially strong in international statistics and statistics emanating from trade associations and other non-governmental sources. Here, the old boy/girl network comes into play. It is worthwhile keeping in touch with fellow students from library school and undergraduate days, going to meetings, making contacts and helping other librarians with enquiries whenever possible, so that they, in turn, will be happy to help you.

Conclusions

In this area of work, it is impossible to have too many contacts. It is valuable to know people within your company, in your profession and in the community in business, industry and the academic world. The information specialist never knows when a contact may be the best route to a piece of information.

Secondly, although paper sources are worth consulting, they will inevitably usually be out of date. It is, therefore, to online that the information specialist would expect to turn, but overseas market data is poorly represented at present outside Europe and North America. Sometimes the only way to get the data is to commission a market survey or pay an agent to obtain an annual report or a status report.

Embassies and Chambers of Commerce are frequently disappointing as information sources whereas banks often prove to be helpful and efficient information providers. The information situation in this area is improving all the time but, in the meanwhile, the information scientist will find this type of search a real challenge and must rely on building up a mental databank of possible sources including the telephone numbers of contacts, friends and colleagues.

Further reading

Business Information Review publishes useful review articles on the information resources relating to various countries from time to time.

TFPL Training and the British Library Science Reference and Information Service are now running a series of country by country information courses. They have currently covered France, Spain and Portugal and the USA. A seminar on Italy is plannned for January 1990.

Some useful addresses

Economist Publications Ltd, 40 Duke Street, London W1A 1DW. Tel: 071-499 2278

Extel Financial Ltd, Fitzroy House, 13–17 Epworth Street, London EC2A 4DL. Tel: 071-251 3333. Fax: 071-608 3514

Graham & Trotman Ltd, Sterling House, 66 Wilton Road, London SW1X 1DE. Tel: 071-236 8000

Peat Marwick McLintock, 1 Puddle Dock, Blackfriars, London EC4V 3PD. Tel: 071-236 8000

TFPL Training, 22 Peter's Lane, London EC1M 6DS. Tel: 071-251 5522. Fax: 071-251 8318

TRADSTAT Sales, EDS, Queen's House West, Greenhill Way, Harlow HA1 1GR. Tel: 081-861 2233

Chapter Ten

BANKING INFORMATION

Olivia Freeman

What is banking?

The meaning of the word 'bank' is thought to be derived from the Italian *banca* which means a bench, tradesman's counter, a work-table and a money changer's bench. Modern day banking is all about money, although, in many cases, no money ever changes hands. Banking is a service industry which ranges from accepting small deposits over the counter in the bank on the high street to multi-million pound company acquisitions. In between, there are a whole range of banking products available to the personal financial customer and the corporate customer. Services for the personal customer are defined as retail banking while services to corporates are generally defined as wholesale banking. Competition in the financial services industry is very intense and consequently there is more need for up-to-date, accurate information than ever before. It is a very exciting environment in which to work.

The growth of information departments in banks in the UK has been relatively unstructured. This is in contrast to the United States, where the major banks have very large well-established libraries. In this country, libraries have developed because a particular department needed information and the collections developed into libraries. All the clearing banks had libraries attached to their economics department, which were initially maintained by the economists themselves. Similarly, libraries in merchant banks frequently grew out of a collection of files on their corporate clients. There are often several of these in one organisation, all with separate budgets and being managed totally independently: sometimes there is a good reason for this because there must be secrecy between one side of an organisation and the other. Those dealing in securities have a so-called Chinese wall between them and the side of the bank dealing in acquisitions and mergers. They are, for obvious reasons, often separate companies.

The information department could be serving any of the following departments:

— Securities dealing
— Acquisitions and mergers
— Trade finance
— Management and strategic planning
— Training
— Marketing
— Information technology
— Economics
— Whole bank
— Investments

Each department requires a slightly different type of information provision. For example, the credit functions require the latest information on a company/industry, whereas training may require background and text books.

The work of the department will have a great deal of influence on the role of the library. The majority of bank libraries support the corporate finance department. Enquiries are concerned with acquisition and major activity and the information provided is predominantly company and industry related. The service is available for anything from 20–100 people, who require in-depth research into their companies and may themselves work all hours of the night.

The other major customer for bank libraries are the securities analysts. These analysts specialise in particular companies and industries. Their in-depth research and monitoring of companies enables them to advise banks and customers of good and bad buys on the stock market. Analysts are very demanding in terms of information provision and demand personalised files and service. Services provided by a bank library could be any of the following:

— Rapid enquiry service
— In-depth enquiry service
— News bulletin daily/weekly
— Journals circulation
— Journals indexing by subjects
— Publications purchase
— Subject reading lists
— Lists of new additions
— Back-up to training
— Referral service

- — Text books for students
- — Client files/RM function
- — Contacts outside
- — Regular contributions to publications
- — Online searching
- — Advice on information requirements

The stage is set for working in a bank information department; whoever the clientele are, it will undoubtedly be busy. The information needs of bankers are pervasive and may include any of the following areas:

- — Banks, private individuals
- — Customers
- — Corporates, countries
- — Industry
- — Macro and micro economics
- — Banking
- — Finance
- — Payment systems
- — Financing techniques
- — Computers and systems
- — Management
- — Management accounting
- — Marketing
- — Planning

The aim of this chapter is to indicate the major sources of information about banking. This is not necessarily what bankers need to know. Many bankers' information needs are satisfied by knowing about their customers.

Regulatory environment

Since deregulation, the regulatory environment has become more complex. The Banking Act has been in force since 1979. The Bank of England, as the central bank, is responsible for the supervision of all banks. The bank sets guidelines for other banks and maintains a list of authorised institutions, which is updated at intervals. No organisation is allowed to carry on banking business, which is loosely the acceptance of deposits, without the approval of the Bank of England. Building societies are subject to different regulations and function as mutual societies.

The regulation of financial institutions has become further complicated by increased competition which has, in turn, led to financial institutions diversifying from their original lines of business. Since 1986, the banking world has been subject to a complicated set of regulations for investor protection.

Every person or institution, who carries out investment business, must be authorised, not by the Bank of England, but by any one of a series of bodies relating to the Securities and Investment Board (SIB). These authorised institutions are not just banks, but can be finance houses, accountants or solicitors.

Big Bang took place on 27 October 1986. Initially, Big Bang was to be just a change in the method of trading shares on the London Stock Exchange: a simple change from trading on the floor of the Stock Exchange to electronic trading. This change was actually the instigator of a breakdown in the traditional methods of trading stocks and shares and of the end of stockbrokers as independent institutions. There is only one independent stockbroker of any size left in the City of London; virtually all the others are part of banks.

There were many other changes going on concurrently but, finally, the failure of several financial institutions led the government to initiate *A review of investor protection*, which reported in 1985. *A financial services white paper* was published later in 1985 and this formed the basis of the Financial Services Act, 1986. This act forms the framework for investment business and the setting-up of the Securities and Investment Board (SIB). Other bodies are still involved in regulation, including the Bank of England and the Building Societies Commission. Lloyds of London regulates insurance broking, the takeover panel scrutinises acquisitions and mergers and the Department of Trade and Industry oversees listing requirements for public issues.

The SIB not only has regulatory powers, but can take investment businesses to court to obtain the return of monies to clients and can carry out criminal prosecutions. It is financed by the City and is a private company, although the Board is accountable to the Secretary of State for Trade and Industry. The SIB is the top of a pyramid with a number of Self-Regulatory Organisations (SROs) reporting to it. There are five SROs, each producing a rulebook covering the conduct of their members. An institution can choose to register with the SIB or direct with an SRO depending on the type of investment business carried out.

Figure 1 shows the structure of City regulators. Current thinking is that it is too complex and that it must be simplified as soon as possible. The SIB maintains a database of authorised institutions or persons: this is available on magnetic tapes or via PRESTEL. It is an offence to carry out investment business without being authorised and most institutions have put the name of their regulatory organisation on their notepaper.

Insider trading is subject to another regulatory authority and it is to be

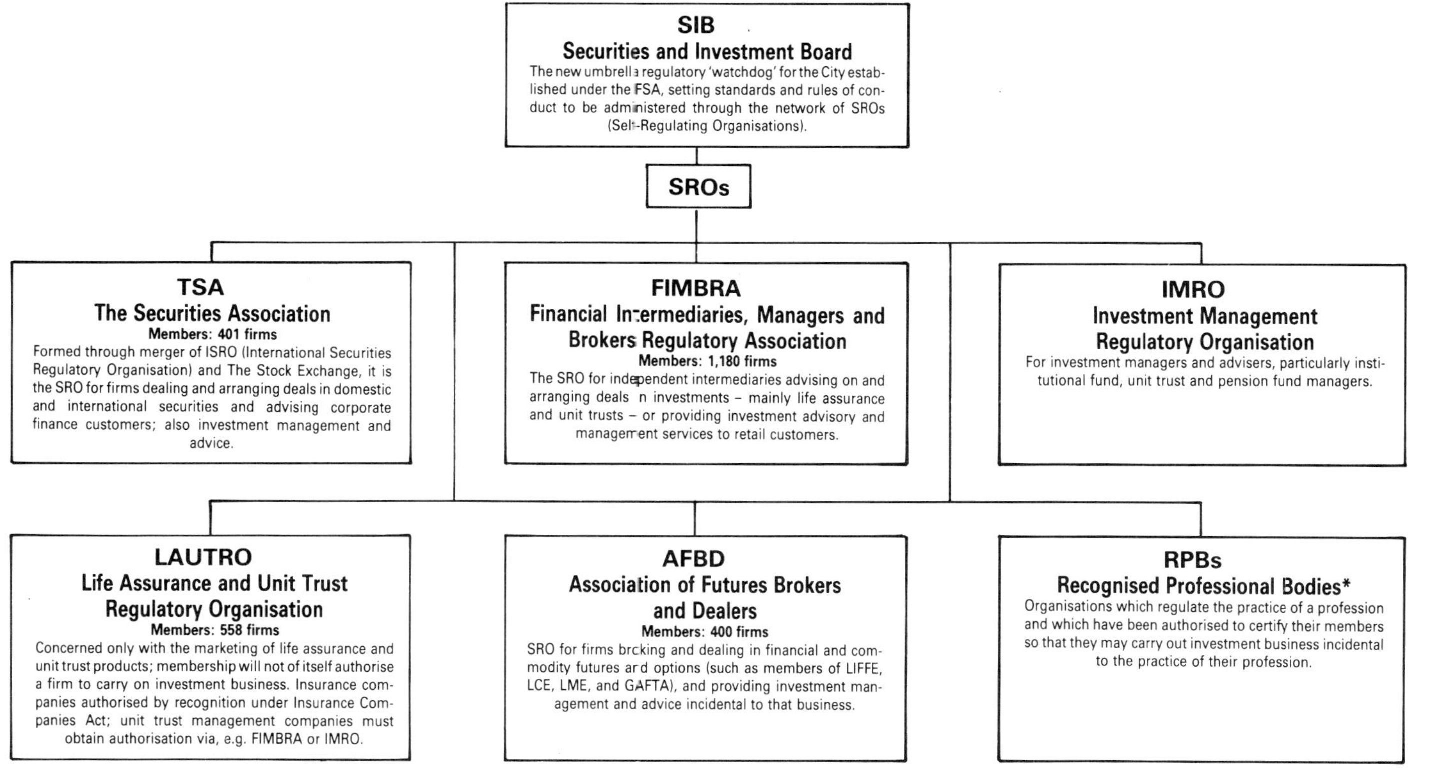

Figure 1: Stucture of City Regulation

hoped that the whole system will be simplified or the City of London may become so hide-bound with regulations that it will not remain competitive.

A final word about the Bank of England may be of value. The regulation of banking is an ongoing process and, from time to time, the Bank issues documents on supervision or capital adequacy. These documents usually start life as discussion documents and are then, after changes, brought into accepted practice. These documents are very important, especially those regarding capital adequacy, but they present a problem for information gathering as they are often semi-published. Normally, documents are commented on in the *Financial Times* and copies of the papers are kept at reception in the Bank of England. Copies of the papers have, of course, been sent to the relevant official within the banks. A similar procedure is followed for papers produced by the Bank for International Settlements or the Committee of London and Scottish Clearing Bankers (CLSB). There is a list of banking organisations at the end of the chapter.

Every country has a supervisory body, which is generally the Central Bank. Although regulations vary from country to country, it is left to the discretion of the regulatory authority as to whether a bank can have a presence in that particular country: this ruling applies to even the largest banks in the world. Having established the regulations, how do we identify banks and their branches? There are over 14,000 banks in the United States alone.

Directories of banks

The *Bankers' almanac* is the most widely used directory in the UK. It is published in January and an updated version is published in July. It is split into two volumes. Volume One is an alphabetical sequence of 3,600 major banks with a separate geographical index. The information provided includes standard address and telegraphic information, a brief history and ownership, details of directors and officials, two years of balance sheet figures, details of branches and correspondents and where possible, the bank's logo is included.

Volume Two is an index to branches, which is probably unique. You can, for example, look up a town in India and identify which banks have a branch in that town. The whole world is covered; addresses are provided, when available.

Other useful features in Volume One are a list of telegraphic addresses, details of association and institutions and details of amalgamations, absorptions and liquidations of banks in the UK since 1700, historical changes in bank rate for European countries and a listing of notes and coins of the world.

There are two American directories which hold information on a greater number of banks. *The Rand McNally bankers' directory* has two volumes devoted to the United States. The volumes are organised by state with a separate alphabetical index. There are listings for every bank head office, branch, agency, representative office and banking Edge Act Corporation in the United States. Each listing, as in the *Bankers' almanac*, contains key marketing, administrative and operational information. The international volume displays listings for all offices of international banks involved in foreign exchange or foreign trade. It is arranged by country and subdivided by town. All volumes are updated every six months.

Polk's bank directory is obviously trying hard to keep its format to two volumes. The North American edition is now over 4" thick. This volume includes the United States, Canada, Mexico, Caribbean and Central America. It is issued semi-annually, whereas the international edition is only annual. The content of the entries is similar to *Rand McNally*.

There are many directories of banks, but special emphasis has been placed on these three directories. Each of them has been published over 100 times and has built up a record of reliability.

There is a variety of reasons for using a directory of banks. In some cases, it is to identify business specialities. Diversification within financial services has given rise to a number of specialist directories.

The City directory, which is now in its eighth edition, is a good source to identify all the players in financial services. The entries only give names and addresses but it can be used to identify members of the London Metal Exchange or equipment leasing companies. In fact, all associations and membership bodies and their members are listed including organisations representing foreign firms in London. In addition, there are lists of ancillary services such as databases, conference facilities and financial market research organisations.

Crawford's directory of City connections is effectively a directory of corporate relationships of the major UK companies and pension funds. For each company, the following are listed; stockbroker, financial advisor (i.e. Merchant Bank), auditor and solicitor. There are separate indexes by these four categories which forms a listing of their major clients. There are additional indexes of insurance brokers, public relations consultants, pension funds and actuaries consultants and institutional investors. Companion volumes are *Crawford's European finance* (formerly *Corporate finance*) and *Crawford's investment research index*.

The Bank register is published by Euromoney. It features 6,000 financial institutions in 175 countries. Its unique feature is that each entry has a section on the specialisation of each bank and the contact names connected with that function. This directory only relates to wholesale banking where there are so many specialist financing techniques that it is important to identify the experts. Stockbrokers are also included.

The Merrill Lynch Euromoney directory is even more specialised and purports to be the only comprehensive reference source to the operating offices at the institutions that arrange, manage, underwrite and provide capital on the international capital markets.

To terminate the section on directories, it is worth mentioning the existence of specialist directories covering particular countries or regions of the world. *Triple A Asia Banking almanac* is the best source of identifying the banks, finance houses, insurance companies and securities companies active in the Asia-Pacific area. Similarly, *The Meed Middle East financial directory* is a useful source of information for Middle Eastern countries and banks with Middle Eastern connections.

Rankings

The major players have been identified. How do they rate in the banking industry? Banks are a little difficult to rank, as there is no actual manufactured product. The majority of rankings are based on assets, probably because it is the best indication of their capital structure. The major bank rankings are published in journals. Probably the best known is produced by *The Banker* which has been compiling league tables for 19 years. The listings appear every year in the July issue and in 1988 the ranking was increased to cover the top 500 banks worldwide. Separate rankings by country are also included. Other rankings are published in the *American Banker* which, in 1988, published a separate supplement of all its rankings, called the *Top numbers 1988: a selection of American Bankers' statistical rankings*, published during the first year. Others appear in the *Institutional Investor* (June) and *Euromoney* (various). Extel Financial produces annually a *Ranking of UK investment analysts*, and there are many others, too numerous to mention.

There are two organisations which take ranking a stage further and analyse the statistics. IBCA and Keefe Bruyette and Woods (US) are both bank credit analysts. IBCA produce an annual publication called *Real banking profitability* and statistical comparisons of banks in UK, Bermuda, Canada, Europe, Australia and Japan. *Real banking profitability* contains a profit ranking based on net income. This produces a completely different list from that based on assets.

Who's whos

Next, we need to find out more about the bankers themselves. A number of eminent bankers merit entries in the general *Who's who*. There are a slowly increasing number of Who's whos dealing just with the financial world.

Becket's directory of the City of London was first published in 1985 and a second edition came out in 1987. The information was collected by questionnaires, so the entries are of varying detail. The third edition will have quarterly updates and also includes an institutional section. The Stock Exchange press published *Who's who in the City: the annual biographical guide to the UK financial community* in 1988. This publication covers the whole financial community with 6,000 biographies and, hopefully, it will be possible to update it annually. The financial world is changing so quickly that it is a mammoth task.

This is well illustrated by *Who's who in international banking* published by the International Insider. The publication started life about four years ago as a small volume. There are now biographical entries for 4,000 senior banking offers worldwide. *Who's who in banking in Europe* was last published in 1984. It is to be hoped that there will be another edition before 1992.

Another useful source are the membership lists of professional bodies. The press and journals are the best source for new appointments and should be used to update and supplement information from *Who's whos*.

Profiles of banks/groups of banks

The information sources listed so far have been specific to financial services but there are some more general sources which should be consulted in order to produce a complete profile of a bank. For further details, refer to Chapter Seven on Company information.

The majority of banks produce an annual report to shareholders and many of the major foreign branches produce separate reports, a fact which is not often realised. Extel cards are also worth consulting in this context.

Stockbrokers comment very often covers groups of banks, for example, the clearing banks. There are always a bevy of brokers' reports prior to the announcement of annual and interim results. There are more occasional reports on merchant banks or banking activity within a particular region of the world. Brokers' reports only analyse banks which are quoted on the Stock Exchange and surprisingly few actually are. Out of the approximately 500 banks in the UK, only 47 are listed in the *Financial Times*' Share Service.

Credit ratings

Credit ratings are of great importance in judging the past and potential performance of a bank. *Moody's bank and finance manual* is in four volumes. It is the most comprehensive and in-depth source of information on financial institutions. The data includes full balance sheet, debt and loan analysis, history, business and credit ratings. Ratings have been of great significance in the USA, where there are, on average, 300 bank failures each year. Their importance in Europe has only been evident in the last few years, as a result of the increased emphasis on bank regulation and problems with Third World debt repayment. Needless to say, banking is a risky business! A bank or branch is normally rated in the country in which it is located. Ratings are normally given for short-term debt, long-term debt and commercial paper. The ratings are an excellent way of applying common standards and comparing a bank's performance with its peer group. The ratings agencies normally have detailed analysis on each rated organisation and maintain them on credit watch. Changes in ratings appear in the *Financial Times*, *Wall Street Journal* and in the weekly *International Financing Review*. The major ratings agencies are Moodys, Standard and Poors, IBCA, Keefe Bruyette and Woods and Dun and Bradstreet.

Market research

Market research is extremely important in the financial environment. It falls into three categories, each with differing degrees of availability and confidentiality.

Publishers such as Mintel and Keynotes produce market research which can be purchased by any organisation. The output is produced either in serial form, for example, Mintel's *Personal Financial Intelligence* or as a separate report on a particular product or sector of the community, for example, credit cards or the over 55s. The research is derived partly from interviews and partly from forecasts of trends and market shares.

The second category is syndicated market research. A group of interested banks or other organisations agree, both to submit data and share the cost of the research between themselves. The results of the research are normally based purely on interviews and the reports are only available to the commissioning organisations. Greenwich Research Associates, National Opinion Polls (NOP) and City Research Associates are typical of the market research organisations that undertake syndicated research. Topics cover such aspects as how corporate treasurers see their banks or public attitudes towards electronic cash management.

The third type of research is undertaken by the bank's internal market research department, usually to research a new product. The research is gathered from interviews and group discussions among potential or existing customers or bank staff. The results are completely confidential. The *Market Research Society's Yearbook* contains a list of recognised market researchers.

Dictionaries

Dictionaries of banking, finance and investment terms are a mushrooming industry. This, again, reflects the rapidly changing nature of the marketplace. They are essential reference tools, but only a few can be selected for inclusion in this chapter. *Thomson's dictionary of banking* is the classic, but it has not been re-issued since the 12th edition which was reprinted in 1977. This has been updated by *Dictionary of banking and finance* (Hanson) 1985. The definitions in these dictionaries relate predominantly to British domestic banking, sometimes with lengthy entries giving case history and examples.

The second edition of *Macmillan dictionary of international finance* was published in 1985. This provides concise but informative definitions of all aspects of international finance; the majority of these definitions also have a further reading list. *Pocket banker* is part of a series of pocket publications published by Economist Publication, again in 1985 and it is well presented and extremely readable. International and domestic finance as well as the organisations involved are included.

Banking and finance has developed not only a myriad of regulations but a terminology to go with it; hence, a *Dictionary of financial regulation, 1988/89*, which contains short, concise definitions on all aspects of the securities and investment business.

Statistics

Banking statistics are collected by the Central Bank in every country. The quality, quantity and timeliness of the statistics varies from country to country. The statistics collected are of an official nature and relate to banking's direct effect on the economy of the country concerned. On the whole, they are not useful for finding out about the banking market in a particular country or the activities of a particular bank or sector of banks.

In most cases, banking statistics are annoyingly incomplete. For example, the Bank of England produces an *Analysis of bank lending to UK residents*, which is split up by industry sectors but the UK manufacturing industry is divided into only 12 sectors, so that it is not possible to produce an accurate correlation of bank lending to all industrial sectors.

Major sources of banking statistics are Bank of England monthly press notices reproduced in the *Bank of England Quarterly Bulletin* and in slightly less detail in *Financial Statistics (CSO)*. The *Financial Times* is the best source of current exchange and interest rates: these are available historically via FinStat. There are other UK banking statistics produced by the Association for Payment Clearing Services (Apacs) and the Committee of London and Scottish Bankers (CLSB), which are confidential.

International statistics are produced by the OECD and published as

Financial statistics and *Financial market trends* and the Bank for International Settlements (BIS), publishes *International banking and financial market developments* and the *Maturity distribution of international bank lending*. The BIS statistics relate to international capital markets activity. Other sources include the European Investment Bank, Central Bank Bulletins and bank economic reports (worldwide).

ECGD and the Committee on Invisible Exports publish statistics which relate to the banks' support of international trade. Ancillary statistical sources are the *IMF international financial statistics* and the *World Bank world debt tables*.

Statistical databanks

Most historical databanks relate to economic statistics and are documented in the chapter on statistics. The very small number which relate purely to banking statistics will be described. The majority of databanks used in the financial environment are real-time services, these are predominantly used by dealers as the tools of their trade. Real-time implies that they are constantly being updated. In other words, every time a foreign exchange rate or a share price changes, the databases will change: this could be every second.

The main historical databank is the Bank of England Databank. It is hosted by ADP and DRI. The databank contains 7,800 daily, weekly, monthly, quarterly and annual time series on UK and overseas banking sectors, discount markets, exchange rates, interest rates and financial transactions. The data is similar to that published in the *Bank of England Quarterly Bulletin* and the *Monthly Banking Statistics*.

The statistics of the other central banks, for example, Germany, Australia, Canada and the United States, are available via the major databank hosts, DRI, WEFA and I.P. SHARP. Equally, these hosts carry long time series of foreign exchange and interests rates, and DRI also includes commodity prices.

CRONOS, the Eurostat databank, has 8,000 time series of intra-European cash flows. Euromoney and IFR produce databases on activity on the International Capital Markets. The Euromoney databases are available on disc and enable the monitoring of loans made on the Euromarkets since 1980. The databases can be searched by borrowers and lenders.

Real-time data

REUTER TELERATE and QUOTRON are the market leaders for real-time information. The data supplied is mostly price information and the terminals are used for electronic trading. The prices relate to equities, commodities and foreign exchange. Subscribers feed in their own prices and the systems work as an electronic marketplace. The services are very costly, largely because there is a captive market; in other words, the dealers cannot deal without subscribing to at least one, if not two, of the services.

The market for real-time price information is starting to open out. CITISERVICE is available from PRESTEL on a pay-as-you-go basis. It is not a trading system, but gives access to continually updated foreign exchange and interest rates, commodities, financial futures, Stock Exchange indices (worldwide), business and financial news. The FTSE 100 share price is updated five times a day. There is a subscription service to STOCK EXCHANGE AUTOMATED QUOTATIONS (SEAQ) to provide real-time updates to share and traded option prices.

TOPIC is the Stock Exchange's own price information service. It is a viewdata system, and since it was first launched in 1980, has been installed by most Stock Exchange members. The service delivers real-time information on the share price of the 2,000 most actively traded UK companies plus 1,500 North American and other foreign stocks.

CITICORP, the American banking corporation, markets a product called GLOBAL REPORT. This database service was originally developed to service the information needs of Citicorps' own executives. It is a mixture of real-time and historical data, again using the viewdata technology. The service provides currency and money market prices; news and commentary on companies and economies; share prices for leading US, UK and European companies. Much of the information is obtained from other banks and news services.

There are many services offering foreign exchange, commodity and share prices. The three described are probably the most applicable to the library information department, even if other parts of the bank are using REUTER and TELERATE.

Journals

It is time to move on to some sources which are actually about banking as an industry. Journals and the press are an important source of up-to-date information. Financial journalism is another growth area.

The *Banker* and *Banking World* (Journal of the Chartered Institute of Bankers) are sources of good background articles on all aspects of banking. *Euromoney* also carries general articles on banking worldwide with a slant towards activity on the international capital markets. The *American Banker* is a daily financial services newspaper. There are numerous other journals monitoring the US banking scene. The *Bank of England Quarterly Bulletin* publishes speeches by bank officials and major articles on current aspects of banking or credit control.

There are a very large number of newsletters in the banking and financial area. In contrast to newspapers, newsletters are usually written for the expert in the area. They contain a mixture of news, informed comment and gossip. To some extent, the gossip is the most important element. Newsletters are very costly and it is important that they are received in good time by the people who can make best use of them. Most newsletters are weekly and no more than about 10 pages long. The exception to this is *International Financing Review* (IFR) which is about 50 pages long and between glossy covers. Newsletters are published on nearly all aspects of financial services. They either come from very small publishers or, as the trend is at present, from a larger publisher who produces a series of newsletters. *Financial Times* business publishing produces *Euromarket Letter*, *International Trade Finance*, *International Banking Report* and others covering Insurance, Taxation and Accountancy. These newsletters are all available full-text via PROFILE or DATA-STAR.

Other newsletters, such as *International Insider* only relates to the Euromarkets. Lafferty Publications are specialist publishers for banking and financial services who are aiming at niche markets within banking. Their publications include *Retail Banker International*, *Financial Services International*, *International Electronic Payments* and *Private Banker International*.

Newsletters and journals can be identified from *Willings* and *Benn's media guide*, advertisements from journals and are covered by databases such as NEWSNET PREDICASTS NEWSLETTER DATABASES and FINANCIAL TIMES BUSINESS REPORTS.

There are other journals which carry in-depth articles on every aspect of banking. They tend to be specialised: good examples of this type of journal are *Euromoney's Trade Finance* and *Corporate Finance* journals. Other specialist journals cover the retail area, for example, *Planned Savings*, *Money Magazine* and *Money Observer*. There is an increasing number of publications covering the technology side, for example *Banking Technology*, *Bank Systems and Equipment*, *Cash Management News*, *Online Finance* and *Cashflow* which also carries some good, more general, articles.

These titles are a mixture of American and British although there are many more American journals. They are often quite applicable to the UK market which is usually running behind the US. For instance, articles on credit cards in the US can have a lot of applications for market planners in this country. As yet, there is not much evidence of European journals becoming available in this country.

Abstracting services and databases

Journals and newsletters have two major purposes, initially current awareness and secondly, informed comment to lead to changes or research and development. It is in this second aspect that abstracting services and databases are invaluable.

The library of the Chartered Institute of Bankers keeps a wonderful collection of paper-based subject files. This is slowly being superseded by the growth of and simplicity of use of online, especially full text retrieval services.

World Banking Abstracts commenced in 1985 to fill a gap in the bibliographic control of banking. It is produced by the Institute of Finance at the University of Wales. It is easy and quick to use. Each issue follows the same format which is a series of broad chapter headings, which reflects the way banking is organised. The abstracts are brief and there is also a subject index. The service is also available as part of the REUTER TEXTLINE BANKING AND FINANCE DATABASE (special subscription of £1,000).

The TEXTLINE database is a good starting-point from which to retrieve press and recent articles on banking. It has its limitations because some of the indexing is imprecise and consequently there is always the risk of retrieving irrelevant information. The *American Banker* is available full text via the following hosts: DATA-STAR, DIALOG, MEAD DATA CENTRAL, TEXTLINE and NEWSNET. The database is updated daily and, although largely American in content, there are a number of features covering international banking. It is good for comparisons and surveys, which are included in the database.

PROFILE is well-supplied with specialist banking databases. It has the *Banker* in full text and the *Financial Times Business Reports* which includes the following specialist banking newsletters; *Business Law Brief*, *Euromarket Report*, *Financial Regulation Report* (monthly guide to regulatory developments in banking, securities and fund management), *International Banking Report*, *International Trade Finance*, *World Accounting Report*, *World Commodity Report*, *World Insurance Report*, *World Tax Report*; *Mintel Financial* and *Euromonitor* research reports. There is also MCCARTHEY'S ONLINE and the general press databases, plus SPEARHEAD, the 1992 database which gives information on potential banking directives in the European Single Market. There is also the output of banks such as the *World Bank: International Business Opportunities Database*.

FINIS is the database of the American Bank Marketing Association and is extremely useful for data on retail and wholesale banking products available in the USA. There is some European coverage. Records are purely bibliographic and it is available on DIALOG, BRS and PERGAMON FINANCIAL DATA SERVICES.

FIND (Financial Institutions Database) is available via PERGAMON FINANCIAL DATA SERVICES. It is comparatively new in database form and is produced by Tekron Publications. FIND contains accounts and general information on UK financial institutions. The database covers banks, building societies and insurance companies. The major elements relating to banks and banking are accounts and general information on UK registered banks from 1982/3 to date. There are separate sections on financial news, advertising expenditure and various rankings by financial performance.

ABI/INFORM deserves a separate mention. Although it is a business management database, it is particularly good for information on banking. It is available on DATA-STAR.

The database of Société Générale de Banque (SGB) is also available from DATA-STAR. It is a bibliographic database with good European coverage of banking, politics and world economy. Its English language sources tend to be duplicated by other databases, but it should become increasingly useful in the hunt for European material, provided one can read in French, German or Dutch.

There are obviously other databases which should be used, such as the more general press databases: TEXTLINE, PROFILE and BIS-INFORMAT. It is also worth using the stockbroker databases, INVESTEXT and ICC STOCKBROKER RESEARCH, both available on DIALOG and DATA-STAR. These databases can all be used to retrieve information by named organisations or by product.

The customers of banks

Customers are either private individuals or organisations, such as schools and hospitals or companies. Banks provide these customers with many different services and each service involves money and some element of risk; therefore, banks need to know the credit-worthiness of their customers.

Information on private individuals and non-corporate organisations is not well-documented but the remainder of banking customers are companies, countries (at local and national government levels) and other banks. They probably account for more than half the customers, as some banks have no private customers or only very few.

Companies

For more details on sources of company information, you should refer to Chapter Seven on Company information. Some company information is specifically of interest to banks and banks certainly require to look at companies in a different way from other organisations.

Company information needs fall into the following categories: credit, corporate finance, securities analysis and marketing. On the whole, the sources used are no different from those in other information departments, in fact most of the sources were initially developed for use by bankers or investment analysts. The difference is in the degree of information required. Information for credit purposes can be extracted from all the normal sources such as annual reports, Extel cards or Companies' House or any of the databases based on Companies' House data, such as INFOCHECK or ICC. A banker will analyse the balance sheet and use ratios according to the bank's own method. They are likely to be interested in the mortgages and charges, details of which can be found on the Companies' House fiche.

The bankers involved in the corporate finance area, dealing with mergers and acquisitions, need to know every possible detail about a company and its subsidiaries. They need to look at a company's performance at least over a 10 year period in contrast to the banker making a lending decision, who will only need three years of figures. Information departments serving the corporate finance function keep a collection of loan prospectuses and Stock Exchange documents. There is no bibliographic control for these publications and they are obtained by systematically ringing round the lead bankers. The Stock Exchange fiche are produced daily and include a copy of every document issued on the Stock Exchange. It usually involves a great deal of filing.

There are two recent services, which have been developed with the Corporate Finance department in mind: both are online services. The first, ANALYSIS, covers 2,800 UK quoted companies. Its aim is to provide a clear, concise and pertinent report on each of these companies. The service pulls together in one very well-presented, easily readable report, 1,200 variable data elements per company. The database is constantly being updated and there is an alerting service for Stock Exchange activity.

The second service is the acquisitions and mergers databases available on PROFILE. The database is based on the monthly printed newsletter FT Mergers and Acquisitions International. It can be searched by date, target and bidder companies, status, currency and industry sectors. The printed section of the magazine will be added to the McCarthy press cuttings file.

Both corporate finance and the lending bankers will want to know the relevant Moodys, or Standard and Poors debt ratings available for both companies and countries (expanded in the section called Credit Ratings).

Analysts working on the securities side of banking monitor the companies for whom their organisation acts as professional advisors. They tend to work on a short-term basis in relation to the current stock market price of a company. Their use of information differs but they will use similar sources. A number of information services, such as Extel Cards and DATASTREAM have been set up specifically to serve the needs of the analysts. They will, of course, use the analysis published by other brokers. The analysts must brief the brokers working in their organisations, who will, in turn, alert their clients to good and bad purchases on the Stock Market. The alerting is done either by written research or verbally at a morning meeting.

The fourth area where banks need information on companies is for marketing, where information is required on actual and potential customers. The most important piece of information is to identify existing relationships between bankers and professional advisors and their customers. *Dunsfiche* or *Dun and Bradstreet Registers* are the traditional publications used to identify a company's clearing bank. The banks supply the information to Dun and Bradstreet. *Dunsfiche* are updated monthly and supply the name and address of the company, telephone number, parent company details, number of employees, the sorting code of the bankers, credit ratings, a turnover band and a description of business. *Crawford's directory of City connections*, which was mentioned in the section on Directories, is the best source of identifying the professional advisors. Databases such as KOMPASS, ICC or ELC are used for producing target lists depending on the products involved and the size of company to be targetted. Skillful use of databases and picking the right criteria on which to search can produce almost any target list which might be required.

Countries

At the beginning of this section, countries were also mentioned as customers of banks. In many cases, the customer is either a commercial bank or one of the international or regional development banks and, in some cases, it is the government. For detailed information on overseas countries, you should refer to Chapter Nine of this book, Worldwide market resources. There are a number of sources and it is not hard to find information on overseas economies. It is more a problem to find up-to-date information which can be used for comparative purposes. Regular sources are the *IMF International Financial Statistics*, the *OECD Economic Surveys* and the twice-annual *Economic Outlook*, the *Economist Intelligence Unit*, published quarterly, *Country Reports* and *Annual Profiles* on 92 countries or country groupings. There are useful articles in the Europa Yearbook series and the World of Information series. *IMF Exchange Arrangements and Exchange Restrictions* gives the current exchange control arrangements for every country in considerable detail. The publication includes details on central bank powers and whether funds can be repatriated. In addition, two vitally important sources are the bulletins from Central Banks and from commercial banks in each country. TEXTLINE and PROFILE are both good for updating information on overseas economies. Prospectuses are another useful source of data on countries. Whenever a loan is made on the international capital markets, a prospectus must be issued; this often contains information which may not be found elsewhere.

Information published by banks

Passing reference has been made to the publications of banks. Banks supply and publish several different categories of information. A brief synopsis of this seems to be a useful addition to this chapter.

Every month, banks supply statistics to the Bank of England which are published in the Banking Statistics. Banks also supply a variety of rates to databases (both real-time and historical) and journals. These rates range from general exchange rates to specialist rates, for example, relating to forfaiting (a trade finance technique). Banks publish economic bulletins in which their economists air their views on the current state of the economy and connected issues. This type of publication is well-indexed by *World Banking Abstracts*, which also contains a list of titles.

Banks' analysts publish research on companies, industries and countries to make recommendations for the stock market, hence in the UK, they are known as stockbrokers' reports, whereas the American equivalent are known as investment bank reports. The analysts have in-depth and sometimes first-hand knowledge of the companies and industries. This makes them very useful sources of information outside the stockbroking community, although circulation is limited and there is no source to check all the reports produced. Two databases, INVESTEXT and IC BROKERS REPORTS (ICC) and their companion paper publications – *New Industry Reports* and *New Additions to the Database* are a good indication.

Another very useful aspect of bank publishing is their product brochures and newsletters for particular categories of customers. For instance, the Midland Bank produces a four-page report known as *Tradebrief*; this publication gives little snippets of information on exhibitions, trade delegations and new regulations, all of value to the exporter. The National Westminster Bank produces a similar publication for exporters and another one aimed at the small businessman or woman. Most banks produce product brochures on each of their specialist products. These are aimed at customers, but are very useful sources of information on the products as well as being a form of advertising.

It has already been mentioned that banks produce prospectuses in support of every loan on the international capital markets and issues on the Stock Exchange. These documents are usually very detailed as they have been written with the intention of raising capital. Large banks publish a house journal, which is intended as a means of communication to employees. They are on the whole easily available and serve as a good indication of the current strategy of the bank.

Not every aspect of bank publishing has been covered, but enough to serve as a reminder not to forget it as a source of information.

EC single market

1992 will have an effect on both banks and their customers. Cross-European acquisitions and mergers have already started happening. The harmonisation of the banking laws will open up the marketplace for financial services throughout Europe.

The advent of 1992 has spawned a number of publications. The best hard source of information at present are the directives which can be identified either from the press, by contacting the EC Information Office or the European Documentation Centres. The SPEARHEAD database is a Department of Trade and Industry initiative to monitor proposed legislation. It, along with CELEX, which contains the text of adopted legislation, is available from PROFILE.

There are a number of abstracting publications to assist in monitoring 1992. BIS-INFORMAT produce a weekly 1992 Alert of article summaries. The same information is also input to the INFORMAT database and they have a special code for articles on 1992 which is aseec.pn. There are a number of other current awareness services, some of which are very specialised. Two of a general nature are monthly publications from the University of Warwick Business Information Service and Chadwyck Healey.

The aspects of 1992 which will specifically affect banking and financial organisations in planning their future strategy are details of the existing markets in the other EC countries. The planners will want to know what they can or cannot legally do in any particular country and if there is an existing market for a certain financial product. *Europe and the future of financial services* was published by Lafferty Publications. It is organised on a county basis as is *EEC: a guide to banking and sources of finance*. This publication is now in its third edition and gives very detailed descriptions of the banking systems in each country. This can usefully be used in conjunction with a looseleaf publication published by Business International. This publication, *Financing Foreign Operations* is updated annually. Each country is arranged by numbered sections, the same for each country. Its chief usefulness is that it gives an indication of basic legal requirements and is updated regularly.

The GT guide to world equity markets is published by Euromoney and has become an annual publication. Its coverage is rather wider than the EC as the book includes information on the Stock Exchanges of 41 countries. The information is uniform for each country and includes stock market performance, the history and organisational structure of each market, market size, types of shares available, a profile of the investors, tax, reports and research information.

Publications of this type are extremely useful when looking at the European market, as Europe is made up of countries with so many different customs. It is much easier to compare like with like.

Firms of accountants are offering different types of help and advice either to their clients or for a fee to outsiders. Spicer's Centre for Europe is a telephone advisory service. Deloitte Haskins and Sells have developed a database on EC policy, monitoring, particular industry sectors, one of which is banking.

The advent of the market will certainly change the face of financial services, in terms of wider markets and increased competition. That, in turn, will affect the work of the information department in the bank. It will be necessary to either have knowledge of or have access to all the sources of information throughout the EC countries.

Conclusion

The aim of this chapter has been to provide an introduction to working in a bank library or information department and to give a broad overview of the sources of information. A list is appended of the major banking organisations, many of whom are useful sources of information.

List of useful banking organisations

Association for Payment Clearing Services (APACS), Mercury House, Triton Court, 14 Finsbury Square, London EC2A 1BR. Tel: 071-628 7080

The Association of International Savings Banks in London, c/o TSB England & Wales plc, St Mary's Court, 100 Lower Thames Street, London EC3R 6AQ. Tel: 071-623 6000

Bank for International Settlements, Central Bahn-Platz 2, 4002 Basle, Switzerland. Tel: 061-208111

Banking Federation of the European Community, Rue Montoyer 10, 1040, 1150 Brussels, Belgium. Tel: 02 511 91 10

Banking Information Service, 10 Lombard Street, London EC3V 9EL. Tel: 071-623 4001

British Merchant Banking and Securities Houses Association, 6 Frederick's Place, Old Jewry, London EC2R 8BT. Tel: 071-796 3606

Building Societies Association, 3 Savile Row, London W1X 1AF. Tel: 071-437 0655

The Chartered Institute of Bankers, 10 Lombard Street, London EC3V 9AS. Tel: 071-623 3531/5071

The Committee of London and Scottish Bankers, 10 Lombard Street, London EC3V 9AP. Tel: 071-283 8866

EFTPOS UK Ltd, 12 Finsbury Square, London EC2A 1AS. Tel: 071-628 3070

Finance Houses Association, 18 Upper Grosvenor Street, London W1X 9PB. Tel: 071-491 2793.

The Financial Intermediaries, Managers and Brokers Regulatory Association (FIMBRA), Hertsmere House, Marsh Wall, London E14 9RW. Tel: 071-538 8860

Foreign Banks Association, 4 Bishopsgate, London EC2N 4AD. Tel: 071-283 1080

Institute of Chartered Accountants in England and Wales, PO Box 4333, Chartered Accounts' Hall, Moorgate Place, London EC2P 2BJ. Tel: 071-628 7060

Institute of European Finance, University College of North Wales, Bangor, Gwynedd LL57 2DG. Tel: 0248 351151

Investment Management Regulatory Organisation Ltd (IMRO), Centre Point, 103 New Oxford Street, London WC1A 1PT. Tel: 071-379 0601

Issuing Houses Association, Granite House, 101 Cannon Street, London EC4N 5BA. Tel: 071-283 7334

LIFFE—London International Financial Futures Exchange, Royal Exchange, London EC3V 3PJ. Tel: 071-623 0444

Life Assurance and Unit Trust Regulatory Organisation (LAUTRO), Lautro Ltd, Centre Point, 103 New Oxford Street, London WC1A 1QH. Tel: 071-379 0444

Securities and Investments Board (SIB), 3 Royal Exchange Buildings, London EC3V 3NL. Tel: 071-283 2474

The Society of Investment Analysts, 211–213 High Street, Bromley BR1 1NY. Tel: 081-464 0811.

The Stock Exchange, London EC2N 1HP. Tel: 071-588 2355

Further reading

ANTHONY, K. and RENNIE, J. Finance and investment newsletters: a study of their content and use. *Business Information Review*, 5(3), January 1989, 24–36.

BALL, S. The Directory of International Sources of Business Information, Pitman, 1989.

BYLAND, T. *Understanding finance with the Financial Times*, Harrup, 1988.

Financial services in the United Kingdom. A new framework for investor protection, Cmnd 9432, HMSO, 1985.

FOSTER, A. Online numeric databases: four years later ... *Business Information Review*, 5(3), January 1989, 3–12.

GOODHARD, C., KAY, J., MORTIMER, K. and DUGUID, A. *Financial Regulation – or over-regulation?* Institute of Economic Affairs, 1988.

MOWAT, M. Information sources in accountancy and finance. *Business Information Review*, 3(2), October 1986, 3–9.
NICHOLAS, D. *Commodities Futures Trading: a guide to information sources and computerised services*. Mansell, 1985.
Online business sourcebook, Headland Press, Spring, 1989.
REID, M. *All-change in the City: the revolution in Britain's financial sector*. Macmillan, 1988.
Review of investor protection, Cmnd 9125, HMSO, 1985, Parts 1 and 2.
Sources of world financial and banking information, Gower, 1981.

Chapter Eleven

PATENTS AND STANDARDS

Jo Haythornthwaite and **Diana Edmonds**

Patents

Patents are often seen only as a source of technical information but they have also considerable utility as a source of business intelligence. The granting of a patent gives an inventor monopoly rights in the invention but, in return for these rights, the patent must disclose how the invention works. There is a great deal of skill involved in patent writing since the inventor frequently does not wish to reveal too much! Patents are supposed to describe the claimed invention in sufficient detail to make it clear to a hypothetical person of ordinary skill how the invention works, but they are also written with an eye towards the eventual need to defend them in the law courts against any infringement of the patent rights. Patent applications are drafted by patent agents and attorneys using generic language rather than specific language, for example, a spade might be described as a 'digging instrument'. This quaint wording seeks to give the inventor the widest possible protection but is singularly unhelpful since it makes free text searching difficult.

In the UK, patents are administered by the Patent Office and anyone wishing to patent an invention can apply to that office and pay a fee. Patents can be obtained for any invention concerned with the composition, construction or manufacture of a substance, article or apparatus or with an industrial process. Schemes of business, mathematical methods and artistic creations, in general, cannot be patented. A patent provides protection for 20 years from the filing date, providing fees are paid. Inventors can write their own patent specification but it is usual to employ a Registered Patent Agent, since a patent is, in fact, quite a complex legal document. If an inventor wants to obtain overseas protection, it may be necessary to apply to the Patents Offices of each country individually, but it may be possible to submit a single international application which covers the contracting states who are signatories to the Patent Co-operation Treaty (PCT). Most countries have their own patents offices and, indeed, over three-quarters of a million published patent specifications appear each year.

Details of patents can be located in two weekly publications, *Official Journal (Patents)* and *Patents for Inventions: Abridgements of Specifications*. The Patent Office also produces a range of informative pamphlets including the especially relevant *Patents: a source of technical information* which is especially aimed at industry. Other regularly updated leaflets include:

Basic facts about patents for inventions in the UK, Patents Office, Department of Trade and Industry, 1988.
Introducing patents: a guide for inventors, Patents Office, Department of Trade and Industry, 1989.
The Patent Office: an introduction to the services of the Patent Office and trade marks and designs registries, Patent Office, Department of Trade and Industry, 1988.
How to prepare a UK patent application and then apply for a patent, Patent Office, Department of Trade and Industry, 1988.
What is intellectual property? Patent Office, n.d.
In addition, there are free leaflets on *Applying for a trade mark and the protection of industrial designs*.

For researchers using patent documents, the two most important sources of information are the *patent specification* and the *patent abstract*. The Patent Office classifies and indexes the abstracts and the specifications in order to facilitate patent searches. While the specification provides a detailed description of the invention, the abstract is a short statement printed on the front of the specification which identifies the technical subject of the invention and the advance it represents. Unfortunately for researchers, these abstracts, like the specifications, are couched in generic language which can be mystifying. It is not surprising that some of the available patent databases have found it necessary to write their own abstracts.

The main library for patents in the UK is the British Library, *Science Reference and Information Service* (SRIS), which was developed out of the library originally established at the Patent Office in 1855. It holds the specifications and abstracts of every British patent from 1617 onwards. The library also receives patent, trade mark and design publications from the patent offices of 38 countries; in all, over 22 million overseas patent publications. The main UK patent archives are stored in vaults beneath SRIS. The staff have access to a wide range of international patent databases and, for a scale of fees, can carry out patent searches online. The *UK Patent Information Network* (PIN) provides patent information facilities in 26 public libraries around the country. Seven of these act as *Provincial Patent Libraries* and have extensive holdings of patent specifications and indexes, while another 19 libraries are *Patent Information Centres* and hold indexes and guidance material on patents. Liverpool Public Library, which is a Provincial Patent Library, carried out a survey in 1986 which revealed that local business and industry were lamentably ill-informed about patents, their uses and the actual existence of the Liverpool Patents Library[1]. This survey bore out the feeling that industry and business were neglecting a valuable resource which can provide not only technical information but invaluable business intelligence.

There are at least five reasons why patents are of immense value to business and industry. First, they provide the first and often only account of the results of a piece of research. Secondly, they give details of a competitor's products, which is invaluable to the marketing department. Thirdly, patents may present a ready-made answer to a research problem and recourse to them may save the time and money involved in re-inventing the wheel. Fourthly, they provide a record of development and advances in a specific technology. Fifthly, they provide inspiration for a related idea which can be developed and marketed; this can provide inspiration both for the research department and for marketing and long-range planning. Edlyn Simmons confirms this view:

> Patents are invaluable sources of information about technology and most of the information can be used in research without infringing the patent. Patents are rich stores of information about businesses, they identify the areas of research and development activity in industry, allowing the prediction of market changes ... by combining the technical information in patents with the names of inventors and corporate patent owners, it is possible to track the research and business interests of companies and other institutions. With the addition of legal status information, it is also possible to determine which products and processes are being emphasised by competitors and which have been abandoned. Most important, of course, patents tell us which products and processes are the exclusive domain of others[2].

A lapsed patent, of course, may present an unforeseen business opportunity.

Although there is no such thing as a world patent, there is an increasing degree of co-operation and improved bibliographic control as regards patents. The Patent Co-operation Treaty (PCT), 1977, made it possible for a single patent application to be processed by the Patents Offices of several countries, thus saving the time and trouble of lodging applications in a variety of countries. The European Patent Convention has also led to the creation of a centralised European Patent Office based in Munich.

Patents online

Patent searching has been revolutionised by the growth of databases. Online offers a uniquely convenient method of accessing patent literature. Patents are available online via two different types of databases: those concerned solely with patents for example, INPADOC and those databases which contain a wide range of data relating to a specific subject and also include patent information, for example, CA SEARCH (that is, Chemical Abstracts online). A great advantage which some databases have over the printed patents is that many write their own abstracts. These tend to be longer and more informative than those supplied with the patent specifications, are couched in specific language and often cite helpful examples taken from the body of the specification. The content of these abstracts are, therefore, frequently markedly different from the original patent abstract.

The patents of most of the developed countries are now available online. The major hosts that specialise in patent literature are ORBIT, DIALOG and QUESTEL. UK patent information is accessible via the WORLD PATENTS INDEX which is available on ORBIT, QUESTEL and DIALOG. INPADOC is available on a variety of hosts including ORBIT and via a few more specialised databases including EDOC, APITAT, CA SEARCH and CLAIMS. European Patents Office data can be accessed via a database called EPAT which is hosted by QUESTEL which also hosts the French patents database FPAT. It is quite surprising to find that even the People's Republic of China has a patents database called, rather endearingly, CHINAPAT.

WORLD PATENTS INDEX is produced by Derwent Publications of London and indexes a wide range of patent specifications from the major industrial countries of the world. The results are available in hard copy on a weekly basis but are more conveniently used online. Subscribers can purchase print, microfilm and magnetic tape versions of abstracts, indexes and complete specifications. The patent specifications of major countries are indexed in greater depth than those of minor countries. Derwent began the database in 1963 with pharmaceutical patents and has expanded its coverage to other subjects over the years. INPADOC is compiled by the International Patent Documentation Centre which is an organisation run jointly by the Austrian Patents Office and the World Industrial Property Organisation of the UN (WIPO). Fifty-five patent offices submit information to INPADOC which is then reissued in the weekly *INPADOC Patent*

Gazette and integrated into the INPADOC database. INPADOC has a file of current patent status information which includes status information on UK and US patents, and this is searchable although only at a substantial charge.

Standards and specifications

Industry is increasingly accepting and using published standards and specifications. This increased level of usage is due in part to the drive towards quality control: as companies implement standards within their own organisations, they oblige the vendors who supply them with goods and services to comply with the same standards. As all industrial sectors are now adopting an international marketing strategy, UK manufacturers and suppliers frequently require both British and foreign standards. Consumers in the high street have also become aware of standards. They wish to purchase items which are designed and manufactured to a uniform level of quality and safety: they regard a recognised standard as a guarantee of quality. As a result of this increased interest in standards, the harassed business librarian now receives requests for a variety of standards and specifications, produced by a wide range of organisations. The librarian's difficulties are compounded as standards are often referred to only by abbreviations, and it can be difficult to trace the organisations which issue them.

To those who are not familiar with technical documentation, the very terms 'standard' and 'specification' can be confusing: frequently they are used, incorrectly, as synonyms. A specification is a statement of what is needed: the American National Standards Institution defines the term specification as 'a concise statement of the requirements for a material, process, method, procedure or service, including wherever possible the exact procedure by which it can be determined that the conditions are met within the tolerances specified in the statement: a specification does not have to cover specifically recurring subjects or objects of wide use, or even existing objects'. While the specification states the requirements, the standard defines the solution: the ANSI definition of a standard is 'a specification accepted by recognised authority as the most practical and appropriate current solution of a recurring problem'. Within the broad term 'standard', it is possible to define a number of sub-categories:

1. Dimensional standards which specify the dimensions required to achieve inter-changeability or to make things fit.
2. Materials standards which cover the chemical composition, condition, tolerances and mechanical properties of raw materials such as alloys, steels and pigments.
3. Standards of performance or quality which are designed to ensure that a product is fit for its intended purpose.

4. Standards of testing which enable materials and products intended for the same purpose to be compared.
5. Standardised terminology which ensures that a term has a unique, unambiguous meaning. Similarly, symbols must be standardised and several compilations of symbols have been issued by national and industrial organisations.
6. Codes of practice which cover the installation and maintenance of equipment or the correct method of accomplishing a certain task.

So who sets the standards? Within individual countries, there is usually a national standards organisation which issues standards. The British Standards Institution (BSI) is the one with which we in the UK are probably most familiar; established in 1931, it is also the oldest. There are now similar organisations in more than 80 countries. Other leading standards bodies include AFNOR (Association Française de Normalisation) in France, DIN (Deutsches Institut für Normung) in West Germany, ANSI (the American National Standards Institution), CAN (the Standards Council of Canada) and GOST (Gosstandart SSSR), the USSR State Committee for Standards. The national standards bodies act as a focal point for information on standards within the country; many have collections of foreign standards which are available for consultation. The British Standards Institution, for instance, has a very large collection of standards and also provides a loans and sales service.

Due to international interest in national standards, the titles of standards and specifications are usually translated into more than one language. The general series of British Standards have titles in English, French and German while the Russian GOST standards give titles in English and Russian. Many of the DIN and AFNOR standards are issued in an English translation, and both DIN and AFNOR issue separate catalogues of these translations.

A number of agencies are responsible for issuing standards which are accepted internationally, rather than within individual countries. The International Standards Organisation (ISO) issues internationally valid standards, and ratifies, for international use, standards which are issued by the national organisations. A complementary organisation, the International Electrotechnical Commission, issues internationally accepted standards relating to the testing of electrical equipment; these are issued under the initials IEC. With the advent of the Single European Market in 1992, standardisation within Europe is becoming more and more important. The national standards authorities are represented in Europe by two European standards bodies, CEN (the European Committee for Standardisation) which issues EN standards and CENELEC (the European Committee for Electrotechnical Standardisation); CENELEC standards are also issued as ENs but with a different number series.

In addition to the national and international standards, voluntary standards are issued within individual industrial sectors to regulate the activities of companies operating within that sector. These industry-wide standards are promulgated by trade associations involved with a particular industry. Examples of this type of standard include the Institute of Petroleum's Model Codes of Safe Practice for the petroleum industry.

Many American trade organisations issue voluntary standards. As there are so many, ANSI, the American Nation Standards Institution, operates quite differently from the other national standards bodies. ANSI describes itself as 'the co-ordinator of America's voluntary standard system': instead of operating a separate system of technical committees which produce standards, ANSI's committees ratify the voluntary standards issued by trade organisations. The American Petroleum Institute (API) is one of these voluntary bodies, as is the American Society for Testing and Metals (ASTM).

Many major companies produce a variety of specifications and standards which specify the quality of equipment used within the organisation, and the quality of procedures to be undertaken within the company. British Rail, for instance, produces a wide variety of standards. Company standards are primarily for internal use, although they are sometimes issued to suppliers.

Neither standards nor specifications should be regarded as permanent entities: a standard may remain effective only for a limited period, since it may become obsolete as a result of technological progress; better methods of testing may be developed or more suitable methods may be discovered for a specific purpose. This works well for the scientist, for the manufacturer and probably for the consumer, too, but the frequent amending of standards causes considerable problems for the librarian.

For the business librarian, acquiring standards presents particular problems. They are, for instance, sometimes difficult to trace. The tradition of issuing standards under an abbreviation, such as SAE or NACE, makes the task of identification even more complex: it is often necessary for the librarian to identify the organisation from its initials, which has issued the standard, before attempting to trace it. It is often particularly difficult to trace standards issued by trade and industry associations, some of which are small and obscure.

Standards issued by national organisations are usually the easiest to trace and obtain. Most issue annual lists of their publications, with frequent updates to announce new standards. The British Standards Institution, for instance, publishes the annual *BSI Catalogue*; additions and withdrawals are listed in the monthly *BSI News*; the bi-monthly *Sales Bulletin* cumulates the monthly listing and indexes them. ANSI, the *American National Standards Institution*, issues an annual CATALOG, which is updated by supplements throughout the year. Many of the trade associations which issue voluntary standards also issue annual lists of publications.

Purchasing standards can also present a problem as library suppliers and booksellers rarely stock them. Standards issued in the UK can normally be obtained directly from the issuing organisation. For foreign standards, there are a number of specialist suppliers: each one can provide a range of standards, although none provides comprehensive coverage of foreign standards.

Within the UK, the British Standards Institution is undoubtedly the best single source of information on national, international and voluntary standards. BSI sell their own publications, of course, and also stock many foreign and international standards publications, including ISOs, IECs, English translations of DIN standards, APIs and some ASME standards. If the standard which you require is not available in stock, BSI can order the publication of most of the national and international standards organisations. BSI members are offered discount prices on some publications.

Other organisations which sell standards include American Technical Publishers Ltd (68a Wilbury Way, Hitchin, Herts), a company which specialises in obtaining standards issued by US trade and industry organisations. These include the Society of Automotive Engineers, the National Association of Corrosion Engineers, the American Society of Metals and the National Electrical Manufacturers Association. American Technical Publishers Ltd also issues *Standards alert*, which lists new standards both numerically and by subject.

ILI, Infonorme London Information (Index House, Ascot, Berks SL5 7EU) supplies a wide range of standards, including those published by ANSI, API, ASME and NFPA. ILI also produces a useful free newsletter called *Standards express*.

Microinfo Ltd (PO Box 3, Alton, Hampshire GU34 2PG) stock on microfiche all US Military and Federal standards, and copy these onto paper to order. American standards which are not held in stock can also be obtained quickly, either in hard copy or on microfiche, from the United States. Microinfo can also arrange to supply annual sets of standards on a subscription basis.

The majority of libraries obtain standards in hard copy. Technical Indexes Ltd, however, offer a range of British and foreign standards on microfilm or microfiche. International Electrotechnical Commission specifications, Japanese Industrial Standards and the International Organisation for Standardisation publications are all, for instance, available from Technical Indexes. A new set is provided whenever standards are issued or amended: this can save considerable staff time which might otherwise be spent in updating the hard copy version. The disadvantage of the Technical Indexes services is that the microfilm or microfiche are only leased to the customer; if the client can no longer afford to maintain the service, the copies are removed.

If you do not wish to purchase a standard, it may be possible to borrow a copy. The BSI Library holds a collection of over half a million international, British and foreign standards, laws, regulations and technical specifications. The library, which is located in Milton Keynes, is available to all visitors for reference purposes, but only members may borrow documents in exchange for loan tokens. A limited selection of standards is also available from the British Library (Document Supply Centre), including those produced by ASTM. A number of local library co-operatives have recognised the need for rapid access to standards: organisations such as HATRICS, in Hampshire, and NETWORK in the North East, have produced union catalogues of standards to encourage local inter-lending.

A number of standards organisations are currently looking at providing online access to standards material. The majority of interest at the moment is concerned with improving the access to bibliographic details of standards; BSI's STANDARDLINE, for instance, provides improved retrieval facilities to BSI publications. Similarly, SAE and ASTM standards are covered by STANDARDS SEARCH on ORBIT. Both of these databases allow the enquirer to order the full text of the standard online. Other standards issuing bodies have also developed online databases – and some standards are included in general databases covering particular industries – COMPENDEX, for instance, covers some standards. The BSI Library has produced a useful *Brief Guide to Standards Databases* (1988) which is available at a cost of £15 to BSI members.

Details of BSI, DIN and AFNOR publications are now being made available on PERINORM, a CD-ROM product. The CD-ROM format allows the flexibility of online searching, without the telecommunications costs. As it contains information on the publications of the three major European standards organisations, PERINORM will undoubtedly prove useful to those who wish to take full advantage of the Single European Market.

References

1. PARROTT, T. and TAYLOR, P. Patents and the public library: a report of a survey in Liverpool. *Refer*, 4, 2, Autumn 1986, 12–13.
2. SIMMONS, E. S. An introduction to patents. In: ARMSTRONG, C. J. and LARGE, J. A. (eds) *Manual of online searching strategies*. Gower, 1988, 88.

Further reading

PATENT OFFICE. Leaflets listed in the text.

SIMMONS, E. S. An introduction to patents. In: ARMSTRONG, C. J. and LARGE, J. A. (eds) *Manual of online searching strategies*. Gower, 1988, 88–156.

Useful addresses

British Standards Institution, Head Office, 2 Park Street, London W1A 2BS. Tel: 071-629 9000

British Standards Institution, Information Services and Technical Help to Exporters, Linford Wood, Milton Keynes, MK14 6LE. Tel: 0908 320033

Patent Office, State House, 66–77 High Holborn, London WC1R 4TP. Tel: 071-831 2525

Science Reference and Information Service, 25 Southampton Buildings, London WC2 1AY. Tel: 071-404 0406

ORBIT Search Service, Achilles House, Western Avenue, London W3 0UA. Tel: 081-992 3456

Chapter Twelve

PAYING FOR INFORMATION

Jo Haythornthwaite and **Diana Edmonds**

The growth of fee-based information services has been spectacular. In fact, apart from the increase in the online industry, the growth in the fee-based sector can be seen as perhaps the most significant recent development in the information world.

There are two distinct categories of fee-based information services:

1. Those which are based on the resources of an existing library or collection of information in either the academic, special or public library sectors.
2. Those which are provided by an independent information broker, who may obtain information from any source on behalf of a fee-paying client.

Online searching is, of course, a fee-based information service and it could be argued that the development of these services in libraries was perhaps a factor in accelerating the debate on charging. Libraries passed on at least part of the cost of an online search to the researcher, so why not charge for other services also?

A second and more pervasive reason for the growth of the trend towards charging has been the current economic and political climate. Several government publications have made it clear that even public libraries would, in future, be expected to charge for some services and, in doing so, contribute in a small way at least to their own finances[1,2]. Self-financing libraries have been discussed exhaustively and many librarians have expressed fears that such developments could lead to the creation of a new 'information poor', an under-class who remain uninformed because they cannot afford to pay for information.

A third factor that has influenced the growth of commercial information services is a slow but perceptible increase in the awareness by the industrial and commercial community that information can provide a competitive edge. Information is power. It is, therefore, also a marketable commodity.

Finally, many organisations now feel that it is far more cost-effective to pay for expert information gathering when they need it rather than enlarging their headcount with additional information specialists who may not be needed all the time. Furthermore, the use of outside expert help means that the company can use a wide range of specialist information providers depending on the type of enquiry or research project.

Thus, the business information sector has radically altered during the last decade. There has been a dramatic increase in the number and use of commercial information services as a whole, and a growing trend towards charging for some types of information in public and academic libraries. These services range from separate and self-supporting services based in large academic libraries (for example, Warwick Business Information Service at Warwick University Library, London Business School Information Service and HERTIS which is based at Hatfield Polytechnic Library) to services given within the framework of an existing public library service (for example, Westminster Public Library).

Commercial information services

If we put aside those information services which are purely databases, and which have been discussed at length elsewhere, there are really five main types of commercial information service: there are market research-based organisations; general commercial information suppliers, many of whom have a strong business orientation; services based in special libraries; services based in academic libraries and, finally, services based in public or national libraries.

Marketing services

Many of the marketing orientated services are mentioned in the chapter devoted to marketing information. Here it may be helpful simply to mention their general characteristics. Most companies in the market intelligence field have a good deal in common. They usually have a library, they produce market research reports and/or journals and they are willing to undertake some research on demand, Mintel is a typical example.

General commercial information services

Most of these general information services started life as large specialist libraries catering for their own staff in the media world. The best known of these services are the *Financial Times* and the *BBC Data Enquiry*

Service. Both of these organisations had a long history of answering simple enquiries free of charge over the telephone and by letter. As the years passed, however, the volume of enquiries increased and began to place unacceptable burdens upon staff. Furthermore, it became evident that such a service could provide a source of income and, therefore, charges were introduced.

The *BBC Data Enquiry Service* started life as an extensive library and now has a large databank. There is no access to the library for external users but information is supplied by telephone and by post. It is not primarily a source of business information although it can supply a good deal of material in this subject area. The strengths of the service are its ability to provide background information and biographical information and to unearth those obscure pieces of information which the enquirer has been unable to locate elsewhere. A great advantage is that the BBC provides a 24-hour service so that queries can be dealt with by day or by night. The material housed by the service encompasses material gathered by the BBC for use in television, radio and overseas broadcasts. They have the reputation of providing a swift service as regards information and pictures. The sort of questions that the *BBC Data Enquiry Service* have answered successfully include:

— Israeli arms sales to Argentina during the Falklands War
— Company information on Heinz
— Interests of the Duchess of Kent.

The *Financial Times Business Information Service*, as its title suggests, is very much a business-orientated service. Like the BBC, they provided free information for the public for many years but, in 1971, decided to promote their library as a commercial information service. Journalists have priority so external users sometimes have to wait for searches, but usually the service is swift and the material is up to date. Until recently, the FT Library was surprisingly unautomated and, although databases were available, most enquiries were answered from banks of press cuttings in vertical files. Since the FT acquired DATASOLVE and renamed it PROFILE, there have been extensive changes in their approach to information, and the FINANCIAL TIMES BUSINESS INFORMATION SERVICE is now marketed with promises that the world of business information is on tap, online, on fax, onstream.

Commercial information services in special libraries

The provision of commercial information services by special libraries has been quite common in the newspaper world for a number of years as the *FT* and now the *Daily Telegraph* provide information services available to researchers outside their organisations, but the development of such services outside the world of the media is still relatively rare. Undoubtedly, it will increase as companies see the commercial value of the services which they have built up over the years for their own use.

One company that has decided to market their library service is Jones Lang Wootton, a firm of property advisors. Their consulting and research activities led to the establishment of a research library in 1979 which has a substantial reference collection of information related to property, and they also have one of the largest databases on commercial property in the country.

Jones Lang Wootton Consulting and Research undertake special studies for clients and provide a Property Information Service for questions that require an immediate answer. Corporate subscribers pay £450 for 10 hours' access to the library and additional time can be purchased. The glossy brochure lists the type of enquiries that the library can satisfy:

- — Background information on a company
- — Press cuttings or articles on a specific topic or area...
- — A preliminary survey of a town or region...
- — A bibliography for a particular subject, complete with photocopies of important articles.

Commercial information services in academic libraries

Academic libraries have enjoyed a considerable measure of success in moving into the fee-based information sector. The move towards the provision of subscription services has developed for a number of reasons. First, cuts in book budgets, increasing book and journal costs, increases in the staff salary bill and in the cost of maintenance of buildings have led chief librarians to look around for other sources of income. Secondly, there has been political pressure to charge for services where this is feasible, pressure both from the government and at the institutional level. Thirdly, there has been increasing pressure over the years for academic libraries to become part of their local community and break down barriers between 'town and gown'. Many academic libraries have, for many years, admitted bona fide researchers on payment of a small annual fee. Recently, the emphasis has changed somewhat and a consciousness has developed that the best way for an academic library to help the local community may be to provide information services for industry. This is especially vital where no large public business library exists in the vicinity. Even where one does exist, it is good economic sense not to duplicate services but rather to complement each other. Where this happens, it may well be that the shorter 'free' enquiries will be handled by the public library while the longer research projects, probably involving online searches, will be passed to the polytechnic or university library. A scheme of this type involving Leicester Polytechnic Library and Leicestershire Libraries and

Information Service is under discussion at present. A fourth factor is that, over the years, like the BBC and the *FT*, many academic libraries have seen a steady increase in the numbers of external users and the time spent by staff in handling their enquiries. Many librarians saw this as presenting a threat to the level of service that they were able to give to their own staff and students. An obvious solution was to charge external users, especially those emanating from companies, a realistic subscription fee. This made it possible to hire additional staff who, in some cases, now work exclusively for the commercial information service part of the operation and are paid entirely or partially out of its income.

Finally, the very success of the *Financial Times*, the *BBC Data Enquiry Service* and other commercial ventures has led many academic librarians to the conclusion that this was a type of service which they could provide just as efficiently as did the media-based libraries, and the success of some academic libraries in this field has proved them correct.

It may be helpful to describe the development and current activities of a small selection of these services, and I therefore intend to discuss the work of three of the most successful information services which are based upon academic libraries; HERTIS, London Business School Information Service and the University of Warwick Business Information Service.

HERTIS is one of the longest established of these services and is based at Hatfield Polytechnic Library. It is, however, also a co-operative venture and can call upon the resources of 11 Hertfordshire college libraries. Their 'Information for Industry' service now operates on two levels. Until 1989, HERTIS supplied free commercial information, being funded by the County Library for this purpose; and it serviced companies who wanted more than brief enquiry work on a subscription basis. The new system provides for all information services to be handled by an integrated team and establishes a scale of charges with brief basic queries still being answered free of charge. Charges are made for in-depth enquiries, online searches, enhanced document delivery, consultancy projects and desk research.

HERTIS staff use a wide range of databases and also utilise other fee-based services and information brokers when it seems appropriate. A factor in rethinking their charging system was a wish not to be accused of undercutting the private sector, although even more important was the directives from the County Council to eliminate any losses on fee-based services.

HERTIS has developed a business databank which holds information on Hertfordshire businesses and a Patents Information Service is also available. They have achieved a high profile over the years and market a wide range of services to companies outside the boundaries of Hertfordshire. While some public and academic libraries fail to sell their services effectively, HERTIS produces an elegant folder with regularly updated information sheets inside. Marketing is all important in inspiring confidence in the professionalism of the services which are offered.

The Library of the London Business School has always been used quite substantially by external users, partly because of its convenient London location and partly because ex-students tended to return to the library service that had given them able assistance in the past. Gradually, the numbers of individuals and companies using the library facilities increased to a point where the library staff began to feel that LBS staff and students were suffering as a result. In 1984, a decision was taken to set up a completely separate *London Business School Information Service* with a separate staff who would do nothing but provide the information service. Brochures were sent out to ex-students and, to this day, many of the companies using the subscription service are those in which ex-London Business School students are involved. All the staff employed in the information service are paid for out of the profits and any additional finance that is generated is ploughed back into the service. Companies use LBS mainly for general reference enquiries and online searching, especially searches of an economic and financial nature. A great deal of business is done over the telephone and LBS staff themselves sometimes obtain information over the telephone on behalf of clients. In addition, HERTIS, LBS and Warwick now run seminars.

The *University of Warwick Business Information Service* was originally called the Warwick Statistics Service but the name was changed in order to make it clear to potential subscribers that not only statistical data was available. All the same, the service's great strength is the extensive holdings of statistical series which constitute a valuable supplement to the collections at the Export Market Information Centre (EMIC) and the Business Statistics Office (see chapter on British Official Publications). Warwick is strong in unofficial statistics (that is, the statistics produced by trade associations, banks, local authorities, etc.) and in international statistics. They charge corporate members a subscription which entitles them to a certain number of hours enquiry time; alternatively, users can pay by the hour. The service has been operational since 1972 and all staff salaries and associated costs are paid for out of the income generated by the service. They have access to a number of databases which are heavily used on behalf of clients and which supplement the existing hard copy in-house resources.

All these services have relatively small numbers of corporate subscribers but seem to be heavily used by these companies. When they were testing the waters in the early days, all offered subscribers rather cheap rates. Now all have taken steps to increase their charges in order to achieve better profit margins and so that they are not seen as undercutting the purely commercial organisations in the field. HERTIS serves a wide range of business and industrial concerns throughout Hertfordshire and outside the county boundaries. Warwick finds most of their use is not specifically local and, although they have widened their remit to include company and business information in general, the majority of their enquiries are still statistical. LBS finds much of their work involves financial and numeric data online, but they are frequently amazed by the simple general reference queries which they also receive.

Business information services in national and public libraries

The same pressures that have influenced academic libraries in establishing fee-based information services have affected our national library service and the public libraries. The British Library came under pressure to become finance-generating as a result of the economic climate and the move was also somewhat influenced by the consciousness of the staff, at the Science Reference and Information Service (SRIS), that many freelance information brokers and employees of market research companies were using their stock, staff and services free and then selling on the assembled information product at a high price. A subscription service was launched in October 1987 offering 10 hours research time for £400, or £50 an hour for occasional use. Individual users can still obtain help with brief enquiries free of charge and people who visit the library and make use of the materials themselves are not charged. Fifteen minutes of searching time costs £12.50 and this constitutes the minimum charge. Such charges are comparable with those at Warwick, LBS and HERTIS.

Public libraries have long thought, like the British Library, that their free business information services were, to some extent, exploited both by wealthy companies who could afford to pay and by market researchers and information brokers. This was frequently the case where online was concerned as many public libraries tended to provide online searches at a heavily subsidised rate.

Public libraries, therefore, are now considering charging the economic rate for online searching and some are beginning to look at the potential of providing a subscription service for local companies or charging for specific searches which involve anything over a minimum period of time.

Westminster Public Library launched a fee-based business information service for local industry in July 1986 charging an annual subscription of £100. Marketing proved difficult and, therefore, interest was initially disappointing. Most of the companies who use Westminster also use other services such as Mintel and LBS, and they take their more detailed and complicated work to these services. Initially, at any rate, Westminster found it was used primarily for quick reference enquiries.

The Mitchell Library in Glasgow has recently announced a new fee-based service entitled the *Business Users Service* (BUS). They are offering an enquiry service, research, advice and assistance with research, a free monthly newsletter for subscribers, a company directory which will be a free advertising medium for subscribers, special monitoring of industries and companies on request, telex and fax facilities and rooms available for hire.

The way forward for public libraries may well be the provision of a co-operative service utilising both their resources and those of a neighbouring polytechnic, college or university library. The needless duplication of staff, stock and effort should be avoided. Some libraries have dipped their toes rather half-heartedly into the deep water of commerce. It is essential to plan thoroughly before launching a service, therefore, a user survey is obviously essential. Secondly, the service must be marketed effectively and this can be difficult. Westminster found the press were not interested while LBS found journals did provide welcome publicity. Marketing materials must be professional-looking. The confidence of the business community will not be inspired by a dingy photocopied leaflet. This is an area where it is truly worth spending money in order to make money. Librarians also have to improve their image in the marketplace. They are frequently, and unfairly, thought of as slow, living in a dream world and likely to produce out of date and badly presented data.

If the job is done well, there is no doubt that British business is at last beginning to grasp the value of information and is happy to pay for speedy and expert service and accurate well-presented and up-to-date data. For the business information specialist, this situation can present a whole new world of job opportunities.

The independent information broker

In addition to the fee-based information services which are provided by libraries, there is an increasing number of independent information brokers who are providing business information on demand for clients. Hardly a week seems to go by but another pamphlet hits the doormat announcing that J. Bloggs, BA, LA, MIInfSc, is now providing a wide range of information services. The target market for these services is often the seemingly lucrative business world with its insatiable demand for business information.

The term 'information broker' has been bandied about for a number of years, although there still seems to be considerable confusion about its meaning. In his booklet on *Information broking: a new career in information work*[3], Marshall Crawford refers to a helpful definition which was included in a special issue of the *American Society for Information Science Bulletin*[4]. In the *Bulletin*, the information broker was described as 'an individual or organisation who – on demand – seeks to answer questions using all sources available and who is in business for profit'.

So, the information broker is truly in the business of providing information in response to a client's query. This function is rather different from that undertaken by the information consultant. In their book on *Information consultancy*, Gurnsey and White defined the consultant's role as providing 'advice'[5]. While the broker provides information, the consultant provides advice. Sometimes, certainly, a consultant needs to obtain a great deal of information to be in a position to provide advice for the client, but this information-gathering exercise forms only part of the consultancy process. Timescales vary considerably between consultancy and brokerage, for while consultants tend to work on projects which take at least a number of days and, more often, weeks or months if not years, brokers usually work on short-term projects which take hours, or days at the most.

This difference in timescales is reflected in the difference in charge rates; brokers usually charge by the hour while consultants normally charge a daily rate. Different brokers have different charging policies, with the larger brokerage firms requiring clients to pay on a subscription basis, offsetting the costs of work undertaken against the initial subscription costs. Smaller brokers may be prepared to charge individually for one-off projects, although this method undoubtedly causes more problems for the broker who has to spend time raising an invoice for each job, and risks having to spend further time chasing the client for payment.

Despite these differences, both brokers and consultants work for clients in the business community. Indeed, some consultants specialise in providing advice relating to business information and might advise the client on matters such as the provision of business information by an in-house information service, or a range of external business databases which should be accessed by the client.

Marshall Crawford lists a range of services which might be undertaken by the information broker. Research is surely the most central service and the most commonly provided. The research process normally involves undertaking desk research using either hard copy or online sources; it may also involve interviewing or sampling to obtain original data. The skill of the broker lies in tracing all pertinent information, and in presenting this information 'in a style which is useful and meaningful to the client'. Other services which may be provided include abstracting, the preparation of bibliographies, the provision of current awareness services and the compilation of directories. Some information brokers also undertake translation work. Having laboured the distinction between the information broker and the information consultant, it must be admitted that many organisations will undertake a wide range of services as long as they get paid for doing them. Many brokers perform a variety of library and information-related tasks, such as cataloguing and classifying stock, producing abstracts for journals or online services and organising training courses.

Individual brokers tend to specialise in particular subject areas or industry sectors. Vital Information, for instance, provides specialist information on health care, biotechnology, food, agriculture, and the environment, while Chancery Lane Information Brokers have particular experience in the areas of construction and architecture.

The expansion of fee-based information services has resulted in a corresponding development in the publishing world: there are now a number of directories which exist simply to list these services. In 1987, Christine Smith compiled a *Directory of consultants and researchers in library and information science* on behalf of the British Library[6]. The directory lists 262 organisations and individuals who claim to be acting as consultants and researchers within the UK. Business information is clearly a hot-spot: 71 out of the total of 262 (27 per cent) list business information among their areas of expertise. The *Directory of information brokers and consultants* is produced on a regular basis by Marshall Crawford and Mary Moody: two editions have been published so far and the third will be published in July 1989. The second edition, produced in 1987[7], listed 150 fee-based services in the UK, of which 112 were independent individuals or organisations, while the remainder were linked to large institutions or organisations. The *Directory of fee-based information services*[8], published annually by Burwell Enterprises based in Houston, Texas, provides international coverage of the information consultancy/brokerage/freelance librarian market – and interestingly, the latest edition includes 47 UK-based businesses.

Online information services are now, of course, extremely important in the provision of business information, and a number of information brokers are particularly involved in online sources of information. Several of the online host systems compile lists of approved information brokers who are experienced in searching their systems; a European directory of information brokers is also available as BROKERSGUIDE on ECHO, the European host system.

It is, of course, difficult to know how many of those listed in these directories really make a living out of their work, and how many are doing a little freelance work as a sideline. It is obvious from a quick glance at the contents that many of those listed are employed on a full-time basis in library schools around the country, and presumably undertake individual projects as and when their work loads permit. It is more likely that these will be acting in a consultancy capacity rather than providing brokerage. The broker's clients require a fast response and it would be difficult for someone doing another full-time job to provide this.

Brokerages are normally small businesses: most information brokers work either as sole traders, in partnerships, or with a few employees. In the UK, the majority of information brokers are based in and around London; 98 of the 150 brokers and consultants listed in the 1987 *Directory of information brokers and consultants* are located in London and the South East. Probably the longest established information brokerage business is SVP which first opened its doors to the paying public in Paris in 1935 (hence the name S'il vous plait) and now has branches in 18 countries. SVP United Kingdom Ltd was established in 1983 and now is larger than most independent brokerage firms with 12 full-time members of staff providing tailored business information services for clients. It is unusual, too, in that it has a wide range of hard copy resources in addition to access to online sources; it has effectively created a business information library in order to provide brokerage services. SVP also has excellent international contacts because of the multi-national coverage of its associated companies.

The majority of independent information brokers have fewer members of staff, and also rely heavily upon libraries to obtain hard copy information, although the majority, of course, have access to online sources in-house. One of the best-known firms in the brokerage business is Chancery Lane Information Brokers which was established by Marshall Crawford in 1981. Chancery Lane Information Brokers specialise in providing business information in the widest sense of the term. Clients frequently require company information and company profiles: published market research is often requested, too. Staff will undertake research for clients and also provide document delivery services. The firm has a number of international clients and frequently obtains American documents for clients in the UK or Scandinavia or, conversely, provides documents produced in the UK for American clients. Chancery Lane Information Brokers have particular expertise in the areas of construction and architecture, and also in the petroleum industry.

First Contact is a more recent arrival on the brokerage scene; it was established in 1987 by Jill Cousins. Its literature claims that it provides 'all the benefits of your own information service with none of the overheads'. First Contact specialises in business information and offers a range of services such as the monitoring of companies or people using online databases and press clippings, the provision of profiles of companies, industries, markets and countries, the preparation of biographies of businessmen and women and the ranking of companies within industrial sectors. In the list of its information resources, First Contact emphasises online sources, and also mentions a number of major libraries such as the City Business Library, Westminster Central Reference Library and Manchester Business School. First Contact was one of six fee-based information services surveyed by *Business Information Review* in 1988[9]; customers interviewed during the course of the survey were reported to be 'more than happy with the resources, the speed of service, the cost and the level of individual attention they received'. It is interesting to note that, at the time the article was written – in 1988 – most of the services surveyed had a relatively small client base, with First Contact having between one and 25 clients while SVP had between 76 and 100; at that time, SVP received between 140–145 enquiries each week, while First Contact received 'up to 6'.

Despite the predominance of the financial sector within the City of London, there are information brokers and consultants operating in other parts of the country. Instant Library was established in 1988, operating from a base in the East Midlands. Instant Library provides both on-site and off-site services, undertaking library reorganisation and automation on the client's premises and providing research and document delivery services from an off-site base; again, online services are emphasised in the brochure which advertises the firm's services. Although Instant Library is based in the East Midlands, clients are located throughout the country, with many in the London area, and some as far north as Scotland.

Kendrick Research Associates, based in Norwich, advertises that it provides 'information support for business' and offers a range of services including company profiles, market evaluations, desk research and online searching. Clients have included management consultancies, industrial counsellors and a local authority, in addition to industrial companies.

Information brokers cannot hope to carry the resources of the major libraries in the office, and it is inevitable that they must depend to some extent upon the stock of major libraries. In a number of areas, this dependence has become formalised and libraries have agreements to refer in-depth enquiries to external information brokers who will answer the query for a fee. Public libraries in particular are interested in developing their business information services by providing an in-depth enquiry service in addition to a range of business directories, but many are restricted by a lack of staff from developing the service in-house. Suffolk County Information and Library Service was the initiator of the relationship between the public library service and an external broker who makes heavy and effective use of the stock held by the public library. The BL Research and Development Department provided funding for a two-year study undertaken in the county of Suffolk between 1984–1986 to identify the information needs of small firms and the relevance to those firms of a public information service. The research officer employed on the project, Fiona Trott, worked with a sample of 43 firms to answer information enquiries[10]. At the end of the project, she established BCIS Associates, to provide a commercial information service for local industry on behalf of Suffolk County Council; the public library service deals with quick reference enquiries, while all in-depth enquiries and requests for market research are referred to BCIS Associates to be answered on a fee-paying basis. BCIS Associates exploits the stock of the local public library service and uses any other sources when appropriate. They concentrate on providing value-added services and 'tailor-made' packages of information.

Similar relationships with private sector information brokers are now being developed by other public library systems. Norfolk County Library service has established a formal relationship with Kendrick Research Associates, based in Norwich; again, extensive enquiries are passed to the information broker who may use material in the public library in addition to any other services which might be required. Devon County Library Service is also considering this type of relationship. At the beginning of 1989, Devon County Library Service commissioned Mary Moody Associates to survey the requirements of firms in Devon for specialist information services, in addition to the free Business Information for Devon service which is located in Plymouth Central Library. It is proposed that a new value-added service should be established; this new service would be separate from the existing public library service and fixed charges would be made for information provided to companies.

Fee-based information services provide the business community with a cost-effective way of obtaining business information – without the need to establish an in-house information service. As the business world is becoming more aware of the value of information, the future looks bright for these services. In the 1990s, we shall undoubtedly see many more partnerships between the independent information broker, who has the time to devote to detailed enquiries, and libraries, which have the stock required to answer them.

References

1. CABINET OFFICE: Information Technology Panel. Making a business of information. HMSO, 1983.
2. *Financing our public library service: four subjects for debate.* HMSO, 1988. CM 324 Green Paper.
3. CRAWFORD, M. J. *Information broking: a new career in information work.* Library Association Publishing, 1988, Library Association (Pamphlet No. 41).
4. The information brokers – can they succeed? *American Society for Information Science Bulletin*, 2, 7 (special issue), February 1976.
5. GURNSEY, J. and WHITE, M. *Information consultancy.* Library Association Publishing, 1988.
6. SMITH, C. *Directory of consultants and researchers in library and information science.* British Library Information Guide 8, British Library, 1987.
7. CRAWFORD, M. J. and MOODY, M. E. *Directory of information brokers and consultants*, 2nd ed. Information Marketmakers Ltd, 1987.

8. *Directory of fee-based information services.* Houston: Burwell Enterprises. Annual.
9. McGROTHER, C. Paying for business information: a survey of fee-based services. *Business Information Review*, 4, 4, April 1988, 3–15.
10. TROTT, F. *Information for industry: a study of the information needs of small firms and the relevance of public information services.* Library and Information Research Report 51, British Library, 1986.

Further reading

CRAWFORD, M. J. *Information broking: a new career in information work.* Library Association Publishing, 1988, Library Association (Pamphlet No 41).

Financing our public library service: four subjects for debate. HMSO, 1988. CM 324 Green Paper.

GURNSEY, J. and WHITE, M. *Information consultancy*, Library Association Publishing, 1988.

McGROTHER, C. Paying for business information: a survey of fee-based information services. *Business Information Review*, 4, 4, April 1988, 3.

Office of Arts and Libraries. *Joint enterprise.* HMSO, 1987.

TROTT, F. and MARTIN, J. An information service for small firms and the relevance of public information services. *Aslib Proceedings*, 38, 2, February 1986, 43–50.

Some useful addresses

Services based in academic libraries:

HERTIS – Information for industry, Hatfield Polytechnic Library, College Lane, Hatfield, Herts AL10 9AD.Tel: 07072 79817. Fax: 07072 79670

London Business School Information Service, Sussex Place, Regent's Park, London NW1 4SA. Tel: 071-724 2300. Fax: 071-706 1897

Warwick University Business Information Service, University of Warwick, Gibbet Hill Road, Coventry CV4 7AL. Tel: 0203 523251/523051

Information brokers mentioned in the text:

BCIS Associates, Friday House, White Horse Road, East Bergholt, Suffolk CO7 6TR. Tel: 0206 298205. Fax: 0473 230758

Chancery Lane Information Brokers, 1st Floor, 35 Piccadilly, London W1V 9PB. Tel: 071-439 8985. Fax: 071-439 0262

First Contact, 9 Granard Business Centre, Bunn's Lane, Mill Hill, London NW7 2DQ. Tel: 081-906 3719. Fax: 081-906 4886

Instant Library, 7 Pytchley Drive, Loughborough, Leics LE11 2RH. Tel: 0509 268292. Fax: 0509 232748

Kendrick Research Associates, 91 College Road, Norwich NR2 3JP. Tel: 0603 57718

SVP United Kingdom Limited, 26 Whiskin Street, London EC1R 0BP. Tel: 071-837 6666.

Vital Information Limited, 30 Hockcliffe Street, Leighton Buzzard, Bedfordshire LU7 8HE. Tel: 0525 38297. Fax: 0525 382308

Chapter Thirteen

BUSINESS INFORMATION: QUO VADIS?

Diana Edmonds

This book has attempted to provide an introduction to the practice and to the sources of business information. The end-product is effectively a snapshot of the current situation for, in the real world, business information is far from static: it is a fast-moving scenario, in which the sources seem to change by the moment, and the style of business information provision changes with them.

In 1980, one of the sessions at the LA/Aslib/IIS Joint Conference at Sheffield was devoted to the problems faced by business librarians in the provision of information, and in particular to those difficulties experienced by librarians 'north of Watford'. The speakers focused on a number of problems which resulted from their isolation from London and from the information resources which were available only in the English capital city. At that time, one of the major issues which concerned the business information community was the lack of access to company data deposited at the Companies Registration Office, records which were available only to those who could visit one of the CRO offices in person, or who used an agent to obtain them. Accordingly, the primary source of company information was often inaccessible to business librarians and their clients. The availability of some secondary sources was limited too. Market research data was particularly difficult to obtain as most of the published reports were too expensive for libraries to purchase.

Librarians working outside London were particularly disadvantaged because the major collections of business material were almost exclusively concentrated in the London area. Business librarians operating outside London had to aim for self-sufficiency and often failed in the attempt: although they were aware of relevant sources of information, they were often unable to obtain them because of resource constraints. Nor could they refer an enquirer to another business library; there probably was no other business library in the area.

Less than 10 years later, the availability of business information sources has expanded considerably. Thanks largely to the campaigning efforts of Edwin Fleming, the Commercial Librarian in Liverpool City Libraries, we now have postal access to the company information held by Companies Registration Office: company records can be posted to an enquirer, or indeed can be faxed or sent by courier if they are required urgently. It was an important victory, although a few years on, most of us now access CRO data online as and when we require it, using commercial host systems. Somewhat ironically, Companies Registration Office has recently allowed Birmingham Public Library direct online access to its own database, on an experimental basis. The thorny problem of market research data has been tackled to some extent, too; the public availability of hard copy market research reports has improved significantly with the development of the British Library's Science Reference and Information Service, for SRIS has gathered together a good reference collection of market research reports. Again, online services have considerably expanded their coverage of market research data, and for many, online databases are now the starting point in any enquiry relating to market information.

Almost 10 years after that conference in Sheffield when speakers and delegates complained of the concentration of business information in the London area, most of the major business libraries are still located in central London. In recent years, there has, however, been some improvement in the geographical coverage of business information services. As industry itself has decentralised and moved to green field sites out of London, public and academic libraries have experienced greater demands for business information, and have responded by improving their business coverage. A number of public libraries in English counties, such as Devon and Dorset, have, for instance, improved and expanded their holdings of business material.

This expansion in the geographical spread of business libraries still does not do a great deal to improve the general availability of expensive business sources, but rather creates a number of small units working hard to serve the needs of industry in their local community. It does not create a central pool of business material from which the smaller libraries can draw, to supplement their own resources. Certainly, the British Library (Document Supply Centre) has made some valiant attempts to acquire business sources to lend to those who are unable to travel to the major business libraries: in the area of market research reports, for instance, BLDSC has endeavoured to make the most popular series available via their interlending service. What is still lacking, however, is a thorough review of the present availability of business information in the UK, an analysis of the unmet needs of the business community and the co-ordinated development of a Business Information Network throughout the country. This could be undertaken in the form of a sectoral Library and Information Plan (a Business Information Plan, perhaps?). In local areas, a great deal has been achieved by local libraries working in co-operation. Even more could be achieved if this were undertaken, with the proper planning, at a national level. This could lead to a truly national Business Information Network in the UK rather than the patchwork quilt of information services which exists at present.

This Business Information Plan should include in its coverage not only the public and academic institutions but also the private sector. The range of fee-based services has expanded rapidly in recent years, while there has been a corresponding increase in the number of independent information professionals who are providing services to the business community. In the future, the businessman or woman who is able and willing to pay for information will undoubtedly have a wide choice of brokerage services to call upon. Those libraries who lack the staff to develop a fee-based service using in-house staff will increasingly develop partnerships with the private sector, perhaps licensing freelance librarians to undertake detailed enquiries, and taking a percentage of the profit from any introductions. Ten years ago, we might have doubted the business community's willingness to pay for information; now, as industry becomes increasingly aware of the value of information, it looks as though there will be a ready market for the sale of business information. As the UK enters the Single European Market in 1992, clients may be European rather than British; in the next decade, the business librarian may require language skills as well as a good knowledge of information sources.

While the business community may be willing to pay for information, it will not be prepared to wait for that information. The ability to disseminate data quickly has been greatly improved with the development of telex, electronic mail and, of course, fax. Audio-conferencing and tele-conferencing are also now increasingly being used by the business community. The pace of life will certainly not slow down for the business librarian in the 1990s, as the enquirer will expect information-on-demand even more than he or she does in the 1980s!

If the provision of business information is likely to change in the next decade, what can we predict for the sources of information? Increasingly business information is online information, and the business librarian of the future will be even more dependent on electronic data sources. The marketplace supplying online systems will alter over the next few years: economics necessitate that the number of host systems will decrease, leaving fewer, larger, companies to dominate the online business. In order to ensure an adequate cash flow, those online suppliers will increasingly supplement the traditional 'pay-as-you-go' charging structures with additional subscriptions.

The business community has been targetted as a growth marketplace by the online host systems in recent years, and the range of online business sources available for the paying customer has expanded from traditional bibliographic databases to include online, and improved, versions of hard copy directories, databanks of company information and the full text of stockbroker reports and business journals. There are, however, still relatively few of the specialist product databanks available online, and many of the best sources of trade and technical information are available only in hard copy. This gap in online coverage will hopefully be filled in the near future. It is also likely that we shall see an expansion in the range of databases which provide information on European companies and markets: as we enter the Single European Market, business information will need to concentrate increasingly on the European marketplace. The demands of the marketplace will hopefully encourage the suppliers to provide new and improved information sources covering European industry.

What other developments can we expect in online services? Online suppliers will certainly face pressure from their customers to improve the currency of data available, as business information, to be of value, must be up-to-the-minute. The range of full text business databases must also expand, as the end-user grows dissatisfied with references and abstracts and demands the full text of the article 'now'! And with the full text, we shall increasingly also have graphics capabilities, to give a total visual presentation to the user. The business librarian of the 90s will not only be able to provide biographical details of the client who is being entertained to lunch, but will also be able to supply a recent photograph, retrieved from the databank.

And what of the electronic journal that we heard so much of in the 1980s? Will the business community be rushing to their terminals each morning to read the latest article on management techniques, hot from the keyboard? While the business community will probably be content to wait for academic journals to be circulated to them in hard copy, they will certainly wish to see time-sensitive stockbroker reports on TOPIC or one of the other screen-based systems before their competitors receive the printed version in the post. Business librarians will increasingly need to know about real-time information systems which were until recently the preserve of the financial gurus.

Business librarians in the future will require an in-depth knowledge of online sources. Increasingly end-users, too, will be developing expertise in accessing online databases. The French appear to have become a nation of end-users as LE MINITEL, a videotex system, has encouraged a national passion for obtaining information electronically. MINITEL offers a wide range of databases appropriate for use by the general public, including for instance all French telephone directories and yellow pages;

MINITEL also provides a gateway to other online systems, and is well-used by the business community, too. In the UK, we seem to have missed out on the French videotex revolution. Videotex or viewdata systems are used extensively within specific industry sectors, such as the travel trade and the insurance business; they are also often used as a medium for local authority information services. However PRESTEL, the British public viewdata system has been less persuasive in its marketing than some of the European videotex services, and has had a relatively small impact on the business community.

For the end-user, the major benefit of videotex is that it is menu-driven and easy to use. In the UK, several of the online hosts are now promoting their services to the end-user by offering simplified, user-friendly search commands which can be used with relatively little training. Both PROFILE and the TEXTLINE/NEWSLINE databases are, for instance, simple to use, and can be searched by an end-user with little experience. DIALOG has recently announced the availability of menu-driven search procedures, again in an attempt to attract the end-user, and it seems likely that, in the near future, other host systems will also develop simplified command structures or menu interfaces to encourage the end-user to make direct use of their products.

So will the expansion of these systems – aimed at the end-user – result in a do-it-yourself approach to business information? Could the end-user dismiss the information intermediary and go it alone at the keyboard? Certainly some databases appear particularly appropriate to end-user access; those which are accessed frequently, as a regular routine within a particular job, could clearly be searched by the end-user as easily as by a librarian. Specialist financial systems such as DATASTREAM are almost always searched by subject specialists. Product databases also seem ideally suited to end-user access, as the end-user knows precisely which products are required, and can save time explaining to the librarian the difference between one manufacturing process and another. But online searching seems unlikely to prove attractive to the end-user who requires information relatively infrequently, from a variety of databases which use different, albeit simple, command languages. The business librarian who has a wide knowledge of both hard copy and online sources will still be able to offer a valuable service to the user.

Online databases widen the resources available to the individual library, and provide improved retrieval facilities which allow the data to be searched more effectively. CD-ROM (Compact Disc Read-Only-Memory) provides the retrieval facilities of the online systems, but eliminates the need to access a remote database using telecommunications links; data from the CD-ROM disc is accessed using a special disc-drive which is installed on a local PC. The discs are updated on a regular basis by the database publisher, and new issues are sent to the subscribers.

At present, most use of CD-ROM appears to be made by academic organisations whose students can search databases such as ABI/ INFORM to their heart's content (and to their tutor's satisfaction) without incurring extensive telecommunications costs. Increasingly, however, CD-ROM will become a medium of more general use within the discipline of business information. Hard copy allows multi-user access to information, but does not provide the search flexibility provided by online retrieval techniques; CD-ROM could provide the solution by providing material to which libraries need access on a regular basis, together with powerful retrieval facilities. Jordans have recently produced an interesting CD-ROM product in the form of FAME (Financial Analysis Made Easy); FAME is the CD-ROM version of JORDANS FINANCIAL database which comprises information on some 125,000 companies, with a five year financial history on some 70,000 of the entries. The data may be searched using a large number of search criteria, while the results can be sorted in a variety of structures. Results can be printed or transferred onto the hard disc of a PC to allow further manipulation of the data using specialist software which allows facilities such as the computation of ratios, the ranking of companies and the analysis of trends.

Company directories could soon be available in a CD-ROM format too; Kompass have announced that their European directories are soon to be produced as a merged file on CD-ROM, which will allow the user to search an integrated European database to trace suppliers within the Single European Market. CD-ROM has tremendous potential within the area of business information; the level of market penetration by this relatively new medium clearly depends largely on price, both of the hardware and of the CD-ROM product. If librarians feel that the investment in CD-ROM gives good value for money, it will become an important medium within business information in the future. As a relatively new mass storage device, CD-ROM is itself likely to be enhanced in the near future, to provide greater storage capability; the availability of CD-ROM juke-boxes will also allow several users on a network to access CD-ROM discs.

Within many companies, there is an increased use of office automation procedures including word processing, electronic messaging and electronic filing. As the use of high density storage media such as optical disc becomes more widely and more cheaply available, workers will become more used to relying on the information available directly from their own PC, maybe networked to other computers within the organisation, or linked to a mainframe facility. It seems likely that more material will be made available in a form in which it can be added to the information store within the PC; so we have seen an increasing number of services made available on disc, to enable the data to be manipulated using specially designed software packages on the in-house PC. Material from external sources will be merged with in-house data – and this will increasingly include text and graphics. During the next decade we shall see an expansion in the availability of soft business information, information which can be loaded onto internal computing facilities, and manipulated using standard software. A number of disc-based services are now available: one of the most interesting is Micro-EXTAT, a flexible company database, which can be tailored by the customer who specifies both the company coverage and the frequency of updates.

The business librarian in the 1990s will obtain information not only from hard copy and online databases, but from a variety of electronic sources. The distinction between internally generated data and external publications will diminish, with the potential to integrate data extracted from external sources into internal databases. The business information librarian operating within companies will increasingly need to mix and match information, taken from a variety of sources, both internal and external. Extra care will need to be taken to ensure that these activities are within the law, and do not contravene copyright or data protection legislation.

The sources and the supply of business information have altered considerably during the last 10 years, and will undoubtedly alter again during the next decade. In the 1990s, the business information specialist will make even greater use of electronically-generated sources of information, perhaps using CD-ROM and disc-based products to obtain historic and semi-current data, and supplementing this with online access to current and real-time information. The data, whatever the source, will increasingly be amalgamated within in-house databases, incorporating both text and graphics. End-users will access both these in-house resources and external databases; the librarian's knowledge of business information resources will still, however, provide a value-added service to the business community.

In this technological dream world of the 1990s, business information providers could easily be divided into the technology rich and the technology poor. If publicly-funded organisations are to continue to provide an effective business information service during the next decade, the business information services within the UK must be effectively co-ordinated and developed into a powerful business information network. The business community needs information in order to develop and prosper; as business librarians, it is our job to ensure that we can provide the information service which industry deserves.

BIOGRAPHICAL NOTES

Sharon Barker started her career with the British Library Reference division and has subsequently worked in academic, public and special libraries in London and the Midlands. She has been in her present post of Information Systems Manager with the Management Information Centre of the British Institute of Management since January 1984.

Diana Edmonds graduated in history from the University of London and then studied library and information studies at the Polytechnic of North London. After working for a number of years as a librarian in a variety of situations, she became the commercial and technical librarian with Aberdeen City Libraries, providing a wide range of business information, primarily for the oil industry. Diana is now a library and information consultant working mainly for corporate clients.

Olivia Freeman started her career at the BBC and then moved on to be librarian of a political/economic research institute in Paris. On returning to this country, she worked briefly for Barclays International before going to Midland International to set up a marketing information library. She is now Manager of the Group Business Library, Midland Bank plc.

Jo Haythornthwaite has worked in a variety of academic, public and industrial libraries both in the United Kingdom and in the United States. She also taught library and information studies at Strathclyde University and at Loughborough University before returning to library management in 1989 as Chief Librarian of Glasgow College.

Michael Hopkins is Deputy Librarian at Loughborough University of Technology. He is a past Chairman of the Association of EDC Librarians and has written and lectured widely on matters concerning the nature and use of EC documentation.

Bob Norton has worked in a number of business information posts in both industrial and service organisations. Formerly Head of Library and Information services in INSEAD, the European Business School in Fountainbleau, France, he is now responsible for information services development at BIM.

Index

A-Z of UK Brand Leaders (directory) 135
A-Z of UK marketing information sources (directory) 128
A-Z of UK retailing (directory) 142
ABI/INFORM database 99, 178, 218
Abstracting and indexing services 96-100
Academic library business information services 10-12
Academic library commercial information services 200-203
Accountants firms as business information sources 183
Acquisitions and Mergers database 179
Acts of Parliament 54
Advertisers Annual 137, 147
Advertising (periodical) 140
Advertising Association 140
Advertising information 133-143
  agencies & rates 136-137
  journals 138-139
  market size 134-136
  online sources 139, 143
  sources 139-143
Advertising journals 138-139
Advisory Conciliation and Arbitration Service (ACAS) 57
AFNOR (French standards body) 192
African business information sources 150
Africa, South of the Sahara (directory) 148
American Banker (periodical) 170, 175, 177
American Technical Publishers Ltd. (standards suppliers) 194
ANALYSIS database 179
Analysis of Bank Lending to UK Residents (statistics publication) 173
Analysis online service 120
Anbar abstracting service 96-97, 138-139
Annual Abstract of Statistics (publication) 60
Annual Profiles (EIU periodical) 180
Annual reports (companies) 114-115, 152-153
ANSI (USA standards body) 192, 193
ANSI Catalog 193
APITAT database 190
Asahi News Service 157
Asia's 7, 500 Largest Companies (directory) 151
ASIA-PACIFIC database 150

Associated Press newswire service 44, 45
Association for Payment Clearing Services (APACS) statistics service 173
Austria's 10, 000 Largest Companies (directory) 151

Bank libraries 163-168
Bank of England databank 174
Bank of England Quarterly Bulletin 173, 174, 175
Bank Register (directory) 169
Bank Systems and Equipment (periodical) 176
Banker (periodical) 170, 175, 177
Bankers Almanac 159, 168
BANKING AND FINANCIAL database 177
Banking in ... series (Peat Marwick McLintock) 159
Banking information 163-183
  abstracting services 176178
  as an overseas business information source 159
  credit ratings 171-172
  customers 178-181
  dictionaries 172
  directories 168-170
  directories of bankers 170-171
  for marketing 180
  implications of European integrated market 182-183
  journals 175-176
  market research 172-173
  online sources 174-175, 177-178
  rankings 170
  regulatory constraints 165-168
  statistics 173-175
Banking Technology (periodical) 176
Banking World (periodical) 175
Banks *see* Banking information
Banks as information producers 181-182
Basic Facts about Patents for Inventions in the UK (publication) 188
BBC Data Enquiry Service 143, 199, 201
BBC Summary of World Broadcasts 157
BCIS Associates (information brokers) 208-209
Becket's Directory of the City of London 170-171
Benn's Media Directory 35, 176
  hotline service 35, 36
BIM HELPLINE gateway service 23
BIM Short Courses database 103
BIS Infomat database *see* Infomat database

BLAISE-LINE online service 51, 58
BRAD (British Rate and Data) 35-36, 137
Brief Guide to Standards Databases (BSI publication) 195
Britain's Privately Owned Companies: The Top 4000 (directory) 117
British Business (journal) 55, 65, 129, 155
British Exports (directory) 112, 147
British Humanities Index 40
British Institute of Management (BIM) databases 97-98
British Institute of Management 101
  see also BIM
British Library 66-67, 83, 203
British Library Document Supply Centre 67, 133, 195, 214
British Library Official Publications Library 67
British Library Research and Development Department 20
British Library Science Reference and Information Service (SRIS) 3, 214
    Business Information Service 67, 131, 133
    Patents Collection 188
British Market Research Bureau 143
British Overseas Trade Board information services 55-57, 155
British Standards Institution 192, 194
  library 195
BROKERS REPORTS database 181
BROKERSGUIDE database 206
BSI *see* British Standards Institution
BSI Catalogue 193
BSI News 193
BSI Sales Bulletin 193
Business and Finance (periodical) 151
Business information
  concentration of sources in London 2, 213-214
  defined 2-3
  future prospects 213-219
  impact of EC 74-84
  information providers 3-4
  overseas sources 147-160
  overview of field 1-13
Business Information for Devon service 209
Business Information Network (proposal) 214
Business International (periodical) 156
Business International - Country Forecasting Reports 158
Business Monitors (publications) 64-65, 129, 154
Business Opportunities in ... (series of business guides to Middle East countries) 149
Business Periodicals Index 96

Business Spain (periodical) 149
Business statistics 58-69
Business Statistics Office (Newport, Gwent) 3, 67, 202
Business Traveller: guide to business cities of the world 156
Business Users Service (Mitchell Library, Glasgow) 203-204
Business Week (periodical) 39

CA SEARCH database 190
Campaign (periodical) 138
  online version 157
  library 140
CAN (Canadian standards body) 192
Cash Management News (periodical) 176
Cashflow (periodical) 176
Catalogue of British Official Publications not Published by HMSO (Chadwyck-Healey) 52, 66, 128
Catalogue of Community Legal Acts and Other Texts Relating to the Elimination of Technical Barriers to Trade for Industrial Products (EEC publication) 81
Catalogue of United Kingdom Official Publications (UKOP) 52
CD-ROM 22-23, 34, 37, 42, 217-218
Ceefax (teletext service) 119
CELEX (EC database) 77, 182
CEN *see* European Committee for Standardisation
CENELEC *see* European Committee for Electrotechnical Standardisation
Census (UK) 129, 141
Central America (directory) 148
Central Statistical Office 59
Centres for European Business Information 83
Chambers of Commerce as an overseas business information source 160
Chancery Lane Information Brokers 206, 207
Charging for information *see* Fee-based information services
Chartered Institute of Bankers library 177
Chartered Institute of Marketing Management 102
CHINAPAT database 149, 190
CIFAR International Annual reports Collection 125
Citiservice *see* Prestel Citiservice
City Business Library (London) 3, 153, 160
City Directory (London) 169
City Research Associates (syndicated market research service) 172
Cityline (Financial Times telephone information service) 121
CLAIMS database 190
Clippings files *see* Press cuttings files

Clover Newspaper Index 39-40
Co-operative information centres 10
COMEXT databank 79
Commerce International (periodical) 156
Commercial information services 197-209
Committee of London and Scottish Bankers (CLSB) statistics service 173
Companies House 115, 179
Companies Registration Office 114, 115, 213-214
Companies Registration Office Directory of Companies 10
Company addresses 110-113, 123-126
Company Data Supplement (periodical) 39-40
Company directories 111-113, 218
Company information 2, 8, 38, 107-126, 207, 213-214
  banks 178-180
  credit ratings 117
  directories 111-113
  European companies 123-126
  financial data 114-121
  local directories 113
  locations (addresses) 110-113, 123-126
  online sources 43, 112-113, 122-123, 152-153
  overseas companies 40-41, 150-153
Company information (continued)
  ownership 113-114
  share ownership data 121-122
  share price data 117-121
  specific industry sectors 113
  see also PROFILE, TEXTLINE and individual databases
Company information units *see* Information units in companies
Company ownership 113-114
COMPENDEX database 195
Compendium of marketing information sources 128
Consumer market information 147-160
Consumer markets in Central America (directory) 149
Consumer markets in Central and Eastern Africa (directory) 149
Consumer markets in Latin America (directory) 149
Consumer markets in North Africa (directory) 149
Consumer markets in the Far East (directory) 149
Consumer markets in the Indian subcontinent (directory) 149
Consumer markets in the Middle East (directory) 149
Consumer markets in the USA (directory) 149
Consumer markets in West Africa (directory) 149
Consumer research information 128-130, 147-160
Consumer statistics 63, 153-154

Co-operative business information services 10, 204
Copyright 219
Corporate Finance (periodical) 176
Country Reports (EIU periodical) 180
Crawford's Directory of City Connections 169, 180
Crawford's European Finance (directory) 169
Crawford's Investment Research Index 169
Credit rating services 117 *see also* Bank credit ratings
CRO Directory of Companies 110-111
CRONOS databank 79, 174
Current African Directories 151
Current Asian and Australasian Directories 151
Current awareness services 7, 18, 34-35
  for banking 182
  for EC matters 77-78
  for official publications 52
  for management information 97
Current British Directories 113
Current European Directories 151
Current Serials (British Library publication) 94

Daily Express (newspaper) 39, 43
Daily Mail (newspaper) 39, 43
Daily Telegraph (newspaper) 32, 39, 41-42, 55, 140, 155, 199
Data protection legislation 219
DATALINE (database) 43
Datasolve *see* PROFILE
DATASTREAM database 26, 68-69, 120-121, 154, 179, 217
Deloitte Haskins and Sells database on EC policy 183
DELPHES database 100
Demographic Yearbook (UN publication) 153
Department of Trade and Industry publications 55
Descriptive information sources for overseas countries 155-156
Devon County Library 209, 214
Dial Industry Directories 112
DIAL information service 135
Dictionary of Banking and Finance 173
Dictionary of Financial Regulation, 1988/89 173
DIN (W.German standards body) 192
Direct mail campaigns 142
Directory of Chinese Foreign Trade 151
Directory of Community Legislation in Force (EC publication) 76
Directory of Consultants and Researchers in Library and Information
  Science 206

Directory of Directors 112
Directory of Fee-based Information Services 206
Directory of Information Brokers and Consultants 206
Directory of International Sources of Business Information 147
Directory of Management Training 103
DISCLOSURE FINANCIALS database 151
Document delivery services 18, 52, 207, 208
Documents (EC catalogue of public documents) 74
Dun and Bradstreet credit rating service 172
Dun and Bradstreet Registers 180
DUNS MARKET IDENTIFIERS database 112-113
Duns Marketing online database 143
Dunsfiche information service 180
Dunsprint information service 150, 152

ECCTIS (Education Counselling and Credit Transfer Information Service) database 102
Economic information on overseas countries 153-154
Economic Outlook (periodical) 180
Economic Trends (publication) 62
Economist (periodical) 34, 39, 43, 156, 157
Economist Intelligence Unit 155, 157
EDOC database 190
EC business information 73-84
  official sources 82-83
EC legislation information 76-78
EEC: a Guide to Banking and Sources of Finance (publication) 182
Electronic journals 216
ELECTRONIC LIBRARY SERVICE (newspaper database) 42
Electronic mail 18
Embassies as an overseas business information source 159
EMIC *see* Export Market Information Centre
Employment Gazette 129
Encyclopaedia of European Community Law 76
End user online searching 7, 25-27, 216-217, 219
Enquiry handling, methodology 18-21
EPAT database 190
Equal Opportunities Commission 57
EQUITIES 2000 database 120
ESPRIT database 120
Essential guides (BIM series) 93
Eurodoc (microfilm service) 81
Euromarket Letter (newsletter) 176
Euromarket Report database 177

Euromoney database 174
Euromonitor 132, 133, 135, 157, 177
Europa Yearbook 180
Europe (EEC legislation alerting service) 77
Europe and the future of financial services (publication) 182
Europe's 15, 000 largest companies (book and database) 124
European alert (current awareness service) 77-78
European Business Information Centres 3, 148
European Committee for Electrotechnical Standardisation 192
European Committee for Standardisation 192
European companies information 123-126
European Country Information: EEC countries (book) 123
European Directory of Marketing Information Sources 148
European Documentation Centres 83
European integrated market 56, 73-84, 215, 216, 218
EUROPEAN KOMPASS database 125
European Motor Business (market report) 158
European Patent Office 190
European Report (EC legislation alerting service) 77
European Trade Association Statistics 154
Export (periodical) 156
Export Direction (periodical) 156
Export Intelligence Service (EIS) Online database 157
Export Market Information Centre (EMIC) 3, 66-67, 153, 160, 202
Exporting to Spain (guide) 155
Extel card service 115-116, 125, 152, 153, 178, 179
Extel Over the Counter Service 116
Extel Third Market Service 116
Extel Unlisted Securities Market Service 116
Extel Unquoted Companies Service 116

Facts on File (news digest service) 41
FAME (Financial Analysis Made Easy) CD-ROM product 218
Family Expenditure Survey 61, 63-64, 129
Far East business information sources 149
Fee-based information services 12, 19, 34, 41-42, 135, 197-209, 215
  see also Freelance information workers
Finance from Europe (booklet) 80
Financial information 2, 17, 38, 43, 62
  companies 111-113, 114-121, 151
  EC 78-79
Financial institutions as an overseas business information source 159
Financial Market Trends (publication) 174
Financial Regulation Report database 177

Financial Services International (newsletter) 176
Financial Statistics (CSO publication) 173, 174
Financial Times (newspaper) 31, 32, 34, 37, 38, 39, 40, 41, 43, 44, 55, 121, 155, 168, 171, 172, 173, 199
index 37-38
FINANCIAL TIMES BUSINESS INFORMATION SERVICE 4, 8, 34, 140, 176, 177, 198, 201
see also PROFILE
Financing Foreign Operations (publication) 182
FIND database 177
FIND/SVP (business information research firm) 158
Findex: the Directory of Market Research Reports, Studies and Surveys 131, 136
Finding Export Markets: a Guide to Methods and Information Sources in the UK and Worldwide 147-148
FINIS database 177
Finstat (financial statistics service) 173
First Contact (information brokers) 207-208
Food Growth Markets (publication) 134, 135
Food Monitor International Business Reports 158
FORECASTS database 159
FPAT database 190
Freelance information workers 4, 8, 215
Frost and Sullivan current market research reports 132
Frost Phillips Russell (marketing organisation) 143
FTBR Business/Finance database 157

General Household Survey 63, 129, 134
Glasgow Herald (newspaper) 32, 33, 38
Glasnost (newsletter on Eastern Europe business opportunities) 149
Global Report database 175
GOST (Soviet standards body) 192
Government Statistical Service 59
Government Statistics: a Brief Guide to Sources (publication) 66)
Grants and Loans from the European Community (booklet) 80
Greenwich Research Associates (syndicated market research service) 172
GT Guide to World Equity Markets 182-183
Guardian (newspaper) 32, 37, 39, 40, 55, 155
Guardian Index 37
Guide to Business Mailing Lists (publication) 142
Guide to Marketing Research 128, 136
Guide to Official Statistics (CSO publication) 59-60, 65, 128
Guidebook on Trading with the Peoples' Republic of China 151

HARVEST database 139, 143
HATRICS library cooperative 195
Helpline (BIM) online service 98
HERTIS information service 11, 198, 201-202, 203
Hints to Exporters (series) 155
HMSO publications 50-51, 128
  subscription service 54
HOPPENSTEDT database 152
House of Commons Library 66, 67
House of Commons Public Information Office 53
Household Food Consumption and Expenditure: National Food Survey (annual report) 64, 129
How to Prepare a UK Patent Application and then Apply for a Patent (publication) 188

IBCA credit rating agency 172
ICC database 23, 116, 178, 180
  see also SHAREWATCH
ICC Industry Sector Reports
ICC Regional Company Surveys 141
ICC Status Reports 152
ICC STOCKBROKER RESEARCH database 178
ICC viewdata service 122
IFR database 174
IMF Exchange Arrangements and Exchange Restrictions 180
IMF International Financial Statistics (publication) 174, 180
In-house databases 4, 6, 7, 33, 219
Independent (newspaper) 32, 39, 40, 42-43, 55, 155
Independent information brokers 204-209, 215
Industrial Innovation: a Guide to Community Action, Services and Funding (EC book) 80
Industrial Market Locations (publication) 142
Industrial Short Term Trends (Eurostat publication) 154
INDUSTRY DATA SOURCES database 131
INFOCHECK database 117, 179
INFOMAT database 125, 132
Infonorme London Information (ILI) (standards suppliers) 194
Information brokers 12, 19, 204-209, 215
Information consultants 205-206
Information units in companies 4-9, 12-13
Information, charging for 10, 12, 19, 22-23, 41, 197-209
  see also Fee-based information services
INFOSEARCH gateway service 23
INPADOC database 190, 191

Inpadoc Patent Gazette (publication) 190
Instant Library (information brokers) 208
Institute of Administrative Management 101
Institute of Directors 101
Institute of Management Services 101
Institute of Marketing 140
Institute of Personnel Management 101
Institute of Practitioners in Advertising 140
Institute of Sales & Marketing Management 101
International Banking and Financial Market Developments (statistics publication) 174
International Banking Report newsletter 176, 177
International business information 147-160
  companies 150-153
  descriptive information on overseas countries 155-156
  market reports 156-159
  non-traditional sources 159-160
  online sources 157-159
  production figures 154
  statistics 153-154
INTERNATIONAL BUSINESS RESEARCH database 115
International Dictionary of Management 93
International Directory of Marketing Information Sources 148
International Directory of Published Market Research 130
INTERNATIONAL DUN'S MARKET IDENTIFIERS database 125
International Electronic Payments (newsletter) 176
International Electrotechnical Commission (standards body) 192
International Financing Review 172, 176
International Insider (newsletter) 176
International Motor Business (market report) 158
INTERNATIONAL RISK DATA database 157
International Standards Organisation (ISO) 192
International Tourism Reports 158
International Trade Finance newsletter 176, 177
International Who's Who 148
Introducing Patents: a Guide for Inventors (publication) 188
INVESTEX database 178, 181
Investment in ... series (Peat Marwick McLintock) 159
IP SHARP (online service) 68, 154
Italy's 2, 000 Largest Companies (directory) 151

Japanese Motor Business (market report) 158
Japanese Software Alert (periodical) 150
Jones Lang Wootton property information service 200

JORDANS FINANCIAL database 218
Jordans Shareholder Service database 122
JORDANWATCH database 116
Journal libraries 140-141
JUSTIS database 77

Keefe Bruyette and Woods credit rating agency 172
Keesings Record of World Events 40-41, 157
Keesings UK Record 40
Kelly's Business Directory 111, 112
Kendrick Research Associates (information brokers) 208, 209
Key British Enterprises 112, 143
Key Data (publication) 60
Key Facts (publication) 129
Key Note Reports 136, 157, 158, 172
KOMPASS Database *see* EUROPEAN KOMPASS database
Kompass directories on CD-ROM 218
KOMPASS online service 125, 143, 152, 180 *see also* EUROPEAN KOMPASS database
Kompass Regional Sales Guide 141
Kompass UK (directory) 112
Korean Fortune (periodical) 150
Kothari's Economic and Industrial Guide (to India) 151

Latin America business information sources 150
LEISURE FUTURES database 157
Leisure Intelligence (publication) 134, 135
Library Association Government Libraries Group 58
Library Association Information Services Group 58
Local government publications 57-58
Local newspapers as a business information source 33
London Business School Information Service 4, 11, 123, 143, 153, 198, 202, 203

Macmillan Dictionary of International Finance 173
Macmillan Dictionary of Marketing and Advertising 127
Macmillan's Unquoted Companies (directory) 117
MAGIC online service *see* PROFILE
MAID database 133, 135, 137, 138, 139, 157-158
Mail order selling 142
Maintaining a Press Clippings File (factsheet) 7
Major Companies of Europe (directory) 124, 151
Major Companies of Latin America (directory) 148, 150, 151
Major Companies of Nigeria (directory) 151

Major Companies of the Arab World (directory) 151
Major Companies of the Far East (directory) 151
Major Companies of the USA (directory) 151
Making a Busines of Information (report) 12
Management & Marketing Abstracts 97, 139
Management Contents database 99-100
Management information 3, 89-104
  abstracting & indexing services 96-100
  classification 92-94
  defined 90-91
  news services 100-101
  online sources 96-100, 102-103
  specialist journals 94-96
  specialist publishers 94
  training information 102-103
Management Today (periodical) 101
Management Training Directory 103
Management training information services 102-103
Manpower Services Commission 57
Manual of Business Library Practice 31
MARIS-NET (Materials and Resources Information Network) database 102
Market Assessment (marketing organisation) 143
Market Assessment (publication) 134, 135
Market Direction Reports 158
Market Eye information service 119
Market Forecasts (publication) 135
Market information 147-160
  about EC countries 78-79
  about specific foreign countries 55-56, 149-150, 156-159
Market Intelligence (publication) 134, 135
Market Intelligence Europe (publication) 157
Market reports for overseas countries 156-159
Market research information 130-143, 157-158, 207, 213, 214
  advertising information 133-143
  banks 172-173
  market size determination 134-136
  overseas information 147-160
  sources & indexes 130-134
  statistics 131
Market Research Abstracts 132
Market research by banks 172
Market Research Europe 157, 158
Market Research Great Britain 134, 135

Market Research Society 140
Market Research Society Yearbook 172
Market Research Sourcebook 128
Market Research: a Guide to British Library Holdings 133, 156
Marketing (periodical) 138
Marketing and Advertising Reference Service (MARS) database 132, 138, 139
Marketing and Management Abstracts 132
Marketing Directory 127
Marketing in Europe (periodical) 157, 158
Marketing information 3, 127-143, 147-160, 198
  advertising information 133-143
  consumer research 128-130
  market research 130-143
  online sources 131-136, 139, 152, 157-159
  overseas sources 147-160
  sources 128-136
  statistics 131-133
Marketing Pocket Book 127
Marketing Surveys Index 131, 156
Marketing Week (periodical) 138
Marketsearch (directory) 130
MARS *see* Marketing and Advertising Reference Service
Mary Moody Associates (information brokers) 209
Maturity Distribution of International Bank Lending (statistics publication) 174
McCarthy information service 34, 44, 123
  European card service 125
MCCARTHYLINE database 44, 100
MEAL Quarterly Digest 133, 137
Meed Middle East Financial Directory 170
MERGERS AND ACQUISITIONS INTERNATIONAL (FT) database 179
Merrill Lynch Euromoney Directory 169-170
MicroEXSTAT database 116, 219
Microinfo (standards supplier) 194
MID EAST database 149
Middle East business information sources 149
Middle East Economic Handbook 149
MINITEL videotex system 216-217
Mintel 8, 134, 143, 157, 172, 177, 198, 203
MIRAC microfiche service 115
Mitchell Library, Glasgow, Business Users Service 203-204
Money Magazine 176

Money Observer (periodical) 176
Monthly Banking Statistics 174
Monthly Digest (statistics publication) 60
Monthly Index to the Financial Times 37
Moody's Bank and Finance Manual 171
Moody's credit rating agency 172, 179

NATIONAL DEVELOPMENT PLANS database 157
National Opinion Polls (syndicated market research service) 172
National Training Index (for management) 103
NETWORK library cooperative 10, 194
Newcastle Business and Technical Library 10
News services 40-41, 44, 45, 100-101
NEWSFILE database 139
NEWSLINE database 17, 43, 53, 158
NEWSNET database 44, 132, 176
Newspaper libraries 41-42, 140-141
Newspapers as a business information source 17, 31-45, 122, 151
  directories 35-41
  indexes 37-41
  online access 42-45
  storage & conservation 33-34
NEXIS database 43-44, 132, 151, 155
NIKAI ONLINE database 151
Non-Food Growth Markets (publication) 134, 135
Non-library business information sources 4
Norfolk County Library 209
Nottingham Business Library 10

OECD Economic Surveys 180
OECD international statistics service 173-174
Official Journal (Patents) 188
Official Journal of the European Communities 76, 81
Official publications 49-69
Online Finance (periodical) 176
Online information 4, 6, 10, 15-28, 34, 215-216
  advertising industry 139, 143
  banking 174-175, 177-178
  command languages 21, 23
Online information (continued)
  companies 43, 112-113, 122-123, 152-153
  costs of 22-23
  end user searching 7, 25-27, 216-217, 219
  international business information 157-159

management information 96-100, 102-103
marketing & market research 131-136, 139, 152, 157-159
menu-driven searching 217
newspaper texts 42-45
patents 190-191
resistance to 21-24
selecting hosts & databases 24-25
share price information 122-123
standards 195
statistics information 67-69
telecommunications 25
training & user support 21, 22, 24-25, 27, 44
user friendliness 217
see also individual databases and host services
Online Public Access Catalogues (OPACs) 21
Operations of the European Community concerning Small and Medium-sized Enterprises (booklet) 80
Overseas companies information 150-153

Patent Co-operation Treaty 189
Patent Information Centres 189
Patent Office: an Introduction to the Services of the Patent Office and Trade Marks and Designs Registries (publication) 188
Patents *see also* UK Patent Information Network
Patents for Inventions: Abridgements of Specifications 188
Patents information 3, 6, 187-191, 201
online sources 190-191
Patents; a Source of Technical Information (periodical) 188
Paying for information *see* Fee-based information services
PERGAMON FINANCIAL DATA SERVICES (PFDS) 18, 45
PERINORM CD-ROM 195
Personal contacts as an overseas business information source 159, 160
Personal Finance Intelligence (publication) 134, 172
PICKUP (Professional and Industrial Commercial Updating Training Directory) database 103
PIN *see* UK Patent Information Network
Planned Savings (periodical) 176
PLANNING CONSUMER MARKETS database 157
Pocket Banker (publication) 173
POLIS database 53, 58
Polk's Bank Directory 169
Population Projections (publication) 129
Population Statistics 141
PREDICASTS database 23, 44, 176

Press and Information Offices (EC) 82-83
Press cuttings files 6, 7, 33, 34, 44, 199
Press Register 137
Press releases as a business information source 55
PRESTEL 10, 51, 103
PRESTEL CITISERVICE 120, 175
PRICELINK (Pacific business information service) 149
Principal International Businesses (book) 124
Private Banker International (newsletter) 176
Private sector libraries & information units 5-9
Product information *see* Market research information
Production figures sources for overseas countries 154
PROFILE online service 17, 21, 32, 42, 44, 56, 58, 122, 123, 131, 132, 133, 136, 137, 138, 149, 151, 152, 155, 157, 178, 180, 199, 217
PROMT database 100, 125-126
Provincial Patent Libraries 189
Public library business information services 3, 9-10, 214-215
Publications of the European communities (catalogue) 74-75

QUOTRON database 174-175

Rand McNally Bankers' Directory 169
Ranking of UK Investment Analysts 170
Real Banking Profitability (statistical analyses) 170
Reality of Management (book) 93
REGIO databank 79
Regional Trends (publication) 61, 63
Reports Index 131
Research Index 38-39, 123, 132, 138
Research projects 8
Retail Banker International (newsletter) 176
Retail Business (publication) 134, 135
Retail Intelligence (publication) 134, 135
Retail Monitor (market report) 158
Retail planning information 142-143
Reuter news service 43
Reuter TEXTLINE *see* TEXTLINE

Sales and Marketing Information Ltd (SAMI) 142
SCIMP (index to management periodicals) database 98-99
Scottish Abstract of Statistics 62
SDI services 7, 18, 24
see also Current awareness services
SEAQ (Stock Exchange information system) 118-119, 120, 175

Securities and Investment Board (SIB) database of authorised institutions 166
Selective Dissemination of Information *see* SDI services
Sell's Directory: products and services 111-112
Setting up a Company in the European Community (book) 123
Share ownership information 121-122
Share prices information 117-121
Sharecall (telephone information service) 121
SHAREWATCH (ICC database) 121-122
Shop Equipment Display and Shopfitting Directory 143
Shopping Centre Trade Area Reports 142
SHOPS database 142
Single Market News (EC newsletter) 78
Social Trends (publication) 61, 63, 129
Société Générale de Banque database 178
Sources of Unofficial UK Statistics (book) 66
South America (directory) 148
South America, Central America and the Caribbean (directory) 150
South American Economic Handbook 150
SPEARHEAD database 56, 58, 77, 177
Specifications information 191-195
  for EC countries 80-81
Specifications produced by individual companies 193
Spicers Centre for Europe (telephone advisory service) 183
Standard and Poors credit rating agency 172, 179
Standard Trade Index of Japan 151
STANDARDLINE database 195
Standards Alert (catalogue) 194
Standards Express (newsletter) 194
Standards information 3, 6, 191-195
  acquiring information 193-195
  for EC countries 80-81
  online sources 195
Standards produced by individual companies 193
STANDARDS SEARCH database 195
Statesman's Yearbook 153, 155
Statistical data 3, 174-175
Statistical information 58-69, 78-79
  digests 60-61, 62
  government-produced 58-65, 68
  on overseas countries 153-154
  online sources 67-69
Statistical News (publication) 60
Statistical Office of the European Communities 78-79

Statistical Yearbook (UN publication) 153
Statistics and Market Intelligence Library *see* Export Market Information Centre
Statistics and Market Research: a guide to current periodical articles 131
Statistics: Asia and Australasia (research guide) 153-154
Stock Exchange Daily Official List 120
Suffolk County Information and Library Service 208
Survey of UK Statistical Sources and their Role in Business Information (1984 report) 67
SVP United Kingdom Ltd.(information brokers) 206
Syndicated market research services 172

TAP (Training Access Points) database 102
Target (periodical) 142
Telephone directories (as a business information source) 113, 125
Telepictorials (advertising library) 138
TELERATE database 174-175
Telesales campaigns 142
Television Register 137
TENDERS ELECTRONIC DAILY (TED) database 79
TEXTLINE(database)17, 21, 26, 27, 32, 4245, 52, 58, 100, 122, 125, 132, 133, 138, 149, 151, 152, 155, 178, 180, 217
Textline Outlook International (market report) 158
Thomson's Dictionary of Banking 173
Times (newspaper) 31, 32, 33, 36, 37, 39, 40, 42, 52, 155
Times Index 37, 39-40, 52
Times of India Directory and Yearbook 151
Top 400 UK Markets (publication) 135
TOPIC videotex system 119, 122, 175, 216
Towards 1992 (EC newsletter) 78
Trade Associations as an overseas business information source 160
Trade Finance (periodical) 176
Trade statistics sources for overseas countries 154
Tradebrief (report) 181
TRADSTAT database 154
Translators 7, 205
Travel and Tourism Analyst (market report) 158
Triple A Asia Banking Almanac 170

UK Balance of Payments (statistics book) 62
UK Facsimile Directory 113
UK National Accounts (statistics book) 62
UK Patent Information Network 189
UK Telex Directory 113

UK Trade Names (directory) 112
Ulrich's press directories 36-37
Unit for Retail Planning Information Ltd. 142-143
US Embassy Library 153
USA Monitor (market report) 158

Vade-mecum of Community Research Promotion (EC book) 80
Videotex 216-217 *see also* PRESTEL; MINITEL; TOPIC
Vital Information (information brokers) 206

Wall Street Journal 31, 172
Warwick Business Information Service 11, 66, 67, 160, 198, 202, 203
Weeks Financial Diary (Financial Times) 114
WEFA Group (online service) 69, 154
Welsh Economic Trends (publication) 62
Westminster Public Libraries 198, 203
Wharton Econometric Forecasting Associates Group *see* WEFA
What is Intellectual Property? (publication) 188
Whitaker's Almanac 153, 155
Who Owns Whom 17, 125
Who Owns Whom: Continental Europe 125
Who Owns Whom: United Kingdom and Republic of Ireland 114
Who's Who 170
 see also International Who's Who
Who's Who in Banking in Europe 171
Who's Who in International Banking 171
Who's Who in the City: the annual biographical guide to the UK financial community 171
Willings Press Guide 35, 176
Wilsonline online service 96
World Accounting Report newsletter 177
WORLD BANK INTERNATIONAL BUSINESS OPPORTUNITIES database 157, 177
World Bank World Debt Tables (publication) 174
World Banking Abstracts 177, 181
World Commodity Report newsletter 177
World Insurance Report newsletter 177
World of Information (periodical) 180
World Patents Index 190
World Reporter database *see* PROFILE
World Tax Report newsletter 177
WORLDCASTS database 159
Worldwide Marketing Opportunities Digest 156

Yearbook of international trade statistics 154

1992: Single market monitor (EC newsletter) 78
1992: Single market news (EC newsletter) 78